# HOMOSEXUAL ISSUES IN THE WORKPLACE

## THE SERIES IN CLINICAL AND COMMUNITY PSYCHOLOGY

*CONSULTING EDITORS*
**Charles D. Spielberger and Irwin G. Sarason**

**Auerbach and Stolberg** Crisis Intervention with Children and Families
**Burchfield** Stress: Psychological and Physiological Interactions
**Burstein and Loucks** Rorschach's Test: Scoring and Interpretation
**Diamant** Homosexual Issues in the Workplace
**Diamant** Male and Female Homosexuality: Psychological Approaches
**Erchul** Consultation in Community, School, and Organizational Practice: Gerald Caplan's Contributions to Professional Psychology
**Fischer** The Science of Psychotherapy
**Hobfoll** Stress, Social Support, and Women
**Krohne and Laux** Achievement, Stress, and Anxiety
**London** The Modes and Morals of Psychotherapy, Second Edition
**Muñoz** Depression Prevention: Research Directions
**Olweus** Aggression in the Schools: Bullies and Whipping Boys
**Reisman** A History of Clinical Psychology, Second Edition
**Reitan and Davison** Clinical Neuropsychology: Current Status and Applications
**Rickel, Gerrard, and Iscoe** Social and Psychological Problems of Women: Prevention and Crisis Intervention
**Rofé** Repression and Fear: A New Approach to the Crisis in Psychotherapy
**Savin-Williams** Gay and Lesbian Youth: Expressions of Identity
**Spielberger and Diaz-Guerrero** Cross-Cultural Anxiety, Volume 3
**Spielberger, Diaz-Guerrero, and Strelau** Cross-Cultural Anxiety, Volume 4
**Suedfeld** Psychology and Torture
**Veiel and Baumann** The Meaning and Measurement of Social Support
**Williams and Westermeyer** Refugee Mental Health in Resettlement Countries

## IN PREPARATION

**Auerbach** Clinical Psychology in Transition
**Bedell** Psychological Assessment and Treatment of Patients with Severe Mental Disorders
**Spielberger and Vagg** The Assessment and Treatment of Test Anxiety

# HOMOSEXUAL ISSUES IN THE WORKPLACE

*Edited by*

Louis Diamant

*University of North Carolina at Charlotte*
*Charlotte, North Carolina*

*Johnson C. Smith University*
*Charlotte, North Carolina*

TAYLOR & FRANCIS

| | | |
|---|---|---|
| **USA** | Publishing Office: | Taylor & Francis<br>1101 Vermont Ave., N.W., Suite 200<br>Washington, DC 20005-3521<br>Tel: (202) 289-2174<br>Fax: (202) 289-3665 |
| | Distribution Center: | Taylor & Francis Inc.<br>1900 Frost Road, Suite 101<br>Bristol, PA 19007-1598<br>Tel: (215) 785-5800<br>Fax: (215) 785-5515 |
| **UK** | | Taylor & Francis Ltd.<br>4 John St.<br>London WC1N 2ET<br>Tel: 071 405 2237<br>Fax: 071 831 2035 |

**HOMOSEXUAL ISSUES IN THE WORKPLACE**



1 2 3 4 5 6 7 8 9 0 B R B R 9 8 7 6 5 4 3

This book was set in Times Roman by Taylor & Francis. The editors were Amy Lyles Wilson and Susan Connell; the production supervisor was Peggy M. Rote; and the typesetter was Wayne Hutchins. Cover design by Michelle Fleitz.
Printing and binding by Braun-Brumfield, Inc.

A CIP catalog record for this book is available from the British Library.
♾ The paper in this publication meets the requirements of the ANSI Standard Z39.48-1984(Permanence of Paper)

**Library of Congress Cataloging-in-Publication Data**

Homosexual issues in the workplace / edited by Louis Diamant.
p. cm.
Includes bibliographical references and index.

1. Homosexuality—United States. 2. Gays—Employment—United States. I. Diamant, Louis, date.
HQ76.3.U5H644 1993
305.9 #0664—dc20 93-399
ISBN 1-56032-038-9 CIP
ISSN 0146-0846

# Contents

## PART 2: CORPORATE OUTLOOK



## PART 3: SPECIAL PLACES, SPECIAL ROLES

## PART 4: AIDS IN THE WORKPLACE

# Contributors

CLINTON W. ANDERSON, Ph.D.
American Psychological Association
750 First Street, NE
Washington, DC 20002-4242

ROBERT L. BARRET, Ph.D.
Human Services Department
University of North Carolina at Charlotte
Charlotte, NC 28223

ROGER G. BROWN, Ph.D.
Department of Political Science
University of North Carolina at Charlotte
Charlotte, NC 28223

KIM BUCH, Ph.D.
Department of Psychology
University of North Carolina at Charlotte
Charlotte, NC 28223

JUDITH CARMAN, Ph.D.
Department of Clinical Biochemistry
Royal Prince Alfred Hospital
Missenden Road
Camperdown, NSW 2050
Australia

LOUIS DIAMANT, Ph.D.
Department of Psychology
University of North Carolina at Charlotte
Charlotte, NC 28223

JOHN E. ELLIOT, M.A., M.S.W., (Ph.D. cand.)
Department of Education and Counseling Psychology
University of Kentucky
245 Dickey Hall
Lexington, KY 40506-0177

RUTH E. FASSINGER, Ph.D.
Counseling and Personality
College of Education
3234A Benjamin Building
University of Maryland
College Park, MD 20742

JOHN C. GONSIOREK, Ph.D.
111 West 22nd Street
Room 210
Minneapolis, MN 55045

JO ANN LEE, Ph.D.
Department of Psychology
University of North Carolina at Charlotte
Charlotte, NC 28223

GARY THOMAS LONG, Ph.D.
Department of Psychology
University of North Carolina at Charlotte
Charlotte, NC 28223

RICHARD D. McANULTY, Ph.D.
Department of Psychology
University of North Carolina at Charlotte
Charlotte, NC 28223

MICHAEL H. McGEE, J.D.
Two First Union Center
301 South Tryon Street
Charlotte, NC 28282

J. R. McSPADDEN, Jr., M.S.S.W., Th.M.
The Saluda Psychology Service Center
P.O. Box 68
Rock Hill, SC 29731

SUE MARGARET NORTON, Ph.D.
University of Wisconsin at Parkside
School of Business
900 Wood Road
Box 2000
Kenosha, WI 53141-2000

MICHAEL W. ROSS, Ph.D.
School of Community Medicine
National Center in HIV Research
The University of New South Wales
2nd Floor, 345 Crown Street
Surry Hills, New South Wales 2010, AUSTRALIA

NANCY L. ROTH, Ph.D.
Department of Communication
Rutgers University
4 Huntington Street
New Brunswick, NJ 08903

RITCH C. SAVIN-WILLIAMS, Ph.D.
Department of Human Development and Family Studies
Cornell University
NG-10B MVR
Ithaca, NY 14853-4401

H. RON SMITH, Ed.D.
American Psychological Association
750 First Street, NE
Washington, DC 20002-4242

# Foreword

I was asked to write the foreword to this book because I am a lawyer who managed the prosecution of employment discrimination with the U.S. Equal Employment Opportunity Commission for 15 years and am a student of family law (McGee, 1984). I am not gay but doggedly oppositional, intellectually and temperamentally, to the discrimination against gays and lesbians, who are mostly unprotected in the workplace.

There will not be much change in the laws or in the culture with regard to gays and lesbians until the heterosexual majority sees the need for change. Groups with minimal voting power fare poorly in a democracy unless allied with other blocs of voters. Up to now, few blocs of voters have wanted to be identified with or support gay/lesbian issues. As a lawyer, I know one thing very clearly about the issues raised here—that gay/lesbian issues will remain solely in the *political* forum until and unless the U.S. Supreme Court chooses to interpret the Constitution to protect gays and lesbians. Currently, the condition of being gay or lesbian is considered in much of the country to be criminal in nature, such persons being placed in the same category as, for example, child molesters or flashers.

The majority needs to see that freedom is a singular word. There can be no long-term stability for freedom until all, other than those who are actually harming society, are free. A policeman who is permitted to club a gay man for no reason will later feel much more free to club you or me for no reason when he has a bad day. This word *freedom* has a lot to do with what a society does and does not choose to define as criminal behavior. In many countries, for example, it is a crime to publish in a newspaper an article that is critical of the government in power. In other countries, it is a crime for a black person to live in an area reserved for white persons. When I was in Vietnam, it was a crime there to dance socially; the penalty was imprisonment. This is not so in the United States, but it is very clear that the legal definition of criminality is a primary key to the meaning of the word *freedom.*

The prime example in the United States is the Supreme Court's 1973 decriminalization of abortion. When you get down to it, the only thing the Supreme Court did in the *Roe v. Wade* case was to decriminalize abortion. In doing so, the Court attempted to fit the Constitution into present day conditions; and, at the same time, the Court added to the definition of the word *freedom.* The Court also took the debate over abortion out of the voters' hands. There is a great deal of controversy now, 20 years later, about whether that was a wise extension of freedom. The fact remains, though, that the abortion debate is a debate about the definition of freedom and the nature of criminality, pure and simple.

In my experience with employment issues, the federal discrimination laws provide no civil rights or employment rights for gays or lesbians, and very few state laws do so. In recent years, the Supreme Court has gone so far as to say that the constitutional definition of freedom does not apply to gays and lesbians and that the continued criminalization of gay/lesbian behavior by state and local political bodies is within those bodies' discretion. Therefore, the Court has left the issue in the political forum.

Further, beyond the issue of criminalization, it has always been true that *employment* rights, as distinguished from basic human rights, can be established for the most part only by Congress and state legislatures and are not inherent in the Constitution. The race, sex, age, and handicap discrimination laws were established by Congress and the state legislatures. If these laws are repealed, it is likely that most of the protection for all of these groups would disappear, except for blacks, who have some minimal nonpolitical protection inherent in the Fourteenth Amendment. The majority, however, sees the need for freedom for blacks, women, older persons, and the handicapped in the area of employment, and its political decisions reflect that observed need.

The problem is that eliminating discrimination against gays and lesbians involves undoing a very complex web of laws in many areas of life, considerably beyond the decriminalization of gay/lesbian activity per se. For example, there is no statutory framework for a gay/lesbian couple or family structure. The current structure of family and divorce laws is geared in such a way as to create a separate cause of divorce for behavior loosely revolving around sexual orientation, and there are many laws on the books of states that criminalize certain sexual behaviors without regard for sexual orientation, which are most often applied to suppress gays and lesbians. The situation is much like that of Gulliver, who was held down as a prisoner of the Lilliputians by many, many thin strings that were placed across his body while he slept.

Consider the plight of an employer who for whatever reason would like to volunteer to stop discriminating against gays and lesbians and be an "Equal Opportunity Employer—Gay/Lesbian." In most states, there is no legal framework within which any such employer may establish that kind of policy. Such employers would feel at risk of being attacked and denounced, or even boycotted, for employing such persons or for having such a policy. Employers may even feel that they could be subject to suspicion for condoning criminal behavior or immoral conduct within the workplace. Without a constitutional pronouncement or an antidiscrimination law on the books, the *employer* has no support for having a policy or practice of having such persons on the payroll, and because it may affect their bottom line, most employers would not take the risk, even when inclined to do so. It is not unexpected, nor is it contrary to human nature, for employers to be unwilling to take that step alone.

I will bring this foreword to a close with a proposed legislative agenda, which is of course in the political forum. Even if the Supreme Court chooses to tackle the issue of expanding the definition of freedom in the context of gay/lesbian issues, most of the items on this agenda will still require legislative approval.

(1) Amend Title VII of the Civil Rights Act of 1964, 42 U.S.C. 2000e et seq., to include sexual orientation as a protected group, and to prohibit discrimination in the workplace based on sexual orientation to the same degree that discrimination based on race, color, religion, sex, national origin, age, and handicap status is now prohibited. A section could also be added that would specifically prohibit any law or regulation that would purport to establish employer hiring or promotion goals or quotas based on sexual orientation, thus defusing one of the major fears of opponents of such legislation.

(2) Repeal all laws criminalizing or otherwise penalizing adult sexual behavior that is private and consenting and does not cause violence or physical harm. Included would be laws that prohibit an unmarried couple of any sex from having sexual relations or occupying a room for the purpose of having sexual relations, and laws prohibiting "the abominable and detestable crime against nature," which is usually interpreted to include oral sex, regardless of whether it is same sex or opposite sex, and anal sex. With the repeal of these

laws, employers would not have to be concerned about condoning criminal behavior, and many security clearance issues would drop away.

(3) Revise state family laws and divorce laws (McGee, 1984) to provide for a civil ceremony uniting any two persons legally for life in the same manner as marriage and to provide for all of the benefits and burdens of marriage, including rights to descent and distribution of estates and rights of property division upon severing the relationship. DO NOT call it "marriage." That word has significant theological implications, and there is no need to tread upon theology in creating these new structures. The churches have a perfect right—protected by the Constitution—to define marriage in the traditional manner and to marry only those persons who fit their standards. Do not try to force the churches to agree with what is happening, or to accept the new structure as having any theological validity. Allow the new structure to be totally civil in nature. Under these circumstances, employers would not have to struggle with such things as family coverage on health insurance, or inviting same-sex couples to family picnics and other events.

(4) In the divorce laws, look at redefining the term *adultery* and restructuring the grounds for alimony and divorce. As of now, in almost every state, adultery is given a specific interpretation dictated solely by theological imperatives. Establish a new ground for divorce or alimony that would encompass any sexual relations with any other person. This would be broader than adultery, and would clarify and solidify family structure considerably. Also, in North Carolina, for example, there is one ground for alimony that reads: "The supporting spouse has engaged in an unnatural or abnormal sex act with a person of the same sex or of a different sex or with a beast," N.C. GS 50-16.2(3). If that doesn't lump a lot of divergent concepts into one great sweep, then I don't know what does. It also leaves it entirely up to the judge to determine what is unnatural or abnormal. Further, if you read this language closely, it implies that there might be such a thing as a *normal or natural* sex act with a beast. Such absurd possible constructions of 19th century laws point to the need for review and revision of these concepts and a rewriting of these laws. These changes would probably be necessary in order to implement the third recommendation above and would give employers more of a sense of peace that they are not a party to adultery or family conflict. There are some employers who will not tolerate adultery or other unlawful family-related behavior in their ranks. Give these employers more of a comfort zone in this area if they are to be expected to employ gays and lesbians.

I urge the reader to thoughtfully consider the analyses that have been brought together in this book by Dr. Diamant, with an eye to how the legal system currently and legitimately (i.e., with approval of the courts and the legislatures) perpetuates discrimination against gays and lesbians, and further with an eye to whether this Lilliputian system of ropes and strings in the legal system should be undone; and, if so, exactly what needs to be done to rewrite the laws and to bring about a reinterpretation of the Constitution.

## REFERENCE

McGee, M. H. (1984). *Separation and divorce in North Carolina.* Charlotte: East Woods Press.

*Michael H. McGee*

# Preface

The question that probably must occur to or, more seriously, plague any author or editor of a volume that is intended to be scholarly, timely, and socially significant, is: is it? Thus prefaces often try to compel to the affirmative. Long before I structured the contents of the divisions and chapter topics of this book, I was certain that the subject, homosexual issues in the workplace, was timely and of such social importance that I brought the notion to the publisher in the barest form. I am grateful to say that they rushed an agreement to me on a title that represented an idea whose time is now. I soon received final confirmation in terms "Yes, do it" from an array of professionals whose views and abilities had been enriching in the past and, I am thankful to say, continue to be so in this book.

That there is stress in the workplace for your very "normal" white Anglo-Saxon Protestant heterosexual Jane and John is acknowledged by uncountable papers, books, articles, and workshops that do not even consider minority status. That there will be an intensification of stress situations for minorities is a pseudo-social given. That gays and lesbians have special minority status has been described elsewhere and in this book. So, if it were for nothing but exploring the stress of gay and lesbian workers within the work world, this book would deserve its place on a list of recommended mental health, psycho-social health readings. However, more than this major factor merits consideration. Issues that are core to the identity of any person must be examined from the particular position of the homosexual worker and career seeker, and include such fundamental concepts as fairness, self-esteem, economics, survival, the need and right to participate in the work force, and the need and right for a voice and basic identity in vocational systems. The list could continue with considerations that are vital to health, well-being, comfort, and security, which is not incompatible with that historical promise: the right to life, liberty, and the pursuit of happiness. In no way is the focus of this book trivialized, even in the seemingly most humble of its case illustrations. Perhaps James, the handsome, Chaplinesque, delicatessen waiter, is as compelling to that concept of the American dream as is Hollywood star Brad Davis or running back Dave Kopay or Congressman Barney Frank. Threatened in his workplace by the refusal of a "prominent" minister to be served by a homosexual, James recalls his anguish in terms of the fear of loss of job, loss of face, and loss of opportunity.

No one who opens this book will be surprised that there is an ongoing psycho-social crisis for gay and lesbian workers in most occupations, corporations, and institutions. The reader of this preface will have read this time and again in journals, magazines, and newspapers. I have used several news articles, pulled from a drawerful, to make some points in the first chapter and left many, perhaps better, illustrations unmentioned. Television has picked up on some of the more attractive cases, and on the day that this is being penned, Magic has quit professional basketball for good under pressure from a small (perhaps?) but intense group of players.

Is AIDS a homosexual issue in the workplace? This book says that it is in a number of chapters, all of which lead us to say that we (the editor *and* the contributors) wrote this book from a belief that there was a *hole* in the literature as far as such works were concerned and that there was a need for an accretion of research now. There was a need for a gathering of contributors with expertise and some immersion in industrial, clinical, medical, academic, legal, military, and sports settings, and even a deli, when one is attuned.

There are, then, really no lofty victims of historically punitive attitudes (which some would call bigotry or homophobia, and still others, convention—the way one is brought up), and none is insignificant. There are also no special towers of ivory from which one is judged, nor any rough field. So varied are the agencies of execution that you can just let your fingers do the walking through the yellow pages (which even classifies military organizations).

*Homosexual issues in the workplace* speaks to the nature or, perhaps more precisely, the variables that operate as forces when gays and lesbians must, as persons in an industrialized society, operate within the confines of the "heterosexually chauvinistic" shop. In doing so, this book becomes an invaluable centerpiece for papers scattered through the literature that deal with the special vocational issues and problems of gays and lesbians. For professionals, it will provide a major reference focus for scholars, researchers, clinicians, sociologists, legal practitioners, and human resource personnel. It is appropriate to a wide range of graduate and upper-level undergraduate courses in the behavioral and social sciences, counseling, and industrial/organizational psychology. The acuteness of this volume is borne out in the recent publication *Studies in homosexuality: A 13-volume anthology of scholarly articles,* edited by W. R. Dynes and S. Donaldson. The virtual absence of workplace issues and their psychosocial and clinical ramifications in such a dramatically large set of references is worth noting.

*Homosexual issues in the workplace* has enlisted the professional acumen and research talents of authors whose expertise is in the personal and interpersonal psychological reactions to human stress where sexual and social issues are involved. Their sensitivities and intellects are particularly attuned to crucial psycho-sexual issues that involve the problems of gay and lesbian career aspirations.

A foreword by Michael H. McGee, a former supervising attorney with the Equal Employment Opportunity Commission, establishes the seriousness of the matter and the enormity of the vocational plight of the homosexually oriented. The introduction (Part I) provides a review of the historical development of attitudes toward homosexuality, interspersed with anecdotal commentary on current psychological career implications.

The special circumstances that affect the employment of lesbians and gays call for a particular skill, knowledge, and focus. Counseling and the problems relating to discrimination in hiring and firing, and the feelings of victimization that are commonly perceived and ordinarily fact, are the major issues presented in Part II.

The major thrust of Part III comes from the emphasis on workplaces that have been especially troublesome and media attractive. One chapter deals with the helping professions, especially the medical, which has been targeted most recently for investigation and research because of the AIDS crisis. A chapter that may at first appear unusual because it deals with prisoners and homosexuality makes lots of sense when you realize that the place of incarceration is the place of employment.

Other chapters deal with traditional areas of employment that have provided major attention, debate, and anguish (media, church, schools, military, and sports).

A creature borne of our times—the AIDS crisis—is examined in Part IV. It is a crisis that has serious and tragic consequences for both the ill and the service providers. The section on special mental health problems of workers with AIDS is replete with research that explores legal issues as they relate to HIV-positive employees, current corporate practices, and policies related to human resources, mental health issues, and other psychological issues involving workers with AIDS.

The social psychology of homosexuality and the workplace is the focus of Part V. Three major issues are given emphasis: (1) the problem of the older homosexual employee; (2) the issues involved in "coming out" (personal reflections of an academician bring the situation to the forefront in dramatic and enlightening fashion); and (3) mental health and personal adjustment problems of the gay and lesbian employee.

Part V approaches the personality and mental health issues affecting the homosexual worker through the use of cases that reflect the experiences and astuteness of sensitive clinicians and researchers. While it is meant to bring this volume to a closure, it is also meant to be heuristically inspirational to the tasks ahead.

There are so many to thank for helping me get this book done that most, though greatly appreciated, could go unannounced. High on my list of recipients of appreciation are the contributors who have borne with me since the germinant notion. Authorities in their disciplines, they have been tolerant of my ideas and my ways. There are the myriad authors, theorists, and researchers whose works have given all of us reference and guidance and to whom I express gratitude. The library reference staff at the University of North Carolina, Charlotte, has been exceedingly good to me. To the university colleagues who listened to me, to talented students who pitched in, and to a number of activists, I give thanks. I also say thank you to the Psychology Department Chair and to Betty Cook, who made vital things available to me. Then, especially, thanks to Winifred Swinson, whose help in every phase of manuscript preparation has been superb and beyond the call. To Kim Buch who has given immeasurably both intellectual and personal support, thanks. Kate Roach (my former editor) and Ron Wilder (my current editor) were and are great. I extend thanks and respect to *The Charlotte Observer* whose news coverage was an invaluable source of information and to Rolfe Neill for his consideration and for the privilege of quoting him.

Not least, thanks to my family for the love that is the catalyst for anything valuable that may come from my effort.

*Louis Diamant*

Part One

# Introduction

Chapter 1

# Some Historical Perspective

**Louis Diamant**

Before motion picture actor Brad Davis died, and while he was suffering from the AIDS that brought on his untimely death, he remarked to the news media that the film industry was exceedingly repressive with regard to AIDS and homosexuality (and thus of course repressive to reason in these issues). He also reported that he had been, in his younger years, an aggressive drug abuser. For the purpose of this introduction, sorting out whether gay sex or drug abuse brought about his illness is not the most relevant part of that press interview. It is, rather, the surprise that the motion picture industry would be one that lacked tolerance for gay and lesbian sexual orientation because folklore has it otherwise. Cautious about promulgating conjecture, I brought my notions on Hollywood to some social psychologists who agreed with me and voiced surprise at Davis' comment. It is no surprise but rather common expectancy that the Church, the military, or even the Boy Scouts (I read somewhere that national Boy Scout leaders have said the ban on homosexual members rests in part on a section of the scout oath that requires members to be morally straight). But if Hollywood, that font of myths could be a myth itself—what then might work environments, not so imbued with a spirit and aura of sexual freedom, be in terms of repressive forces and stressors to gay and lesbian workers?

Today homosexual is a marginal term. Referring to issues it may have acceptability; as an adjective or noun referring to persons it may be considered pejorative. Current designates for those with the same sex orientation are gay and lesbian, while gay and lesbian issues are homosexual issues. History has shown us that there are differences for men and women, which implies also different explanations for sexual orientations and different outcomes for the genders. Lesbianism has been largely unreported by anthropologists as an institutionalized phenomenon when compared to the studies on male homosexuality. Socarides (1965) wrote that he had found no recorded case of lesbian entrapment such as had been common with males, although lesbian behavior has been prosecuted in the United States (*State of Louisiana v. Young,* 1976). Lesbianism, unlike male homosexuality, has never been a crime in England nor in most European countries. In the United States, most states have had proscriptive laws and many still do. (This includes my current state of residence, North Carolina, which only a decade ago brought a friend and colleague to trial for crimes against nature [homosexuality]). With careful selection of attorneys, the guidance of Julius Chambers, and the progressive attitude of the judge (no humor intended because prison terms for male homosexuality in North Carolina are not meant merely to frighten wayward youths), he pled guilty and received a five-year suspended sentence. He has since moved to California where he has practiced as a licensed clinical psychologist. Certain felonies precluded licensure and practice in the state in which he was convicted.

## THE EVOLUTION OF THE PERCEPTION OF HOMOSEXUAL BEHAVIOR IN THE JUDEO-CHRISTIAN EPOCH

Over the centuries, Western societies, in particular, have labored over the question of homosexuality (gay and lesbian sexual behavior). Under various governments, it has gone from criminal to noncriminal behavior and in religious dominated governments, it has been equated to sin and non-sin. In the domains of medicine, psychology, and psychiatry, the homosexual designation has gone from dementia to character disorder to neurotic to nonneurotic to nonmentioned in Diagnostic and Statistical Manuals (DSM) I, II, III, IIIR (American Psychiatric Association, 1952, 1968, 1980, 1987). All of this might seem like progress, but it has in essence been a nonliberating journey because it, like slavery, would have been better had it never begun. The residue from all these labels of contamination as we shall see, is a noxious burden. We have created a class of citizens always on trial, always suspect, always beggars for one crumb of equal citizenry. Nothing could more tragically dramatize or illustrate the gay person's tenuous grip on belonging than the AIDS-related assaults. Even in sports there is an agonizing ignorance and lack of sportsmanship. Following basketball superstar Magic Johnson's decision to play again, Tom Sorensen (1992) wrote:

> Some NBA players will be afraid to share the court with him, but they probably won't admit it.
>
> There is no disease quite like AIDS. If Magic had cancer, he would be beloved. But there are folks who believe AIDS is a punishment dropped directly from heaven.
>
> Many of them write letters to newspapers. Sometimes, they are illegible, though. Crayon is easily smudged. (p. 1B)

Under continuing player and public pressure, what could Magic do? He resigned, of course.

Each time the notion of social progress appears to signal the end of the sin, crime, and disease, a countermovement may bring out the notion of deja vu again directly related to the issues of this book. Last June, Presbyterian Church (USA) leaders rejected a report recommending that gays and lesbians enjoy full participation nationwide in the church. Reported the *Charlotte Observer,* "In North Carolina, Pullem Memorial Baptist Church was ousted last week from the Raleigh Baptist Association for allowing the formal union of two homosexual men, considering 'that no society can exist without a common core of values and acceptable limits'; the Raleigh Baptist Association concluded its statement on human sexuality. Into that atmosphere comes the Charlotte Area Clergy Association, intent on shifting the debate from whether homosexuality is a sin to how clergy can better care for gays and lesbians. 'Even if you do see it as a sin,' said Reverend Little, 'what are you doing to relate to the sinner?' Reverend Tremann, whose presbytery is not officially involved in the outreach, wanted the focus to be on *equal employment* (italics added) and pastoral care and not whether to endorse the ordination of gay and lesbian ministers" (Crum, May 12, 1992, p. 4A). And from Today's Quote (May 14, 1992): "It is an outrageous invasion of privacy. I want to find out what they think they are doing. I want to make clear to them that they need to stop this." Rep. Barney Frank, D. Mass, an acknowledged homosexual, saying he will ask Federal Emergency Management Agency officials to explain at House Judiciary Subcommittee hearing why they forced an employee to produce a list of homosexual coworkers (p. 7A).

Homosexuality has been reported as being at other times a celebrated event; for example, between males in Ancient Greece (West, 1967). Accordingly, homosexual relationships were encouraged with some restriction of the law in Hellenic society (West, 1967). Regarding lesbianism, the main point of reference for that sexual orientation appears to be the poet Sappho, circa 600 BC. It is from the celebration of female love on the Isle of Lesbos from which the noun *lesbian* came. For the record, and according to Dover (1978), it was probably a romanticized view of female love rather than overt sexual intimacy, that occurred. Nevertheless, if there was freedom for a homosexual ethic those so oriented were to be highly restricted by the Old Testament and the growing prominence of the Judeo-Christian ethic. The Christian Church, as well as the Jews, developed and promulgated attitudes that cast homosexuality in a despicable light (despite recent attempts to challenge the traditional position, Lovelace, 1978), and voiced the need for punishment for this behavior, i.e., Leviticus 20:13 "If a man is with a man as with a woman, both have committed an abomination, their blood is upon them." Szasz (1970) commented that only male homosexuality is forbidden and no references to woman lying with woman are made, which reflects the Bible's treatment of women as less than human. The legal statute of modern Western society, and indifferences to the prosecution of woman for homosexuality support a historical disregard for women (Diamant, 1987).

In more recent times we have seen at least some controversial positions regarding the participation of gays and lesbians in church membership, but ordination of persons with a known gay or lesbian orientation has got to be the rarest of occupational phenomena. Separately, theological Judaism has struggled with the Talmudic homosexual bias and their tendency toward liberalism. According to Matt (1978) this appears to have created a dilemma for the clergy and the homosexual Jew.

In the history of Western civilization, not only homosexuality but all sexual behavior has been restricted within a legal framework. The political control of sexual behavior is in most instances a consequence of the Judeo-Christian ethic. (Currently in the state of North Carolina, for example, not only is homosexual sodomy a crime, but so is heterosexual behavior between unmarried, consenting adults as well as oral sex in the marriage bed.) In Europe, ecclesiastical law incorporated ideas from the Jewish tradition, Christian teaching, and Roman law as a basis for criminalizing and punishing homosexual behavior with the prosecution of homosexuals directed mostly against males. A rare exception to the tendency to avoid entrapment and prosecution of females is seen in the affirmation of the conviction and sentencing of Mary Young and Dawn LeBlanc for unnatural copulation (*State of Louisiana v. Young*, 1966).

But entrapment apparently continues elsewhere. Recently I sat for jury selection for a case in which the prosecutor alleged that the defendant, who acknowledged his homosexuality, had, at a location frequented by gays, approached an undercover police officer for sex. An interesting number of prospective jurors were disqualified by the defense because of admitted prejudice toward gays as sinful or criminal. Interesting, too, was that the racial makeup of the jury shifted from an original nine whites and three African Americans to an exactly reversed final panel. (I was not called.) Only months later, in a restaurant I often frequent, a waiter named James told me that he was going to trial in a similar prosecution related to an incident at a city park urinal at which time he asked, "Are you sure you're not a policeman?" and was told, "Hell, I hate cops." When I asked if this incident was stressful, he said that he was a nervous wreck and that he had already visited a colleague who specializes in such stressed patients. And at the risk of having this sound invented, he also told me of his horror caused by hearing that a prominent minister had told someone in the restaurant owner's family that he did not want to be served by a homosexual who could give him AIDS. I asked James how he reacted when he heard this. "I felt rotten, how would you feel? I could have lost my job, I had just moved into a new apartment, how could I pay the rent? I'm just lucky that the people I work for understand."

In Europe, punitive attitudes toward homosexuality began diminishing under the liberalizing effect of the Napoleonic code. Today, most European countries no longer consider homosexuality in itself a crime if it does not include public indecency, coercion, or minors (West, 1967). Contributing to the change was a modern psychoanalytic theory that until recently said it was a disorder. Krafft-Ebbing (1922) wrote that homosexuality was the result of physical degeneracy and hereditary defects and both constitutional and a disease. Although Freud (1905/1935) did not see homosexuality as a disease or illness, he did think of it as a developmental phenomenon related to infantile sexuality while some disciples pursued it as a mental disorder (Bieber, 1962, 1976; Socarides, 1965; Socarides & Volkan, 1991). Because psychoanalysts and others in the practice of psychiatry were reluctant to give up the notion of homosexuality as a neurotic or personality disorder, its appearance as such may be seen in the first three issues of the Diagnostic and Statistical Manual of Mental Disorders (American Psychiatric Association 1952, 1968, 1980). An influential difference of opinion is not noted until its absence from codification in DSM IIIR (American Psychiatric Association, 1987).

The twentieth century then ushered in the scientific outlook on male and female homosexuality. The illness issue may well have been the scientific issue that brought the application of scientific principles in the fields of neuropsychiatry and clinical personality psychology to test that very concept of illness. The landmark study of Elizabeth Hooker (1956) was followed by scores of researchers using empirical methods that demonstrated, in part, that gay men and lesbians were not any different with regard to personality pathology from heterosexually oriented men and women. For a comprehensive review of the empirical input to the investigation of psychopathology and personality differences between heterosexual and homosexual subjects, I suggest Marvin Siegelman's (1987) review of the literature.

With all the pluses, where do the minuses show? According to George and Behrent (1988), speaking of gay mental health, "In addition to the normal stress in our society, the homosexual male is subject to other internal and external stresses due to homophobia, the irrational fear of homosexuality" (p. 81). According to the laws of homophobia, regardless of its historical journey into and out of diagnostic labeling, most homosexual males have been exposed to the insults accorded to men of such orientation whether addressed to them, someone else, or just overheard. And according to Gonsoriek (this volume) men themselves often buy into the homophobia with self-negation. In a recent personal ad in a Charlotte paper that carries personal ads for relationships of varying orientation, a female asked for a female companion for living, friendship, and intimacy, and stipulated "No Dykes." Sophie (1988) defined homophobia in terms of racism or sexism with emphasis on negative attitudes of all sorts. She elaborated that internalized homophobia represents an internalization of negative attitudes and assumptions regarding lesbianism. She compared this to societal homophobia, which encompasses the negative attitudes expressed by others in the individual lesbian environment.

There is then a consistency of opinion that gays and lesbians are under stress. There has also developed a large literature that says gay men and women are no different than other men and women, not so delineated, with regard to personality and emotional problems and illness. Martin and Hetrick (1988) adopt a minority group label for homosexual men and women, and using Allport's definition declare a minority group as one that suffers from unjustified negative treatment from the dominant group. In other words, the minority group is a victim of prejudice. Now it raises the question, "How can a minority group suffer unjustified negative treatment and remain its equal in mental stability?" For an answer I am reminded of Robert Coles' (1967) observation in *Children of Crisis: A Study of Courage and Fear,* in which he tries to sort out this very question involving African American children at the beginning of school desegregation in the South. (His dilemma comes in striking a balance between study of the contemporary as well as antecedents in the past and the treatment of symptoms, some generated by the present and some with a life of their own that largely ignore racial conflict.)

But prior to any postulates that structure the dilemma is an essential statement that clarifies the difference in an illness concept of Bieber and the stress concept of Gonsoriek. To Bieber and others who cling tenaciously to his point of view, homosexuality is a disorder in and of itself. In appraising their belief, it would be well to remember that in those of the old school and in DSM I, II, and III, there was such a diagnostic category and code. It is the diagnostic label applied to a person with the same sex orientation that is forced into an a priori psychiatric condition for the sake of etiology. Others, since Kinsey (Kinsey, Pomeroy, & Martin, 1948), see homosexuality as a condition of expected variation in orientation. In this view the consideration of a priori pathology is as erroneous as it would be in the condition of heterosexuality.

It might be wise to remember that there are many detractors of gays and lesbians who are not much concerned with crime, sin, or illness, at least not cognitively. Difference alone is enough to create antipathy, ridicule, and discrimination that has much in common with many other applications of prejudice and in many other forms of social distancing. Ross Perot, a billionaire, and an unsuccessful candidate for the U.S. presidency in 1992, did not fall on the undisguised formal defamation to justify, in an interview, his rejection of a homosexual person for a cabinet position, but stated simply that he would not want any person in that kind of position who could cause controversy or make others uncomfortable. Thus gays and lesbians were put on the alert that if their sexual orientation were known and if Ross Perot were to become president, and if they had aspirations for a certain kind of White House connection, they were out of this job market. Later he changed his mind, he said. It is apparent that not every boy or girl who aspires to become president of the United States or a cabinet member has by citizenship the papers in his or her portfolio for those vocations. Nevertheless, the labor to do that goes on. When a group that has been deprived of rights enters the political arena, it is its vow, stated or otherwise, that whatever the Constitution allows one citizen be available for its members. Thus when President Bill Clinton called on his out-of-the-closet long-time friend, David B. Mixner, for support, it did not come unqualified, according to Jeffrey Schmalz at the *New York Times Magazine* (1992). Mixner responded to Clinton: "Before I can get behind this campaign I have to know where you stand on this, where you stand on AIDS and our struggle for our freedom" (p. 18). Fortunately, like African American children (Coles, 1967), homosexual children are also not aware of their despised status until after they have had an opportunity to form some early family relationships that may allow them to face themselves and the stress.

We know that the human condition precludes the absence of stress. Modern corporate America spends a lot of money to reduce stress, the by-product of its occupations. These costs are to a large degree fitness programs to reduce work tensions and improve health (Falkenberg, 1987) and to reduce absenteeism (National Chamber Foundation, 1989). Stress has become a catchall word. It means what one wants it to mean and there is a general concurrence so that the dictionary usage and clinical usage and household usage are not far apart. The waiter I mentioned earlier called his emotional response to the unkind actions of an uninformed minister "stress." It might not be unfair to say that the waiter's presence as a food server caused the reverend some stress also. Of major interest to sports participants, athletes, coaches, and sport psychologists is the role stress plays in athletic performance (Diamant, 1991). It is fair to say that stress may leave one discomforted but not mentally ill. Nowhere is stress itself labeled a disorder but it is possible that stress may result in disorders as well as in death. Hans Selye (1956), to whom modern psychology, for better or for worse, is indebted for its introduction to the world of mental phenomena, did use it originally to deal with physiological phenomena and went so far as to describe an activity on which so many of us are dependent for the relief of stress, as a stress itself. "Even exhaustion does not always have to be irreversible and complete as long as it only affects part of the body. For instance, running produces a stress situation mainly in our muscles and cardiovascular system. To cope with this we have to limber up and get these organs ready for the task at hand'' (Selye, 1956, p. 54). Although originally Selye was basically concerned with stress as measured in physiological terms, he could not discard the role of the perceptual and learning processes and, like others, faced the difficulty of that term. Was stress the cause of an organism's adaptive changes or the thing that happened to a person? He decided that the stimulus was the stressor and that stress was the adaptive reaction. If we look at this syndrome, stressors can create adaptive responses and create a growth situation—provided the organ is not completely thwarted. Thus cold can create intellectual and physical activity in a coping response that creates a warmth seeking response if allowed. (Although it is a painful experience that we would not wish to, nor could endure indefinitely before moving to higher levels of adaptation.)

The point of this discourse is to bring our chronicle to date. Gay and lesbian people confirm as stress the painful experiences that exist occupationally. An unquantifiable portion of the pain reported is related to the negative workplace experiences incurred by the homosexuals oriented to being themselves. But stress, too, is the product of earlier adaptation related to abandoning the closeting and isolation that may be necessary to maintain normalcy, or what we sometimes refer to as mental health.

## THE WORKPLACE AREAN OF IDENTITY: ISSUES OF STRESS AND COMFORT

Savin Williams (this volume) has eloquently and skillfully brought to life and full dimension issues that could be kept suppressed or repressed. He is a scholar and an academician at a university of some renown. "Homophobia exists in my workplace," he says, and yet he discredits the alternative of being closeted, as he was for the first five years of his stay at Cornell. "There are risks," he says, "of being out on the job and they are the ones that every gay man and woman who enters the field of academic scholarship must face.'' I relate this to something that occurred a few years ago. I was invited by a scholarly press to write an Abnormal text. The project fizzled but because I felt the door was open with the publisher, I sent them a prospectus generated from a paper I had presented in Atlanta that related to issues of gay men and women involved in seeking psychological assistance. The editor welcomed the project, sent the prospectus out for review, and received a largely favorable response. Suddenly, and to my surprise, the editor sent me a page from a not-remembered journal that described what I would now call a homophobic attitude toward aspiring gay faculty. Thus, he reasoned, it would be a disaster to publish a book for the academic market. Happily another publisher was not mired in the same homophobic mess.

Of course there is a danger to assume that a reviewer's dissatisfaction with teaching or academic performance is based solely on sexual matters—but there is a good chance it is. I suspect from the above experience that not only is there a highly moralistic and social distancing directed at homosexuality, but also at all sexuality that goes too far beyond Judeo-Christian comfort. A recent and confusing encounter with administration in which I had applied to teach a particular class at a high, but generally acceptable fee, and had expected approval, brought that notion to the front. When I protested the refusal, I was told by chair that complaints by colleagues about my classes (they were always filled to the chandeliers and brought student teaching evaluations that were always enviable) were brought to support the denial. The major complaints were high grades and lack of seriousness. The weekly chair publication, which I have just received (*Headlines,* June 12, 1992), has this quote: "The arrival of a good clown exercises more beneficial influence upon the health of a town than the arrival of 20 asses laden with drugs" (Thomas Sydenham, 17th-century physician). Good for Sydenham, whose major medical work was the syndrome that bears his name (Sydenham chorea). He chastened people not to take too seriously and react not too punitively to the psychological symptoms and behavior disorders that accompany this organic illness (Kolb, 1968). However, the chair, whose views on academic freedom I respect, felt he should tell me of an encounter with higher administration about whom there is consensus that he rules the college fiscal system with an iron and clenched fist. The chair told me that upon discussing with him the course I might teach, that he suddenly and without specific introduction or using my name launched into an emotional discussion about professional morals. The substance was that even tenured professors were not immune from dismissal for immoral behavior and that in fact it had been done already. I know of no such dismissal. I did know from local newspaper accounts that a biology chairman had resigned his professorship following a reported sexual harassment charge against him by a male student. Just prior to putting these words on paper, I called the university personnel director to corroborate my belief about this issue. He concurred that it was the only case of sexual harassment on campus that ended in the resignation (or dismissal) of a tenured professor. The arrangement between the resigning individual and the university was that the details of the case would be unavailable for public information. But he agreed with my contention that male homosexuality raises a red flag to the guardians of academe. In the case of the biologist it would seem that an agreement to resign if lips or files are sealed forever could give some support to the notion of antipathy toward homosexuality, while the psychologists could affirm a more common sexual constringency that, laughingly detoxified, may be relieved in the sanctuary of the locker room.

Recently, and in a not too dissimilar view, a University of South Carolina president who was forced to resign following the reporting of some university fiscal and tax irregularities and illegalities, was later to give up his emeritus status only after newspapers reported that male students on whom some of the money was spent complained that he had patted their rears. When I met with one of this volume's contributors, he said something that surprised me—"When I read your book, and your being in North Carolina, I said, 'that guy's got balls!' " Now it begins to make sense: I, of emeritus age with an adored son of five whose mother is my beautiful partner and one-time student, who writes and does research in a concerned way on sexual orientation, sexual independence, and personal freedom, am "tainted" by my outlook, even though I have been assured I am really liked. It is possible that I am a nonserious teacher by the same codification that made me in a conversation, tangentially immoral.

To paraphrase Savin-Williams' remark (this volume), "I will never know to what extent their sexual phobias and repression have played a role in my academic career." Certainly sexual behavior of certain people has produced anxiety and both phobic and counterphobic reactions among the repressed. At the risk of being cited for throwing in the kitchen sink, I will relay one additional episode that, if not essential to this essay, may make an interesting adjunctive. In a recent visit to the university cafeteria, I was joined at my table by a person who, because of my recent emeritus status, might be called a former colleague. He is considered some sort of genius in science and engineering and as such enjoys, I am told, a very privileged salary status at this institution. We talk only on chance encounters and he is, maybe because of my personality or my profession, always provocative and challenging. When he learned quickly from me that I was still teaching and practicing, he wondered why. I said that I had still to earn a living as I had a preschool aged son. "More power to you" he retorted, with an ebullition far in excess of his usual pace. And rightly or otherwise, I told him that his remark could be considered a condescending and bigoted view of sexuality of older persons (in all fairness he is not young, just not retired). To support my view on the way institutions, customs, and prejudice affect a person's sexual orientation through the life span (older folks' sex is often treated with jokes or exaggerated congratulations that are still jokes), I told him about a reference work I was editing on the psychology of sexual orientation. He rushed in at the words "sexual orientation" with "they are abnormal and mentally disturbed"; to him, as it turned out, orientation meant homosexual. Obviously he was not only unaware of his bigotry and prejudice clusters but was also clinging to the old diagnostic criteria.

Relationships between personality types and bigotry were explored nearly half a century ago (Frenkel-Brunswick & Sanford, 1945; Frenkel-Brunswick, Levinson, & Sanford, 1952). Bigotry and prejudice and their effects, it appears, may be somewhat modified by social action and legislation. However, a question remains for psychology. How much can these personality types that are given to their biased attitudes be changed?

The thrust then of various disciplines in the social and behavioral sciences, in mental health, in education, and in religion, to name some of the areas addressed in this volume, must at least be bifurcated. One, we must work toward the relief of pain and its symptoms brought on by the contextual dissonance of having the gay or lesbian worker in an environment that does not consider and structure its programs, benefits, and social life as though a gay or lesbian had the right to thrive and grow, and two, we must deal with the personality factors and the homophobia that create or contribute to the chronic stress and emotional pain.

## SUMMARY

The preceding has perused the social-psychological history of gays and lesbians through the odyssey of categories from the label of "evil" that found its answer in governmental events as barbarous as the Inquisition in Spain (Szasz, 1970) to a tenuous normalcy in which prejudice without bars, executions, prison cells, and psychiatric denigration has brought homosexuality to near mainstream, but not without occupational hazard and stress. When I first conceptualized this project the plan had irony as its fuel. A young gay minister was referred to me by a colleague. Married, father of two with definite church respectability, a family man, he was on the staff at a church at which several friends, including my former in-laws, were members. This colleague had also referred another of his acquaintances to my practice who was a university dean who would not see anyone around his own base. These two men would and could not come out and maintain occupational tranquility, or as they believed, occupational status or tranquility.

In the ancient regime (before DSM IIIR), gay men in this situation would almost always seek psychiatric help so they could deal with the gayness that they would have been propagandized to believe was an illness, but an illness so akin to evil or blasphemy that it had received the same inquisitional treatment in 13th-century Spain. But the reverend and the dean were not of that cloth. Neither were repentant, neither wished change, only some help in understanding and dealing with the predicament of their social system. But they were different. Freed from the prepackaged diagnostic baggage and of orientation rearrangement it was a fact that one had a personality disorder and the other did not. Both suffered the terrors of a "wetback" waiting to be found and exiled. (I had such a Mexican client, he had become affluent, married with children, whose worst fears were realized when he was discovered and threatened with deportation.) The solution, or nonsolution, for the dean was to break off therapy, which I'd like to say he found threatening but more likely meaningless. I was told that he went back to an even more sexually predatory life and treated his wife even more unkindly and unfairly. The young minister made a very friendly arrangement for a divorce, and kept up his fatherly relationship with his young children even after he moved to Atlanta where he lives a gay life as a gay man. He does not work within the church but works at his second vocation of special education. I have seen him and talked to him a number of times since his move and as much as folks can be OK at his juncture of personal evolution, he is. And the major difference between then and now, according to him, is that he can be mostly who he is where he is. Am I now able to say that staying in the closet will lead to greater personal pathology or that coming out will bring about self-actualization and happiness? In this regard I will talk about another person. G is an excellent business woman, she makes money, and she is as ethically and personally considerate as anyone whom I know. She came to see me a few years ago suffering from tension anxiety and physical symptoms that she attributed to interpersonal conflicts that she could not resolve. Having had a course with me in the seventies, she knew what she was talking about. Out of her talks she brought something that she said was difficult for her to deal with or reveal. As she put it, "I like women." She also liked men. She liked and respected her husband and felt indebted to him for putting up with her moods and periods of heavy drinking (which she attributed to inherited family alcoholism). She really loved her young, athletically gifted son, she greatly admired the corporate head with whom she had a brief and amicably concluded affair. But she liked women with a passion that she did not find with men. She was not ashamed of this feeling but it was something about which she was not going to tell anyone else except the one woman who had been continually in her life since high school and the other, more recently. She was certainly not going to tell her boss and coworkers and deal with those repercussions. It wasn't anyone's business. She was not going to risk her family and security, she felt no push or wish in that direction. What really concerned her was the domination and intimidation she felt at the hands of the two women. The course of the counseling and therapy saw changes in her anxiety and depression in the lesbian affairs and more concern with business and the school and developmental issues concerning her son. The affair with one woman ended. It was an affair that was masochistic and neurotic, and its demise was related to her growing ego strength. As far as the relationship with her lifelong friend, that is at a much higher plane. I know because she came to see me recently after a hiatus of about six years. Her friend had visited her from the West Coast where she now lives, and some stressful things had occurred and she was not sure of her reactions. I thought that she handled the matter in a productively ego-syntonic way, earning the kudos that I uncharacteristically gave her.

At some time during those clinical situations, I read *The David Kopay Story.* It is in some parts a gothic tale of an American football star constantly in fear and constantly in terror of exposure. David Kopay is gay. Upon being taken to a gay bar by a woman when he was playing with the Detroit Lions, he cries out in terror, "How the hell do you have the nerve to bring *me* to a place like this? I realized that Maxine knew, and I suppose that's why I panicked at the bar. I knew I looked like the other football players and there was nothing wrong with my performance on the field, but there was still something about me that told her I was secretly homosexual. And if she could detect this, was it possible that other people could too? I could see myself ruined as a professional football player. I could see this as the end of my friendship with Alex Karas" (former all pro line backer) (Kopay & Young, 1977, p. 129).

In apparent, perhaps similar anguish, Dave Pallone (Pallone & Steinberg, 1990) writes about the letter that terminated his job as a National League baseball umpire. "I was distraught. None of the reasons was valid. . . . The reasons were camouflage for the real reason: I was gay, and they didn't want the publicity surrounding that to tarnish baseball's macho image" (p. 320).

Closer in time and place, all American power forward Christian Laettner of NCAA number one Duke University was questioned about his sexual propensities. "Monday Laettner denied widespread rumors that he is homosexual. Officials for several NBA teams, including the Charlotte Hornets, confirmed Tuesday they had already started looking into the rumors, as part of the usual research they do on potential draft choices. The rumors have followed Laettner much of his career and were raised in a *People* magazine profile and covered in an ESPN interview with him" (*Charlotte Observer,* April 1, 1992, p. 413).

It struck me that anyone in sports and who has changed his shoes in the men's or boys' locker room cannot have missed the ribaldry that not only reflects attitudes toward sex and women but also toward homosexuality. Life in the men's locker room can be torturous for the closeted gay but also for the inhibited non-sexually oriented young male (Diamant, 1970). A few years ago I taught a course on the psychology of sexual orientation that was largely attended by male university athletes with whom I worked and worked out. They are largely good-natured, but the lack of sensitivity with which they questioned the invited gay lecturers brought about some unwelcome tension. However, their reaction did not surprise me as did the reaction in the faculty room to some psycho-social studies I was doing with a group of lesbians. A good part of the faculty who use the locker room regularly are aging jocks, would-be jocks, and fantasy jocks, and outside of the locker room they are rarely if ever salacious. But the crudeness of their remarks concerning my research surprised me more than I anticipated.

*The David Kopay Story* led me to believe that Kopay had a contribution that he could make, a contribution toward understanding the stress factor involved in the volatile formula of sports and the locker room mentality and the gay athlete. I located him in Los Angeles and on the telephone he agreed to meet with Bob Barrett, my colleague and a psychotherapist whose intellect and emotion are especially attuned to conscientiously interviewing and doing the kind of reporting to put together a chapter on homosexual issues in sports (this volume).

Perhaps to this point, it appears that the weight of orientation bias is stacked in sports, education, and religion. That impression is very possible from my weighted experience in education, sports, and clinical psychology. Homosexual issues in occupation are truly quite pervasive and more so in some areas than in others. For example, farther from my guess about the film industry as a place of prejudice toward gays and lesbians, would be the newsroom. That is until Cose (1990) reported "Newsroom Homophobia." It came as a surprise because one of the most open and active pursuers of gay and lesbian rights in the city of Charlotte is Don King, who is a newspaper person and journalist.

I just assumed the newspaper business would not bog itself down in homophobia involving job and reporting discrimination. But on reflection, expecting entirely unbiased reporting defies the facts. Homophobic journalistic and reporting practices represent unstated disdain for homosexuality. So along with the more deliberate ostracism of gays and lesbians in the military and minorities are lesser defined homophobic issues in which the presence or absence of hostility to gays and lesbians has consequences ordinarily given little thought. The hostility need not be conscious and yet it may be. Cose notes that after the *Contra Costa Times* in Walnut Creek, California, gave front-page display to a gay freedom-day parade in Cali in San Francisco, copy editor Bill Walter declared in a memo, "Bad things, disgusting things in human beings happen . . . but we don't have to describe every naked person or show a photo of every dead body. The message was clear 'disgusting' things are better left off the front page." That is a dangerous mindset for a journalist, yet that spirit has affected coverage of gay issues and AIDS in particular. The article also emphasized an American Society of Newspaper Editors (ASNE) survey of gay and lesbian journalists by noting that more than 200 respondents felt their employers were tolerant of gays but nevertheless reported widespread homophobia in the newsroom.

I discussed this report with Don King. He responded from his own personal experiences at *The Charlotte Observer* that he felt no workplace stress once he had come out. I also talked with Mark Calvy, who is a business writer for *The Charlotte Observer* and a member of the National Newsroom Lesbian and Gay Journalist Association, and he said that *The Charlotte Observer* was not typical of newsrooms. This was basically corroborated in a personal communication by Leroy Abrams, who was coordinator of the ASNE project. The newsrooms were, like many other enterprises, some bad and some good, and he had experienced both. *The Charlotte Observer* has added individual rights and sexual orientation to the other equal employment categories and presents it as a workplace that is free from discrimination based on gay or lesbian sexual orientation. This does not, of course, eliminate homophobia, which like all phobias is a matter of personal psychopathology. It does, however, indicate that from the employees' position there is no blanket persecution of gays and lesbians in the newspaper business and that some publishers have come forward to address this aspect of vocational discrimination.

It is not intended that this section of the book review all areas where gay and lesbian issues involve working conditions and relationships. Other chapters look more deeply. It is designed to give some historical perspective to the issues that abound in regard to lesbian and gay people in relationship to vocational existence. Some focus is on the issues facing gays and lesbians who are dealing with the stress of their differences as they involve their career destinies, in another approach it may examine the way some career professionals act toward gays and lesbians. For example, within the church there is the struggle of the gay theologian to find ordainment and pulpit, while on the other hand there is the plight of the homosexual worshiper longing to be accepted and comforted by the denomination of his birth or choice. For example, the Catholic church "recently sanctioned Dignity, a national gay organization with chapters in most cities in the United States" (Diamant, 1987), and yet *The Charlotte Observer* (Stepp, 1992) reports "the Vatican has declared its support for discrimination against gay people in public housing, family, health benefits, and the hiring of teachers, workers, and military personnel." The report further states in a statement to U.S. Catholic bishops that homosexuality is an "objective disorder such as mental illness and that government should deny certain privileges to gay people to promote the traditional family and protect society." A Gallup Poll last spring showed the percentage of U.S. Catholics who favored equal job opportunities for gay people rose to 78% in 1992 from 58% in 1978. A dilemma in the church regarding both the priest and parishioner has certainly become pronounced though it is little researched. The health field, especially since the AIDS crisis, also has a double dilemma where gay patients and doctors appear to be subjected to negative feelings. A study of senior internal medicine and family medicine residents (Hayward & Shapiro, 1991) indicated negative attitudes and fear of AIDS patients, while a study in an underresearched area indicated that many physicians would not refer to a gay colleague (Pritchard et al., 1988). A final note, not because it is a fact but rather because it is an editorial reality. I was reading in the newspaper, "Board advises honorable discharge for gay aviator" (*Associated Press,* 1992, p. 4A) when the busboy looked over my shoulder and said, "Why don't they just keep their mouths shut?" Waiter James, whose case is discussed earlier, asked what he said and I told him. "You know he's gay," James said.

## EPILOGUE

The evidence that there are no final notes came in the form of the following essay by publisher Rolfe Neill just a few days before manuscript mailing (*Charlotte Observer,* August 30, 1992). I have subtitled it "Epilogue" (albeit temporary).

> Leon L. Clark is 72 and has lived here 58 years. For most of that time, he says, he has been a *Charlotte Observer* reader. He writes to protest a Dannye Romine column about a UNC Charlotte professor who left his wife of nearly three decades and three daughters to lead a homosexual life. Dannye's sympathetic conclusion about Bob Barrett: "He struggles with two things we all struggle with—becoming more fully ourselves and remaining true to ourselves."

Reader Clark sees it differently: "The most disgusting article ever published. You insist on pushing the queer lifestyle upon the American people, when less than 1% of the population follows this disgusting lifestyle. Why do we constantly have to be bombarded with what they do? It really is not something that we are interested in."

"My suggestion is to put them back in the closet and let them make a change back to decent ways of living. We don't care to read about it."

Similar letters reach us regularly.

Such reactions are reminiscent of the height of the black civil rights movement, when many whites wrote to say: I'm comfortable with the way things are and most blacks are, too, except for a few rabble rousers. Just ask your maid.

The time is now to confirm gay men's and lesbians' rights. How sad that one of our two major political parties should devote so much of the Republican convention to scapegoating this 5% to 10% of the population. It's not 1%, Mr. Clark.

Nor do gay and lesbian people "choose" their sexual orientation. Rather, as research suggests and most gays will tell you, sexual orientation *chooses them* at birth. Does anybody really think someone would, as a preferential matter, adapt a life fraught with hatred and vilification within his or her own country?

At last, the Christian church is giving compassionate attention to the issue. Not all churches, of course, but a growing number are turning from exclusion to inclusion, from condemnation to comfort. The matter is being conscientiously examined in Sunday schools, pulpits, and conferences. Reader Clark said the Dannye Romine column came up in his class at Oakhurst Baptist Church and that class members were unanimous with his view.

The *Observer* does not wish to offend customers, for they are the only reason we have a job. On any day thousands of readers and we are in disagreement on one issue or another. We try to present our views while respecting yours, giving extra consideration to letters and columns from dissenters.

Yet, we would be false to our heritage if we did not stand for something. One of our beliefs is that all people are equal and should be treated that way. This includes gays, a group of citizens who have long been pariahs. Ignorance and hatred, which are twins, account for much of the misinformation about gay people. When institutionalized through a major political party, gay-bashing is all the more frightening. The Republicans didn't frame an issue; they built a gallows.

The nation was captivated by AIDS victim Mary Fisher's account to the GOP as she sought in quiet eloquence to broaden delegates' understanding of the disease while opening their feelings to *all* so afflicted. Her red ribbon of camaraderie hung from her lapel. So did Barbara Bush's red ribbon show when seated in the presidential box, but it was gone when she rose to speak.

Employment and promotion at this newspaper are not a matter of sexual orientation, and a number of gays work here as they do at every Piedmont business. They contribute without incident alongside heterosexual employees. The almost exclusive majority of sexual harassment cases involving *Observer* employees are about heterosexual, and not homosexual, advances.

One of the myths about gays is that they recruit children. Most gays shun children for the same reason nongays do. A small organization that does advocate pedophilia stains all gays with a point of view most do not embrace.

Every school class contains gays. Yet, we do not teach acceptance. Instead, these young people are left to flounder in confusion as they confront a sexuality different from the majority. Greater understanding comes through articles such as Dannye Romine's. We aren't advocating gayness, but we do advocate knowledge. Especially necessary is the courage of people such as Bob Barret to tell their story. Professor Barret isn't a monster but a useful human being whose story is instructive to any willing to search for truth.

Love is an equal opportunity employer. Think what it would be like to be denied the right to affection and to show it publicly within societal bounds. Gays are our brothers and sisters and our children, literally. How could a party whose platform advocates right to life deny the nature born into that child? It's not really a theological or political question, but one of the heart.*

Since I started proofing this chapter in January 1993, the United States has a new president who has become embroiled in the gays in the military issue, driving home the temporary if not oxymoronic-like character of epilogues in matters of social evolution.

## REFERENCES

American Psychiatric Association. (1952). *Diagnostic and statistical manual of mental disorders.* Washington, DC: Author.

American Psychiatric Association. (1968). *Diagnostic and statistical manual of mental disorders* (2nd ed.). Washington, DC: Author.

American Psychiatric Association. (1980). *Diagnostic and statistical manual of mental disorders* (3rd ed.). Washington, DC: Author.

American Psychiatric Association. (1987). *Diagnostic and statistical manual of mental disorders* (3rd ed., rev.). Washington, DC: Author.

Associated Press. (1992, May 29). Perot: Some cabinet posts not for gays. *The Charlotte Observer,* 2A.

Associated Press. (1992, July 25). Board advises honorable discharge for gay aviator. *The Charlotte Observer,* 4A.

Bieber, I. (1962). *A psychoanalytic study of male homosexuals.* New York: Basic Books.

Bieber, I. (1976). A discussion of homosexuality: The ethical challenge. *Journal of Consulting and Clinical Psychology, 42*(2), 163–166.

Bonnell, R. (1992, April 1). Sexual issues worries NBA official. *The Charlotte Observer,* 4B.

Coles, R. (1967). *Children of crisis: A study of courage and fear.* Boston: Little, Brown.

Cose, E. (1990, April 16). Newsroom homophobia. *Time Magazine, 135*(16), 76.

Crum, D. (1992, May 12). Methodists uphold ban on homosexual behavior. *The Charlotte Observer,* 4A.

Diamant, L. (1970). Premarital sexual behavior, attitudes and emotional adjustment. *The Journal of Social Psychology, 82,* 75–80.

Diamant, L. (1987). In L. Diamant (Ed.), Introduction. In *Male and female homosexuality: Psychological approaches* (pp. 3–20). Washington, DC: Hemisphere.

Diamant, L. (1991). Athletic competition: Stress and performance. In L. Diamant (Ed.), *Psychology of sports, exercise and fitness* (pp. 119–137). Washington, DC: Hemisphere.

Dover, K. J. (1978). *Greek homosexuality.* Cambridge, MA: Harvard University Press.

Falkenberg, L. E. (1987). Employee fitness programs: Their impact on the employee and the organization. *Academy of Management Review, 12,* 511–522.

Frenkel-Brunswick, E., Levinson, D. F., & Sanford, R. N. (1952). The antidemocratic personality in reading in social psychology. In T. M. Newcomb & E. L. Hartley (Eds.), *Reading in social psychology* (pp. 636–646). New York: Holt, Rinehart & Winston.

Frenkel-Brunswick, E., & Sanford, R. N. (1945). Some personality correlates of antisemitism. *Journal of Psychology, 20,* 271–290.

Freud, S. (1905/1935). Three essays on sexuality and other works. In I. Strachey (Ed.), *The standard edition of the complete psychological works of Sigmund Freud.* London: Hagarth.

George, K. D., & Behrent, E. A. (1988). Therapy for male couples experiencing relationship problems. In E. Coleman (Ed.), *Psychotherapy with homosexual men and women* (pp. 77–88). New York: Haworth Press.

Hayward, R. A., & Shapiro, M. F. (1991). A national study of AIDS and residency training: Experiences, concerns, and consequences. *Annals of Internal Medicine, 114,* 23–32.

Hooker, E. A. (1956). A preliminary analysis of group behavior of homosexuals. *Journal of Psychiatry, 42,* 217–225.

Kinsey, A. C., Pomeroy, W. B., & Martin, C. E. (1948). *Sexual behavior in the human male.* Philadelphia: W. B. Saunders.

Kolb, L. C. (1968). *Noyes' modern clinical psychiatry.* Philadelphia: W. B. Saunders.

Kopay, D., & Young, P. (1977). *The David Kopay Story.* New York: Arbor House.

Krafft-Ebbing, R. von. (1922). *Psychopathia sexualis with special reference to antipathic sexual instinct.* A medico-forensic study (F. J. Rebman, Trans.). Brooklyn, NY: Physician and Surgeons.

Legal citation. (1966). *State of Louisiana v. Young*: 193 2a.

Lovelace, R. F. (1978). *Homosexuality and the church.* Old Tappan, NJ: Fleming H. Revell.

Martin, D. A., & Hetrick, M. D. (1988). The stigmatization of the gay and lesbian adolescent. In M. W. Ross (Ed.), *The treatment of homosexuals with mental health disorders* (pp. 163–184). New York: Harrington Park Press.

Matt, H. J. (1978). Sin, crime, sickness or alternative life style? A Jewish approach to homosexuality. *Judaism, 27*(1), 13–24.

National Chamber Foundation. (1989). *Determinants of employee absenteeism.* Washington, DC: U.S. Chamber of Commerce.

Neill, R. (1992, August 30). Gays deserve equal rights. *The Charlotte Observer,* 3C.

Pallone, D., & Steinberg, A. (1990). *Behind the mask: My double life in baseball.* New York: Viking Penguin.

Pritchard, J. G., Dial, L. K., Holloway, R. L., Mosley, M., Bale, R. M., & Kaplowitz,

H. J. (1988). Attitudes of family medicine residents toward homosexuality. *Journal of Family Practice, 27,* 637–639.

Schmalz, J. (1992, October 11). Gay politics goes mainstream. *The New York Times Magazine,* 18–21.

Selye, H. (1956). *The stress of life.* New York: McGraw-Hill.

Siegelman, M. (1987). Kinsey and others: Empirical input. In L. Diamant (Ed.), *Male and female homosexuality: Psychological approaches* (pp. 33–79). Washington, DC: Hemisphere.

Socarides, C. W. (1965). Female homosexuality. In R. Slovenko (Ed.), *Sexual behavior and the law.* Springfield, IL: Charles C Thomas.

Socarides, C. W., & Volkan, V. D. (Eds.). (1991). *Homosexualities: Reality, fantasy and the arts.* Madison, CT: International University Press.

Sophie, J. (1988). Internalized homophobia and lesbian identity. In E. Coleman (Ed.), *Psychotherapy with homosexual men and women* (pp. 53–66). New York: Haworth Press.

Sorensen, T. (1982, September 30). Why wouldn't Magic want to come back? *The Charlotte Observer,* 1B.

Stepp, L. S. C. (1992, July 17). Vatican supports denying certain privileges to gays. *The Charlotte Observer,* 3A.

Szasz, T. (1964). *The myth of mental illness.* New York: Holber.

Szasz, T. (1970). *The manufacture of madness: A comparative study of the inquisition and the mental health movement.* New York: Harper & Row.

Today's Quote. (1992, May 14). *The Charlotte Observer,* 7A.

West, D. J. (1967). *Homosexuality.* Chicago: Aldine.

Part Two

# Corporate Outlook

Chapter 2

# Lesbian and Gay Concerns in Career Development

**John E. Elliott**

## INTRODUCTION

It has now been almost two decades since the public became aware of the issues surrounding rights for lesbian/gay people (hereinafter abbreviated l/g) via the Stonewall Riots in June of 1969 (Adams, 1987). The riots, spontaneous protests, were triggered by a police raid on an l/g bar in Greenwich Village in New York City. This was the beginning of the fight for civil rights for l/g people, a time to come "out of the closet" and become more open about one's sexual orientation. As part of this relatively new openness, there have been some substantial gains in both civil and employment rights (Bamford, 1989); however, despite this, little emphasis is now placed on career counseling with l/g clientele (Hetherington, Hillerbrand, & Etringer, 1989). In fact, the subject is notable in its absence from many of the better known texts in career counseling even though many of the same texts contain excellent sections on counseling culturally different minorities. This book seeks to remove this inequity by treating the problems of l/g people as a totally separate group. This chapter delineates the issues involved in career development and counseling with l/g clients and suggests how counselors can better address the needs of this population.

Before 1969, the subject of l/g clients was not totally absent from the literature. Brown (1975) gives a case review of articles written from the 1940s to the early 1970s and makes an initial attempt to classify l/g clients into four categories of vocational adjustment: the "Successful Professional," the "Under-employed," the "Craftsman," and the "Professional Homosexual (Brown, 1975, pp. 245–246). In the mid-1970s, the author posed many of the same questions that are in the literature today, but, apparently, the social climate was not right for other authors to commit themselves to comment or research on the issue. Brown also reported, as an example of the kind of discrimination that existed before Stonewall, a 1950 investigation of the employment of homosexuals in the government by a U.S. Senate committee. The committee concluded that homosexuals were not suitable for government employment because they were immoral and a security risk. This report was designed to make various government units more aware of the "dangers of homosexuality."

Canon (1973) pointed out that until the era directly following Stonewall, career counselors did not address l/g issues because so few l/g people were willing to be open about their sexual orientation. Canon cited, as an example of one of the reasons why l/g people were so reticent, a convention presentation of a paper on l/g issues. Keeping in mind that this was in the early 1970s, the career counselors and placement officers at this convention were asked to indicate by a show of hands whether they would be willing to have, as a *counselor-colleague,* a qualified individual who happened to be l/g. Approximately 25% of that fairly large group answered affirmatively. If the 75% of this group who answered negatively is considered representative of career counselors as a whole, then it is little wonder that few lesbian or gay clients feel comfortable addressing their sexual orientation with career counselors.

With the changing sociopolitical climate in the last several decades, more l/g people have found it either necessary or desirable to be more open about their sexual orientation on the job. One result of this new accessibility is the possibility of assessing some of the vocational needs and difficulties that pertain to this group and to give some thought to ways to alleviate problems. The career development issues that will be examined are cultural minority status for l/g people, training for students and practicing career counselors in l/g issues, employment discrimination, decisions with respect to openness about sexual orientation in the workplace, differences in career counseling issues among lesbians, nongay women, gay men, and, finally, factors related to age.

Before examining the actual process of career development, this chapter poses a framework for career counselors to consider l/g people a *nonethnic, cultural minority* and to prepare for working with them in similar ways to counselors preparing to work with any minority group. Counselor attitudes toward any minority group should be examined in preparation for working effectively as a cross-cultural counselor. In some regards, l/g people are a separate subculture similar to other racial or ethnic minority group subcultures. Career counseling with l/g clients involves considering the part that minority status plays in the employment discrimination faced by l/g people, the very real impact that this discrimination has on the decision to be open on the job about one's sexual orientation, and the problems faced within the work world by l/g people of different ages and genders. Finally, concrete suggestions will be given for working effectively with this clientele and providing badly needed services.

## CAREER DEVELOPMENT ISSUES

### Cultural Minority Status

Increasing attention has been devoted recently to the needs of minority clients (Herr & Cramer, 1988). It would, perhaps, encourage clearer thinking on the subject for counselors to regard l/g clients as members of a *nonethnic, cultural minority* group, keeping in mind the very real effects of minority status in the workplace. Herr and Cramer (1988, p. 154) commented that it is crucially important for counselors who provide career services to special populations to reduce the "stereotypes, discrimination, environmental barriers, and other forms of bias that typically impede the development of such groups." They further recommended that, in order to counsel a member of a culturally different minority (in this case, an l/g client), counselors should be familiar with the culture of the client. This familiarity is to be accomplished through changes in counselor beliefs and attitudes, education, increases in knowledge, and sharpening of skills. Buhrke (1989) suggested that lesbian women and gay men be included with various minority groups in courses on multicultural counseling in order to facilitate counselor training. In order for any career counselor to adequately be a part of career development with an l/g client, that counselor must be aware of the legal prohibitions (Achtenberg, 1985; Hedgpeth, 1979/1980; Schmitz, 1988) in particular professions, levels of discrimination against l/g people in particular professions, and discrimination at particular levels within professions.

For instance, consider the young person who either shows on an instrument or indicates in another way a preference for military service. In the absence of any information regarding sexual orientation, one set of possible alternatives might be presented to the client; however, if this is an l/g client, an entirely different set of options might be presented. The antipathy with which the military has treated l/g people is well known (McCrary & Gutierrez, 1979/1980) and continues to be a current matter in the news. (President Clinton's views toward lifting the ban on lesbians and gay men in the military may change the advice career counselors have to give l/g clients.) If another l/g client were to show an interest in food service, given the current fears in the food industry over gay employees who may or may not be spreading the virus that causes AIDS, a different course of development may proceed. This in no way implies that a career counselor makes decisions for or discourages a client, only that information regarding discrimination among and within professions be part of a realistic career development process in the same way that information about possible environmental barriers might be provided any other minority client.

Drawing from guidelines set down by the American Psychological Association, Herr and Cramer (1988) indicated that a professional helper who wishes to become culturally skilled as a counselor should become aware of his or her own cultural heritage and the values and biases that arise from that heritage, comfortable with differences (sexual orientation among them) that exist between counselor and client, and sensitive to personal circumstances that would indicate the need to refer a client to someone better able to fulfill that client's needs. For an l/g affirmative approach to career counseling, counselors should become aware of sociopolitical issues (discrimination) of importance to the l/g community, specific knowledge and information necessary to l/g clients (receptiveness in certain professions), and institutional barriers (possible restrictions on l/g people being in the visible, higher levels of certain professions) that oppose l/g people in the world of work. Fassinger (1991) gave a comprehensive list citing concrete suggestions for counselors who wish to become skilled at l/g affirmative interventions with their clients. Most of these are included here. As a group, l/g people have their own history, culture, ethics, jargon, and sense of community. Counselors who have l/g clients need to become aware of both how l/g culture is different and how it is the same as the prevailing national culture.

Fassinger (1991), Hetherington et al. (1989), and Paul (1982) perceived lesbians and gay men as a "nonethnic" minority. Paul noted that l/g people who are recognized as l/g by the straight (heterosexual) majority are treated as a minority whether they wish to be or not. This includes the world of work. Lesbian women and gay men are distinct in some ways from the majority community in which they were raised and suffer the oppression inflicted on many minority groups. Cooper (1989) delineated some of the group characteristics: lack of civil rights, secret or semisecret lives, oppression, rejection or ostracism by family of origin, societal censure, lowered self-esteem due to internalized anti-gay feelings, physical violence, and objectification by campaigns of hatred and vilification. Add to these characteristics the "coming out" process that involves l/g people in coming to terms with the true nature of their sexual orientation and the possibility of disclosing that nature to others. McDonald (1982) viewed coming out as an "arduous developmental process that may extend well into adulthood" (p. 54). It is an ongoing process that must be reexperienced to some degree throughout the life cycle whenever a new person enters an l/g person's life. It is a life event unique among minority groups in one respect: l/g people are probably the only group where the family of origin has to be informed about their family member's minority group status, in other words, membership in the l/g community. This presents a powerful cohesive experience for the group—a rite of passage.

All of these factors affect not only the private lives of l/g people but also their work lives. These factors affect whether an l/g person is willing to change geographic locations in order to accept employment or promotion, to mention one of many possibilities. A person who lives in a liberal, progressive part of the country might well view a job move to a more restricted area where there is more discrimination with great anxiety. This anxiety may be similar to the anxiety faced by other minority groups, chiefly racial. Given the current conflicts over the basic rights of l/g people in the states of Oregon and Colorado, which have recently been in the national news, it might be understandable if one's l/g clients viewed relocating to those states with a sense of uneasiness. Similar initiatives promised in other states may add further geographical considerations.

### Counselor Attitudes

Masters and Johnson (1979, p. 247) have stated that if l/g clients expected the worst of the health-care delivery system "they would rarely be disappointed." The available evidence seems to extend this statement to the mental health delivery system as well. Dulaney and Kelly (1982), Coleman (1982), and DeCrescenzo (1985) all speak to the negative attitudes shown toward l/g clients by clinicians. Numerous studies, both large and small, over the last 20 years consistently point out ambivalent feelings among professional helpers of all disciplines (Gartrell, Kraemer, & Brodie, 1974; Rochlin, 1982; Rudolph, 1988; Thompson & Fishburn, 1977). Canon's (1973) comments extend this back into the early 1970s. Given this data, it should come as no surprise that up to 50% of l/g clients have reported discontent with their professional counseling experiences (Bell & Weinberg, 1978; Rudolph, 1988; Saghir & Robins, 1973). Rudolph (1988, p. 166) indicates that counseling professionals "hold divergent opinions regarding the acceptability of homosexuality, with as many as one-third in many samples expressing negative attitudes."

These negative attitudes are embodied in the concepts of heterosexism and homophobia. Heterosexism is an attitude or set of beliefs that views heterosexuality as the only normal mode of expression of romantic-sexual expression while relegating homosexuality to immoral, inferior, sinful, or perverted status. Homophobia (Weinberg, 1972) is an irrational fear or hatred of homosexuals, same-sex feelings, or the perceived homosexual "lifestyle." Homophobia is sometimes used in a more generic sense to refer to all forms of l/g oppression. (While these are useful definitions, there exist many similar definitions of homophobia and heterosexism.) Such attitudes are part of the environment in which both heterosexual and l/g people are raised and, as such, represent prevalent attitudes in student trainees as well. Commitment to the education and training about l/g people in career counselor training programs is one comprehensive way to deal with such an ingrained, prejudicial mindset.

### Counselor/Student Training

Although the percentage of l/g persons who seek counseling is estimated to be two to four times higher than the rate for heterosexual clients due to the arduous nature of "coming out" and the ongoing experience of persecution (Bell & Weinberg, 1978; Rudolph, 1988; Saghir, Robins, Walbran, & Gentry, 1970a, 1970b), counselors of all disciplines receive little or no training or education in this area. It has been estimated that at any given moment in time, 10% to 15% of the population is predominantly lesbian or gay (Fassinger, 1991; Fischer, 1972; Kinsey, Pomeroy, & Martin, 1948; Kinsey, Pomeroy, Martin, & Gebhard, 1953; Reinisch & Beasley, 1990). A somewhat smaller percentage of the total population has had exclusively homosexual experience for their entire lives; however, a larger percentage has had heterosexual experience early in their lives and gone on to develop their l/g identities in adulthood. Taking all this into account, at any one moment in time, given a population of 250 million in the United States, somewhere between 25 and 37.5 million l/g people reside in this country. If, in fact, 25% to 65% seek therapy (Rudolph, 1988), there may be as many as 15 million l/g clients in the mental health system: however, mental health professionals sometimes report a total absence of that clientele from their caseloads (Dulaney & Kelly, 1982).

Perhaps the first role that career development has is to adequately train its counselors to deal with l/g people. Iasenza (1989), Buhrke (1989), and Buhrke and Douce (1991) commented on the lack of counselor training in l/g issues and called for an integrative approach on issues of sexual orientation both in training and in research. Though their work addressed the counseling community as a whole, it is possible to extend their suggestions to career counseling as well. Inclusion of l/g issues in courses that train career counseling students to deal with minority counseling would contribute to an enlightened educational climate. Provision of inservice programs in practica and internship programs by professionals who are already trained would also be beneficial. Seeking supervision from an educated, enlightened l/g-affirmative career counselor could be most helpful, but obtaining supervision from an openly l/g career counselor who is already working in the field is perhaps the most beneficial educational experience, especially if the student or professional has not previously known an l/g person who is also a professional. This could go a long way toward attitude adjustment.

Extending Iasenza's (1989) and Buhrke and Douce's (1991) suggestions to career counselor education would indicate the value of developing additions to existing course work such as those on counseling techniques, counseling different genders, and counseling minorities. Becoming aware of the jargon of the l/g community and of semantic traps into which one can fall is similarly useful.

Even in enlightened and well-meaning articles like Schmitz [illegible] problems can occur. Schmitz refers to sexual orientation as [illegible] ence'' and as a ''private, personal decision.'' He implies that sex[illegible] is what a client chooses rather than what a client is. The use of suc[illegible] such an idea, no matter how well meaning, may sometimes have un[illegible] consequences when dealing with an l/g client, with the following caveat. [illegible] calling sexual orientation a ''choice'' has been used to oppress l/g people, [illegible] close examination of the literature (Faderman, 1985) and an ear to clients' [illegible] experience, particularly lesbian clients, indicates that there are some l/g identified people who do experience some degree of choice. Generally these choices revolve around the ''politically correct'' stances of some people in the radical feminist movement (Faderman, 1985). This is a complex issue; therefore, to say that sexual orientation is absolutely never about choice is incorrect. In view of the intricacies and complexities surrounding l/g issues, an important task for educators is the location and encouragement of opportunities for career counselor trainees to gain practicum experience working with l/g clients or other l/g professionals. Myths, fears, and stereotypes can then be subjects discussed in supervision. Finally, simply providing an educational environment conducive to l/g faculty and students being able to be open about their identities will yield an opportunity for open discussion among people of differing sexual orientations within the educational setting. Such open dialogue might help to alleviate, both in trainees and faculty, the negative attitudes about l/g people that are so prevalent in our culture.

Buhrke (1989), Buhrke and Douce (1991), and Norton (1982) pointed out the value in educational programs of using lesbian and gay problems as illustrative cases of counseling concerns. Their suggestions can be extended to career counseling. Educational information regarding l/g people can be provided along with specific information regarding specific topics such as AIDS and homophobia. The contribution of both homophobia and heterosexism to career or personal counseling can be discussed. As part of this educational effort, information about the very real problems on the job produced by discrimination is a necessity.

## Employment Discrimination

Hetherington et al. (1989) reviewed the work of several authors who emphasized that career development is one of the most constructive ways that counselors can assist l/g clients in improving their quality of life. Herr and Cramer's (1988) review of Super's theory spoke to the entire concept of the meaning of work with respect to individual self-esteem and quality of life. Work and job satisfaction are seen as cognitions linked to other cognitions such as work alienation, job involvement, and life satisfaction. A client's occupation becomes integrally related to these concepts; therefore, the role of career guidance and development becomes one of the primary means of offering service to this or

Essay use to prove the career discrimination toward Employers & how they r affected.

tegies of preparing to serve any cultural ge base of the concerned professional. In come aware of prejudice as a factor in

ality for l/g clients. Discrimination acts ons. The top three stereotypic gay male decorator, and nurse, and the top three are doctor, engineer, and photographer et al., 1989). Thus, discrimination may g people *believe* are open to them. With at large, a Gallup Poll (1987) revealed veyed believed that l/g people should not be hired as sales persons (20%), armed forces personnel (37%), doctors (42%), or elementary school teachers (60%). Such opinions were strongly conditioned by age, education, and religious affiliation. People under 50, the college educated, Catholics, and nonevangelicals express more liberal views than their opposite numbers. Southerners, on the other hand, "were opposed to legalization of homosexual relations by a 3-to-1 ratio, reflecting the large evangelical population there" (Gallup Poll, 1987, p. 12). Note that in all these statistics l/g people had to have been included in the sample unless some care was taken to eliminate them (no mention is made of this). Little is known, therefore, of what a general, heterosexual sample thinks about l/g people although one could imagine that the negative opinions might be higher for a totally heterosexual population. The importance of geographic consideration with respect to l/g clients was reinforced by findings presented in Hetherington et al. (1989). The authors indicated that certain parts of the country have substantially larger l/g populations than others. They conjectured that this relationship between geography and l/g community size may assume greater importance for l/g clients than for heterosexual clients, in other words, heterosexual clients may be less reliant on geographical issues when selecting careers or employment locations.

Schmitz (1988) indicated that only 16% of the l/g population outside the state of California were covered by personnel policies espousing nondiscrimination on the basis of sexual orientation. Fassinger (1991, p. 162) stated that "employment protection exists for gay people in 13 states, 17 counties, and 63 cities as of this writing." The National Gay and Lesbian Task Force (1986) recognized 11 states as possessing some degree of protection for l/g people. This coverage varied greatly from state to state. For example, recently one well-known restaurant chain that owns more than 90 restaurant/gift shops located mostly along interstate highways in the Midwest and Southeast and that advertises itself as catering to families, fired all of its known l/g or bisexual employees stating that they "fail to demonstrate normal heterosexual values which have been the foundation of families in our society" (Kaupman, 1991). Some l/g employees who were not identified by their employer as being homosexual reported to the author that their decision was whether or not to deny their orientation, and therefore themselves, by crossing the picket lines composed of l/g people, their friends, and their families. These unidentified l/g employees saw their only alternatives to be losing their jobs and thereby remaining true to themselves or keeping their jobs and thereby negating themselves and losing their acceptance by their l/g communities. Fortunately, the pickets prevailed and the company relented, but this is only one story and only partially successful at that. The pain reported by l/g people forced to confront such choices was substantial.

As far as corporate discrimination goes, the National Gay and Lesbian Task Force (NGLTF) maintains a list of companies that have stated a position relative to the sexual orientation of employees (NGLTF, 1989). Beginning in 1976, NGLTF surveyed more than 850 firms: the Fortune 500 (the top 500 American industrial corporations), along with more than 350 leading nonindustrial firms involved in areas such as finance, insurance, retail sales, etc. The purpose of the survey was to encourage major American corporations to adopt nondiscrimination policies based on sexual orientation. To date, 238 companies (28%) have responded, most answering with statements that indicate a knowledge that an employee's sexual orientation is a private issue unrelated to job performance. Though we know little of the 72% that chose not to respond, it is difficult to see this in a positive light. Interested parties can write for this list free of charge to NGLTF, 1517 U Street, N.W., Washington, DC 20009. Anyone doing career guidance with l/g clients should be in possession of this information.

NGLTF grouped the responses into six categories: companies that state specifically that they do not discriminate on the basis of sexual orientation (42%); those that do not discriminate unless sexual orientation interferes with job performance, disrupts other employees, or adversely affects the company (19%); those that say they hire and promote employees solely on the basis of their ability to do the job and make no specific mention of orientation (19%); companies that state they are not aware of or do not inquire about an employee's sexual orientation (4%); those that do not express any willingness to establish a policy against discrimination in those localities where there is no such legal protection of gay employees (13%); and companies that either did not comment directly on the issue or did not provide enough information for categorization (4%). Expressed in terms of numbers of employees, nearly three million of the nine million employees of the Fortune 500 companies are currently not covered by sexual orientation, nondiscrimination statements.

One thing that would provide a great service is for more career counselors to poll local employers on their personnel policies with respect to l/g people and to make their own registries like those listed in Bamford (1989) and Hetherington and Orzek (1989), and to network with other career development professionals to share this information. Just the simple act of having a career counselor check into personnel policies may have a positive effect. At least employers will be aware that the eye of the professional community has been focused on them. Bamford reported that some college counselors have been willing to poll local employers on their own to get an idea of the environment prospective l/g employees face. After increasing the knowledge base concerning the cultural differences between l/g and heterosexual clients and gathering information with respect to job discrimination, the task of dealing with the real client presents itself.

### The First Decision: To "Pass" or Not to "Pass"

Although it is increasingly more common for clients to be forthright about their sexual orientation with career counselors, it is certainly more likely that they will not be. One strategy that can increase the likelihood of openness is to have a published, visually prominent policy in the office denouncing discrimination of all types, including sexual orientation. A posting of a statement of the national organization of which the career counselor is a member (e.g., American Psychological Association, AACD) may be sufficient. Another strategy might be to have books with prominent titles on l/g issues obviously displayed on the bookshelves in a counselor's office. Clients in the author's own experience commonly report scanning the offices of counselors to get some clue as to whether they would be receptive to disclosure of the client's sexual orientation. It is also important that career counselors do not assume that their average clients are necessarily heterosexual. If questions asking whether issues surrounding sexual orientation with respect to employment are of concern to the client are made a routine part of any assessment interview, the likelihood of getting that information is increased.

Given that a client is l/g, one of the primary issues becomes whether or not that client wishes to be open on the job about orientation or wishes to "pass." The concept of "passing" embodies the fact that homosexuality can be hidden from others; despite misconceptions to the contrary, few l/g people can be identified by appearance or mannerisms (Goffman, 1963). The decision on whether or not to pass as a heterosexual is a major life task. Every individual must make a decision as to how to manage an l/g identity. With respect to career planning, a counselor can assist an l/g client with this decision, keeping in mind the following information. Berger (1982) commented that passing leads to poor self-concept and other emotional problems. It encourages the internalization of negative concepts (Weinberg & Williams, 1975), but public attitudes toward l/g people make passing a realistic adaptation. It can, however, lead to the development of a belief system that devalues the client. Over the years, these devaluations of self can have a cumulative, negative effect (Fischer, 1972).

Passing is reminiscent of the "pawn" behavior described by deCharms (1975). It is a reactive rather than a proactive measure. In pawn behavior, the locus of control is external in that the client feels at the mercy of environmental forces. The opposite behavior in deCharms' nomenclature is "origin" behavior where the locus of control is internal. In moving a client from pawn to origin behavior, a career counselor can teach decision-making skills. These can be particularly employed at this point by l/g clients with respect to their decisions to be open or not. No matter what the decision, there are attendant risks. Helping the client explore the risks and applying problem-solving, decision-making strategies (Jepsen & Dilley, 1974; Remer & O'Neill, 1980) to the encountered environmental barriers (job discrimination, personal consequences of passing, etc.) is a tremendous contribution that a career counselor can make. Clients may need help with recognizing problems at environmental barriers on the job and at becoming more assertive and setting goals with respect to identity questions in the world of work. Once the basic issue of passing is explored, the counselor can move on to other issues.

### Gender-Related Issues

To some readers who are familiar with the literature on counseling women (cf. Betz & Fitzgerald, 1987; Fitzgerald & Crites, 1980; Harmon, 1978), many of the concepts and suggestions on counseling l/g clients may sound familiar. Of course, lesbian clients have not only the career disadvantages shared by all women, but also the added societal stigma of their lesbianism. Gay male clients, while having the advantages society extends to males, also suffer the stigma of their homosexuality. The many articles that have appeared in the literature in the last several decades with respect to raising counselors' consciousness, combatting stereotypes, encouraging client assertiveness, increasing counselors' knowledge, and dealing with ". . . the obstructive effects of traditional role definitions and reactive decision-making. . ." (Fitzgerald & Crites, 1980) to name a few concepts, apply equally well to l/g career counseling. Browning, Reynolds, and Dworkin (1991), Hetherington and Orzek (1989), and Morgan and Brown (1991) commented on the difficulties that lesbian women have with multiple minority status (female and lesbian), negative stereotypes with respect to status in both minorities, and with issues surrounding both gender and career. If a lesbian is a member of more than two minority groups, if she is also of a different racial or ethnic group, or if she is physically challenged, overlying layers of job discrimination must be taken into account when assessing employment possibilities. There is an obvious need here that can be addressed by counselors in general and career counselors in particular.

L/g people are not a homogeneous group. Neither should gay men and lesbian women be necessarily lumped together when considering them in career development. Etringer, Hetherington, and Hillerbrand (1990) found that in their survey that compared heterosexual women and men with lesbian women and gay men, gay men have the greatest uncertainty about their vocational choices and are also significantly more dissatisfied with their choices than are either nongay men or lesbian women. Lange and Elliott (1990) indicated that for many lesbian women, acknowledging themselves as lesbian involves a total redefinition of self and a rejection of socialized prejudices. It can also mean relinquishing numerous heterosexual privileges acquired through identification with men particularly in relationship contexts, including status and economic advantages. This process is experienced differently by each lesbian woman depending on her specific circumstances. Three of the primary differences between lesbian women and gay men to be taken into account when considering career counseling are: (a) the increased likelihood of the presence of children in the homes of lesbian women; (b) the differences between sex-role socialization of men and women in general; and (c) lower projected earning power of lesbians with respect to gay men. Harris and Turner (1986) cited several studies that indicated that the number of lesbian mothers in the total population ranges from 200,000 to three million. As many as one and a half million lesbian mothers reside with their children as a family unit. The number of households headed by gay fathers is fewer. There may be many reasons for this, but, even though times may be changing, custody still generally goes to the mother. Harris and Turner (1986) indicated that there may be as many as 14 million children of l/g people in the United States; therefore, career counselors should not exclude inquiries into parental concerns or responsibilities with l/g clients under the mistaken assumption that l/g people do not have family responsibilities. Lesbians seem to be more often heads of households than their gay male counterparts. Bozett (1989) commented on the differences in earning power between gay fathers and lesbian mothers. In the studies he reviewed, lesbian mothers made between 52–55% of the salaries of gay fathers. This is supported by the fact that women in general earn less than two-thirds of that of men (Worell & Remer, 1992).

The interdependence of careers and relationships is also an important issue to many l/g people (Browning et al., 1991). Because l/g relationships are not validated by society at large, many l/g couples face this lack of validation in addition to the same dual-career issues that face heterosexual couples. This lack of validation restricts the support or assistance these couples can get to deal with their issues. Career counselors can help their l/g clients explore their occupational options, including dual-career issues, and differentiate between unrealistic and realistic fears.

Hetherington and Orzek (1989) and Morgan and Brown (1991) discussed the difficulties encountered in the work world by both lesbian and heterosexual women. Along with Betz and Fitzgerald (1987), they discussed how the female socialization process trains both groups to be passive, dependent, and other-oriented. Hetherington and Orzek (1989) discussed several unpublished studies that indicated that employers may perceive women as less committed than men to their jobs. Employers may often believe that women in both groups are only temporary workers and will soon leave to pursue family responsibilities. If a lesbian woman counters these assumptions and reveals her identity, she may find herself the object of discrimination based on sexual orientation instead. This is compounded by the lack of role models for successful l/g people as a whole. If to be open about one's orientation, to be "out," is to risk being unsuccessful, then the problems of finding appropriate role models for l/g people as a group become quite serious.

Morgan and Brown (1991) stated that because lesbians have given up the option of being supported by a man, from 85–92% surveyed since the early 1980s are employed. This contrasts to a figure of 50% for heterosexual women in the United States who work outside the home for pay. Morgan and Brown (1991) also presented conclusions from many studies that indicated that lesbians value androgyny and exhibit more gender nonconforming behaviors than do nonlesbian women, value independence more in intimate relationships, and stigmatize highly gender-role stereotyped behaviors in other women. From a career standpoint, because lesbians as a group do not conform to traditional gender roles, they may be more open to seeking nontraditional employment than nonlesbian women. Some lesbian communities may even denigrate the performance of traditional job roles by women. Given that occupations that are stereotyped as male occupations pay considerably more than female-typed occupations, Morgan and Brown (1991) suggested that opting for work in nontraditional occupations may be one way for lesbians to bridge gender-related gaps in wages and "mitigate the effect of living without a man's higher wage and better economic opportunity" (p. 278).

## Age-Related Factors

Herr and Cramer (1988) reviewed the theoretical perspectives related to the development of career behavior and choice with respect to the age of the client. The needs of populations of different ages differ. L/g people share this with some additional complications. The coming out process can be entered into at a variety of ages and not just in adolescence. Of particular importance is the elapsed time since accepting one's identity. Self-concept undergoes a dramatic flux during this time. In Herr and Cramer's (1988, p. 137) review, they commented that "the process of vocational development is essentially that of developing and implementing a self-concept." Thus, self-concept, its development with respect to an emerging acceptance of self, and vocational development are all intertwined life tasks.

Berger (1982), Canon (1973), and Reynolds (1989) all spoke to the varying counseling needs of l/g people at different points in their lives. McDonald (1982) and Coleman (1982), in their study of gay men, found that men can enter into the stress of the coming out process at any age. McDonald cited several studies that placed the average age of self-designation as a homosexual at 21 and initial self-disclosure at 28; however, his elapsed time between awareness of homoerotic feelings and self-labeling ranges from 1–33 years. Thus, for l/g clients, the coming out process emerges as a factor superimposed upon the age and maturational factors experienced by all clients. As such, it also enters into one's career. L/g clients who have just come out may either wish to stay in their home localities where they have recently established themselves in a community, or, if they live in a nonaccepting locale, they may use their emergence as an impetus to find a less restrictive part of the country in which to work. In either case, unless their sexual orientation is known, career counseling with them proceeds without a great deal of valuable information.

One last factor in this area is the epoch when l/g clients went through their formative years and the social climate at the time they came out. The forces acting on a college student who has been out for several years in the early 1990s are vastly different than those experienced by someone who has been out since 1955. The trauma of changing jobs and facing the possibility of self-disclosure to a whole new cadre of coworkers can be very stressful for the middle-aged l/g person who was raised in a much more restrictive time.

## DIRECTIONS FOR CAREER DEVELOPMENT

### Services

Anyone wishing to work with this clientele will have to find a way of reaching the l/g community. One of the best ways is by word of mouth via the first few l/g clients who find satisfaction with one's work and ethos. This is a very network-oriented community because resources both from family of origin and society may have been affected by prejudice. Finding some way to publicly examine traditional career counselor roles, techniques, and values with respect to l/g issues will influence the number of l/g clients who are willing to use an agency's services.

Hetherington et al. (1989) recommended the provision of special programming for l/g clients in the way of workshops, information on resume writing, procurement of relevant information regarding prejudice in careers, and job fairs. They indicated that tapping into the existing l/g community to find mentors for younger l/g people would be very useful. Shadowing, or having a client following one of these mentors throughout a normal work day, could be extremely valuable as a modeling technique, as well as giving the l/g client the valuable experience that shadowing usually provides. Organization of regional efforts in more sparsely populated areas would also be useful. As Bamford (1989) pointed out, counselors who are willing to take the personal risk to poll local businesses with respect to their employment policies concerning l/g people provide an invaluable service.

Bamford (1989) and Hetherington and Orzek (1989) both recommended that l/g clients take some responsibility for doing their own sleuthing about professions in which they have an interest. Certainly some careers, such as the military, have a longstanding discriminatory policy toward l/g people (McCrary & Gutierrez, 1979/1980) although this policy is currently under review by the Clinton administration. Other clients may be interested in investigating their rights under the law. Both Hedgpeth (1979/1980) and Achtenberg (1985) addressed this in detail. Provision of information to clients as to how they can learn which companies protect their employment rights is one way to facilitate clients' taking charge of their own sleuthing. Clients can also request a copy of a company's Equal Employment Opportunity statement or a copy of an employee handbook. This is good policy regardless of the orientation of the employee. At the very least, it is a reasonable precaution to take when considering a job offer. Local l/g advocacy groups may have lists of local companies that have protection policies. Directing clients to resources where they can learn about the discrimination levels in geographic areas where they are considering employment or indicating to l/g clients how they can word resumes so that they can get credit for appropriate employment experience in the l/g community without necessarily revealing their orientation on the resume would also be helpful. Counseling with respect to dual-career issues when there is an l/g partner to be considered is crucial.

Perhaps the best source of information, both for counselors and clients, is the networking provided by many gay community and professional groups. One such group (Bamford, 1989; Schmitz, 1988) is High Tech Gays in San Jose, California. The group has 600 active members who are engineers and scientists working in high-technology companies. Particularly, if geographic location is of prime importance, accessing the local l/g network in the area would be a shortcut to assessing prospects. Lists of networking possibilities published by Bamford (1989) and Hetherington and Orzek (1989) could be most useful in providing clients with professional contacts in selected areas. In addition, many of these networks are connected by electronic mail via computer networks. Information can be disseminated to large numbers of people almost instantaneously.

While realizing that the typical number of visits to a career counselor does not usually comprise more than several sessions, this may be the first time an l/g person has encountered a receptive, l/g-affirmative professional. As such, this contact may prove pivotal. So many decisions regarding partners, dual-career issues, geographical differences in discrimination, social interactions, openness on the job, familial support systems, family responsibilities, and styles of living may be involved.

## Research

Even with the information gathered by NGLTF (1989), very little is known about relative levels of prejudice that exist not only within different companies but also in different professions as a whole. There is a critical need for investigations within companies, professions, and geographical areas before a complete picture emerges as to the receptivity of occupations to l/g people and to points in the system where change agents can be effective. There is room here for counselors on local levels to conduct their own research projects on a small scale and to share the information with NGLTF, with the professional community via publications, and with individual clients. Hetherington et al. (1989) outline other areas of research such as the effects of sexual orientation on career decision-making processes, social stereotypes about "homosexual" occupations, employment discrimination as a result of the AIDS crisis, and unique life issues of l/g people relative to relationships and the transition from school to work. This group needs advocates in the counseling community.

## SUMMARY

Lesbian women and gay men comprise a unique cultural minority in this country with the attendant problems of minority status. In addition to the problems encountered with prejudice from society at large, they encounter similar problems from the counseling community. In order to remedy these inequities, counselors must prepare themselves for working with this minority in ways similar to those that the American Psychological Association has set out for working with racial and ethnic minorities. One of the greatest ways to enhance the quality of life of this minority group is the provision of a satisfying career. In light of this, career counselors are in a unique position to alleviate the environmental stress impinging on lesbian and gay people.

## REFERENCES

Achtenberg, R. (1985). *Sexual orientation and the law.* New York: Clark, Boardman.

Adams, B. (1987). *The rise of the gay and lesbian movement.* Boston: Twane.

Bamford, J. (1989). Can you be straight about being gay? *CV, The College Magazine, 1*(1), 66–69.

Bell, A., & Weinberg, M. (1978). *Homosexualities: A study of diversity among men and women.* New York: Simon & Schuster.

Berger, R. (1982). The unseen minority: Older gays and lesbians. *Social Work, 27,* 236–241.

Betz, N. (1991). Implications for counseling psychology training programs: Reactions to the special issue. *The Counseling Psychologist, 19*(2), 248–253.

Betz, N. E., & Fitzgerald, L. F. (1987). *The career psychology of women.* New York: Academic Press.

Botkin, M., & Daily, J. (1987). Occupational development of lesbians and gays. Paper presented at the annual meeting of the American College Student Personnel, Chicago, IL.

Bozett, F. (1989). Gay fathers: A review of the literature. *Journal of Homosexuality, 18,* 137–162.

Brown, D. A. (1975). Career counseling for the homosexual. In R. D. Burack & R. C. Readon (Eds.), *Facilitating career development* (pp. 34–247). Springfield, IL: Charles C Thomas.

Browning, C., Reynolds, A., & Dworkin, S. (1991). Affirmative psychotherapy for lesbian women. *The Counseling Psychologist, 19*(2), 177–196.

Buhrke, R. A. (1989). Incorporating lesbian and gay issues into counselor training: A resource guide. *Journal of Counseling & Development, 68,* 77–80.

Buhrke, R., & Douce, L. (1991). Training issues for counseling psychologists in working with lesbian women and gay men. *The Counseling Psychologist, 19*(2), 216–234.

Canon, H. J. (1973). Gay students. *Vocational Guidance Quarterly, 21,* 181–185.

Coleman, E. (1982). Developmental stages of the coming out process. *Journal of Homosexuality, 8,* 31–43.

Cooper, C. (1989, April). Social oppressions experienced by gays and lesbians. In P. Griffin & J. Genasce (Eds.), *Strategies for addressing homophobia in physical education, sports, and dance.* Workshop presented at the annual convention of the American Alliance for Health, Physical Education, and Dance, Boston.

deCharms, R. (1975). *Personal causation.* New York: Academic Press.

DeCrescenzo, T. A. (1985). Homophobia: A study of the attitudes of mental health professionals toward homosexuality. In R. Schoenberg, R. S. Goldberg, & D. A. Shore (Eds.), *With compassion toward some: Homosexuality and social work in America* (pp. 115–136). New York: Harrington Park Press.

Dulaney, D., & Kelly, J. (1982, March). Improving services to gay and lesbian clients. *Social Work,* 178–183.

Etringer, B. D., Hetherington, C., & Hillerbrand, E. (1990). The influence of sexual orientation on career decision making: An initial investigation. *Journal of Homosexuality, 19*(4), 103–111.

Faderman, L. (1985). The "new gay" lesbians. *Journal of Homosexuality, 10,* 85-95.

Fassinger, R. E. (1991). The hidden minority: Issues and challenges in working with lesbian women and gay men. *The Counseling Psychologist, 19*(2), 157–176.

Fischer, P. (1972). *The gay mystique: The myth and reality of male homosexuality.* New York: Stein & Day.

Fitzgerald, L., & Crites, J. (1980). Toward a career psychology of women: What do we know? What do we need to know? *Journal of Counseling Psychology, 27*(1), 44–62.

Gartrell, N., Kraemer, H., & Brodie, H. K. H. (1974). Psychiatrists' attitudes toward female homosexuality. *The Journal of Nervous and Mental Disease, 159,* 141–144.

Gallup, G. (1977, July 18). Gallup poll on gay rights: Approval with reservations. *The San Francisco Chronicle,* 1, 18.

Gallup, G. (1987, March). Homosexuality: Backlash against gays appears to be leveling off. *Gallup Report,* 258, 12.

Goffman, E. (1963). *Stigma: Notes on the management of a spoiled identity.* Englewood Cliffs, NJ: Prentice-Hall.

Harmon, L. (1978). Career counseling for women. In S. Hansen & R. Rapoza (Eds.), *Career development and counseling of women* (pp. 443–453). Springfield, IL: Thomas.

Harris, M., & Turner, P. (1986). Gay and lesbian parents. *Journal of Homosexuality, 12*(2), 101–113.

Hedgpeth, J. M. (1979/1980). Employment discrimination law and the rights of gay persons. *Journal of Homosexuality, 5*(1/2), 66–78.

Herr, E., & Cramer, S. (1988). *Career guidance and counseling through the lifespan* (3rd Edition). Glenview, IL: Scott, Foresman.

Hetherington, C., Hillerbrand, E., & Etringer, B. (1989). Career counseling with gay men: Issues and recommendations for research. *Journal of Counseling and Development, 67,* 452–454.

Hetherington, C., & Orzek, A. (1989). Career counseling and life planning with lesbian women. *Journal of Counseling and Development, 68,* 52–57.

Iasenza, S. (1989). Some challenges of integrating sexual orientations into counselor training and research. *Journal of Counseling and Development, 68,* 73–76.

Jepsen, D., & Dilley, J. (1974). Vocational decision-making models: A review and comparative analysis. *Review of Educational Research, 44*(3), 331–340.

Kaupman, G. (1991). Cracker barrel waffles on anti-gay policy. *Southern Voice, 4*(1), 1.

Kinsey, A. C., Pomeroy, W. B., & Martin, C. E. (1948). *Sexual behavior in the human male.* Philadelphia: W. B. Saunders.

Kinsey, A. C., Pomeroy, W. B., Martin, C. E., & Gebhard, P. H. (1953). *Sexual behavior in the human female.* Philadelphia: W. B. Saunders.

Lange, S., & Elliott, J. (1990, August). *Counseling lesbian women: A non-linear approach.* Paper presented at the American Psychological Association Convention, Boston.

Masters, W. H., & Johnson, V. E. (1979). *Homosexuality in perspective.* Boston: Little, Brown.

McCrary, J., & Gutierrez, L. (1979/1980). The homosexual person in the military and in national security employment. *Journal of Homosexuality, 5,* 115–146.

McDonald, G. J. (1982). Individual differences in the coming out process for gay men: Implications for theoretical models. *Journal of Homosexuality, 8,* 47–60.

Morgan, K. S., & Brown, L. S. (1991). Lesbian career development, work behavior, and vocational counseling. *The Counseling Psychologist, 19*(2), 273–291.

National Gay & Lesbian Task Force. (1986). *Gay rights protections in the U.S. & Canada.* Washington, DC: Author (1517 U Street, N.W., Washington, DC 20009).

National Gas & Lesbian Task Force Corporate Survey (1989, update). Washington, DC: NGLTF (1517 U Street, N.W., Washington, DC 20009).

Norton, J. (1982). Integrating gay issues into counselor education. *Counselor Education and Supervision, 21,* 208–212.

Paul, W. (1982). Minority status for gay people: Majority reaction and social context. In W. Paul, J. D. Weinrich, J. C. Gonsiorek, & M. E. Hotvedt (Eds.), *Homosexuality: Social, psychological and biological issues* (pp. 351–369). Beverly Hills, CA: Sage.

Reinisch, J. M., & Beasley, R. (1990). *The Kinsey Institute new report on sex: What you must know to be sexually literate.* New York: St. Martin's.

Remer, P., & O'Neill, C. D. (1980). Clients as change agents: What color could your parachute be? *Personnel and Guidance Journal, 58,* 425–429.

Reynolds, A. J. (1989). Social environmental conceptions of male homosexual behavior: A university climate analysis. *Journal of College Student Development, 30,* 62–69.

Rochlin, M. (1982). Sexual orientation of the therapist and therapeutic effectiveness with gay clients. *Journal of Homosexuality, 8,* 21–29.

Rudolph, J. R. (1988). Counselors' attitudes toward homosexuality: A selective review of the literature. *Journal of Counseling and Development, 67,* 167–168.

Saghir, M., & Robins, E. (1973). *Male and female homosexuality.* Baltimore: Williams & Wilkins.

Saghir, M. T., Robins, E., Walbran, B., & Gentry, K. A. (1970a). Psychiatric disorders and disability in the male homosexual. *American Journal of Psychiatry, 126,* 1079–1086.

Saghir, M. T., Robins, E., Walbran, B., & Gentry, K. A. (1970b). Psychiatric disorders and disability in the female homosexual. *American Journal of Psychiatry, 127,* 147–154.

Schmitz, T. J. (1988). Career counseling implications with the gay and lesbian population. *Journal of Employment Counseling, 25,* 51–56.

Thompson, G. J., & Fishburn, W. R. (1977). Attitudes toward homosexuality among graduate counseling students. *Counselor Education and Supervision, 17,* 121–130.

Weinberg, M. S. (1972). *Society and the healthy homosexual.* New York: St. Martin's.

Weinberg, M. S., & Williams, C. J. (1975). *Male homosexuals: Their problems and adaptations.* New York: Penguin.

Worell, J., & Remer, P. (1990). *Feminist perspectives on counseling women: An empowerment model.* Chichester, U.K.: John Wiley & Sons.

Chapter 3

# Hiring, Firing, and Promoting

**Jo Ann Lee**
**Roger G. Brown**

*No person shall be . . . deprived of life, liberty, or property, without due process of law . . .*

*—U.S. Constitution, Amendment V*

The United States is a diverse society, encompassing a myriad of subcultures, opinions, and values. Although the diversity makes our society fascinating, it is threatening to some who prefer to live and work with persons who are similar to themselves. The beauty of America, and what has attracted the variety of peoples who fight to live and stay in the United States, is that it is seen as "the land of opportunity," where dreams can be fulfilled, all persons are treated equally under the law, and anyone can succeed with hard work. However, this image may be an elusive one for U.S. citizens who are nonheterosexual. Gays and lesbians deprived (because of their sexual orientation) of jobs that they find

The authors thank Charles Krugel for his assistance with the research for this article.
Inquiries should be sent to Jo Ann Lee, Department of Psychology, The University of North Carolina at Charlotte, Charlotte, NC 28223.

psychologically and economically rewarding are deprived of achieving and maintaining the quality of life and standard of living they desire.

The world of work is commonly divided into two major categories: the private sector and the public sector. This chapter focuses on gay men's and lesbians' access to and treatment in private sector jobs. Several of the chapters in Part 3 of this book focus on specific occupations in the public sector. The first section of this chapter reviews the legal environment surrounding discrimination against gay and lesbian employees, including federal, state, and local regulations. Personnel actions have become heavily regulated by a network of laws, and the authors included a discussion of both the private and public sectors to highlight the differences between the two. The second section is devoted to a discussion of our society's social environment toward the nonheterosexual community. Public opinions and values influence not only a person's self-concept but also policymakers' decisions regarding needed legislation. The third section describes the authors' views of the current corporate climate toward gays and lesbians. The fourth section offers the authors' assessment of current forces affecting personnel actions in the private and public sectors. Finally, the authors provide recommendations for employers in managing a diverse workforce.

## LEGAL ENVIRONMENT

The legal environment for gays and lesbians is somewhat different in the private sector compared with the public sector. However, government regulations for public sector employment practices often set the benchmark for private sector employers (Decker, 1980). For the purpose of comparison, the laws covering the private and public sectors are discussed separately.

### Private Sector

The legal climate for gays and lesbians in the private sector is not very bright. At the time of this writing there is no federal statute that specifically prohibits employment discrimination based on sexual orientation.

Title VII of the 1964 Civil Rights Act, which is the primary federal statute requiring equal employment opportunity, prohibits discrimination based on race, color, religion, sex, and national origin. "Sex," under Title VII, refers only to biological sex, and does not include sexual orientation (Ledvinka & Scarpello, 1991). Attempts dating back to 1981 to add "sexual orientation" to the list of classes protected by Title VII have failed (Rivera, 1991). Similarly, the recently passed Civil Rights Act of 1991 does not extend protection against employment discrimination to lesbians and gay men.

Lesbians and gay men who have felt they have been victims of discrimination have sought redress under the U.S. Constitution. Based on the Fifth and the Fourteenth Amendments of the U.S. Constitution, two legal arguments have been made: right to privacy and equal protection (Bersoff & Ogden, 1991). To the shock and dismay of the lesbian and gay community (Melton, 1989), the U.S. Supreme Court recently ruled in a 5 to 4 decision that the U.S. Constitution does not provide protection to gay men and lesbians (*Bowers v. Hardwick*, 1986). The Court's decision, based on Judeo-Christian moral and ethical standards, has ramifications for employment practices. Employers wishing to deny employment to lesbians and gays may feel vindicated by arguing same-gender sexual activities are antithetical to our society's established moral and ethical standards.

Ironically, Congress' failure to include same-gender sexual orientation under the Americans with Disabilities Act of 1990 (ADA), despite proponents' arguments to the contrary, may have provided inadvertent justification for civil rights protection for lesbians and gay men. Citing the American Psychological Association's position, it was argued by certain Congressional members that lesbians and gay men should not be covered by the Act because same-gender sexual orientation did not imply impairment in "general social or vocational capabilities" (Conger, 1975, p. 633) and is not a disability. The juxtaposition of these arguments with Congress' inclusion of lesbians and gay men under the Hate Crimes Statistics Act of 1990 seems to argue for protection from employment discrimination based on sexual orientation. Under the Hate Crimes Statistics Act, lesbians and gay men are recognized as having special status, like racial minorities, needing protection from hate-motivated crimes (Morin & Rothblum, 1991).

Despite the lack of federal leadership on civil rights protection for gays and lesbians, legal protections for these persons have been enacted at lower levels of government. The National Gay and Lesbian Task Force (NGLTF), a gay civil rights and public education organization, publishes lists of cities, counties, and states with gay rights laws, covering private sector and public sector employment as well as union practices. The lists are revised quarterly. The appendix at the end of this chapter contains the most recently published list with the types of civil rights protection. It lists 59 cities and counties, four states (Connecticut, Hawaii, Massachusetts, and Wisconsin), and Washington, DC, as having protections for gays and lesbians in private sector employment. Gay and lesbian members of labor unions are afforded the same protection provided all members of the unions; and most national labor unions have policies protecting the rights of their gay and lesbian members (Rivera, 1991).

The current absence of a specific federal statute prohibiting discrimination based on sexual orientation is troublesome to gay rights activists. Without it employees in the private sector have limited recourse. The gay community's cries and demands for equal protection under the law may force the political and legal atmosphere to change. Politicians tend to respond to pressure from their constituents who vote them into power (Lamal & Greenspoon, 1991). The recently enacted Civil Rights Act of 1991 and the Americans with Disabilities

Act of 1990 intimate the influence of certain interest groups and are indications of a renewed public concern for the civil rights of employees. Society's attitudes toward civil rights for all, including nonheterosexuals, may be turning more positive.

### Public Sector

More legal protection exists for gays and lesbians in the public sector than in the private sector. This is revealed in the attached appendix.

Discrimination against gays and lesbians in public employment has occurred within three distinct employee groups: military employees, those in jobs that require a security clearance, and general civil service employees (Harvard University, 1989). Chapter 4 discusses gays and lesbians in the military, and this topic will not be covered in the current chapter.

Persons seeking government security clearances have fared only slightly better than military personnel in avoiding discrimination based on sexual orientation. Courts have accepted several arguments by the federal government alleging that gay men and lesbians are security risks. In *McKeand v. Laird* and *Adams v. Laird,* federal appeals courts agreed that gay and lesbian employees are subject to blackmail from persons who threaten to reveal the identity of the employee or an intimate partner and are untrustworthy to protect classified information (490 F.2d 1262 (9th Cir., 1973); 420 F.2d 230 (D.C. Cir., 1969)). This argument was upheld even in a case where the alleged security risk, a female applicant to the Federal Bureau of Investigation, was openly gay (*Padula v. Webster,* 822 F.2d 97, 104 (D.C. Cir., 1987); Harvard University, 1989).

Herek (1990) argues that extensive research by psychologists, psychiatrists, and others has clearly refuted the claim that gay employees are more unstable, personally unreliable, or impaired in perceiving reality, when compared to the general population. With regard to the threat of blackmail against gay employees in security-sensitive positions, he concludes:

> no cases of security leaks resulting from such blackmail have been documented. As the American social climate becomes more tolerant and gay people feel less pressured to hide their homosexuality, opportunities for such coercion will decrease even further. (p. 1038)

The Department of Defense has asserted that gay men and women are not barred automatically from receiving security clearances. However, a federal district court in California invalidated the military's policy of subjecting gays and lesbians to expanded security investigations and to mandatory legal review (*High Tech Gays v. Defense Industrial Security Clearance Office,* 668 F.Supp. 361 (N.D. Cal., 1987)). The Federal Bureau of Investigation and the Central Intelligence Agency, meanwhile, have policies that suggest a total ban on the employment of gay men and lesbians (Harvard University, 1989).

Limited protection of the rights of gay men and lesbians in civil service employment has been based on (1) the due process and equal protection clauses of the Fourteenth Amendment to the U.S. Constitution, and (2) free speech rights under the First Amendment. Gay and lesbian employees also have attempted to base legal claims on Title VII of the Civil Rights Act of 1964 and on the Rehabilitation Act of 1973, but to date no court has recognized special protection against discrimination based on sexual orientation under these acts.

Court review of the due process and equal protection rights of gay and lesbian civil service employees occurs under one of three standards: "rational relationship" classification, "quasi-suspect" classification, or "suspect" classification (Harvard University, 1989, pp. 1557–1571). Rational relationship review imposes the least burden of proof on the government employer to show why the gay or lesbian person was dismissed from employment or was not hired. The government's actions must be "rationally related to a legitimate governmental purpose" (*Kadrmas v. Dickenson Public Schools,* 108 S.Ct. 2481, 2487 (1988)).

The rational relationship standard is met automatically for virtually all decisions of the military or government security agencies and so provides little or no protection for homosexual applicants or employees. However, the U.S. Court of Appeals for the D.C. Circuit in 1969 provided some due process protection for gay men and lesbians when it ruled that the civil service must establish a rational relationship between an applicant's or employee's sexual orientation and the employing agency's efficiency (*Norton v. Macy,* 417 F.2d 1161 (D.C. Cir., 1969)). The protection was limited, though, when the court emphasized that the plaintiff did not "flaunt" his off-duty homosexual conduct, implying that open or public homosexuality may not be protected (417 F.2d at 1167; Harvard University, 1989, p. 1558).

In fact, the Ninth Circuit Court of Appeals used the distinction between private homosexual behavior and public behavior or advocacy to uphold the dismissal of a federal employee who was "openly and publicly flaunting his homosexual way of life" (*Singer v. United States Civil Service Commission,* 530 F.2d 247 (9th Cir., 1976)). However, Singer ultimately prevailed when the federal civil service regulations were changed. Federal guidelines now state that a person "is not unsuitable for federal employment merely because such person is gay or lesbian or has engaged in homosexual acts . . . . Specific factors such as criminal, dishonest, infamous, or notoriously disgraceful conduct, however, can provide the requisite link between a person's sexual orientation and job performance" (Harvard University, 1989, p. 1559, note 29).

Therefore, the courts continue to allow considerable latitude for the government to argue that work performance is adversely affected when a gay man or lesbian is employed. Consequently, most government actions based on an individual's homosexuality are upheld under the rational relationship standard.

More rigorous standards of court review for government employment decisions affecting gay men and lesbians may be evolving, however. Some recent court decisions have suggested that gay and lesbian employees are treated as a "quasi-suspect" or even a "suspect" class of citizens and therefore are entitled to greater judicial scrutiny of discriminatory personnel decisions affecting them. Traditionally, classifications based on gender, for example, are considered "quasi-suspect" classifications, and they are subject to an intermediate level of scrutiny by the courts, while classifications based on race or national origin constitute "suspect" classifications and require a still higher standard of court review.

Gay men and lesbians in the government workforce meet several of the conditions that courts have used to determine a quasi-suspect or suspect class. They have suffered a history of discrimination. They are prohibited from serving in the military and from participating effectively in the political process. In many states, gay individuals and couples are prevented from rearing children. Classifications that lead to discrimination against gays are based on unfounded stereotypes, including an alleged inability to perform satisfactory work. Gay men and lesbians face harassment and "social ostracism" (Harvard University, 1989, p. 1567).

When courts employ the higher standards of review based on suspect classifications, they require that the classifications be supported by more than a rational relationship to a "legitimate" government interest. For a quasi-suspect classification, the government interest must be "important" (*Craig v. Boren,* 429 U.S. 190 (1976); for a "suspect" classification, the government must show a "compelling" interest in taking the contested personnel action (*Palmore v. Sidoti,* 466 U.S. 429 (1984)).

Overall, most courts have refused to apply a higher standard of review to cases involving discrimination based on sexual orientation. However, some important exceptions have occurred. In the *High Tech Gays* case discussed earlier, a federal district court in California found that gay men and lesbians constitute a quasi-suspect class and therefore overruled the government's policy of subjecting gays and lesbians to extended security investigations and mandatory adjudications (668 F.2d 1361 (N.D. Cal., 1987); Harvard University, 1989).

In *Watkins v. United States Army,* the Ninth Circuit Court of Appeals found that the Army policy of discharging gays and lesbians violated their equal protection rights under the Constitution because they were a "suspect" class (847 F.2d 1329 (1988)). Watkins lost the case on other grounds when the case was reheard *en banc* (847 F.2d 1362 (9th Cir., 1988)).

In 1991, two lower court cases added to the precedents of treating gay and lesbian plaintiffs as members of a suspect class. A federal court in Kansas concluded that "discrimination based on sexual orientation is inherently suspect" (*Jantz v. Muci,* 759 F.Supp. 1543 [D. Kansas, 1991]). A California appeals court ruled that the "compelling interest" standard must be used to determine whether the use of questions relating to sexual orientation in psychological tests given to applicants for security officer positions violated the constitutional right to privacy (*Soroka v. Dayton Hudson Corp.*, 6 IER 1491 (1st App. Dist., Div. 4, Cal., 1991)).

Balanced against these new developments toward more serious treatment in court of discrimination against gays is the finding in *Bowers v. Hardwick* discussed earlier. Although the U.S. Supreme Court ruled that no constitutional protection exists for homosexual behavior, rights have become available to public sector employees in many parts of the nation in the form of state and local legislation. Typically, such legal protection is stated in the terms of the jurisdiction's equal employment policy. One such statement is part of the personnel policies of Orange County, North Carolina:

> The policy of Orange County is to foster, maintain, and promote equal employment opportunity. The County prohibits discrimination in employment on the basis of race, color, national origin, religion, creed, sex, *sexual orientation*, age, disability, political affiliation, and Vietnam Era or disabled veteran status as provided in law (Personnel Policies of Orange County North Carolina, Article II, Sect. 1.0, 10/1/91) [emphasis added].

The existing legal protections for gay men and lesbians in the public sector are more extensive than those in the private sector. Nevertheless, no uniform national standard exists for the legal and constitutional treatment of employment discrimination based on sexual orientation. Congressional action is needed in order to add to the list of prohibited employment practices any unjustified discriminatory action based on a person's sexual orientation.

## SOCIAL ENVIRONMENT

The social acceptance of gays and lesbians has increased over the past 15 years (Morin & Rothblum, 1991). Since Morin and Garfinkle's enlightening article in 1978 about the origins and dynamics of homophobia (the irrational fear or intolerance of gay men), the stigma of same-gender sexual orientation has faded somewhat. The decline in homophobia is probably partially due to the efforts of professional societies such as the American Psychological Association (APA), which in 1974 adopted an official policy statement that "Homosexuality per se implies no impairment in judgement, stability, reliability, or general social or vocational capabilities" (Conger, 1975, p. 633). Similar resolutions criticizing discrimination based on sexual orientation had been adopted previously by the professional societies of the American Sociological Association, the National Association of Mental Health, the National Association of Social Workers, and the American Psychiatric Association (Adam, 1987). APA's efforts in combating discrimination against gays and lesbians include writing amicus curiae briefs in cases concerning gays' and lesbians' civil rights (Bersoff & Ogden,

1991), discouraging heterosexist bias in psychological research (Herek, Kimmel, Amaro, & Melton, 1991), and educating the psychology community about heterosexist language (Committee on Lesbian and Gay Concerns, 1991).

Society's increasing tolerance of gays and lesbians is reflected in the pattern of Gallup Poll (1989a) results collected since 1977. When asked whether "homosexual relations between consenting adults should or should not be legal," 43% of the respondents interviewed in 1977 said it should be legal. In 1989, 47% said it should be legal. The percentage of respondents who think that homosexuals should have equal rights in terms of job opportunities increased from 56% in 1977 to 59% in 1982 to 71% in 1989. However, many people interviewed in 1989 (at least 40%) continued to believe gays and lesbians should not hold teaching positions. In other words, much of the public may still believe that gays and lesbians should be banned from certain types of employment.

Negative attitudes toward gays and lesbians in certain jobs is probably influenced by the abiding misconception that sexual orientation is a product of one's environment or upbringing (Gallup Poll, 1989a). The recent publicity (Gorman, 1991) about research indicating a biological basis of homosexual orientation (LeVay, 1991) in gay men may serve to increase social tolerance of gays and lesbians (Adler, 1991a, 1991b). Although psychologists have argued before that sexual orientation usually is involuntarily acquired and resistant to change (Melton, 1989), religious leaders have convinced many that it is a preference adopted by choice. Strong evidence of a biological basis of sexual orientation may serve as a foundation for legal protection from discrimination.

Compared to 15 years ago, society's tolerance of gays and lesbians may be increasing. However, hate crimes against gays and lesbians continue to occur today (Herek, 1989; Youngstrom, 1991), indicating a need for continued efforts to combat prejudice and hostility against these persons. Special efforts are imperative for the workplace, because gainful employment is integral to one's standard of living.

Our society is in a transitional state, in which pockets of homophobia as well as extreme prejudices and hostilities against other subpopulations exist. For example, as recently as November 1991 David Duke, a former Grand Wizard of the Ku Klux Klan, ran a very strong campaign for governor of Louisiana. Although he was defeated, he attracted a disturbing amount of nationwide support, with 40% of his campaign contributions coming from 46 other states (Riley, 1991).

## CURRENT CORPORATE CLIMATE

A general characterization of the corporate climate as either tolerant of or discriminatory against gays and lesbians is not possible, as one might expect. While some companies have explicit policies that prohibit discrimination based on sexual orientation (Kronenberger, 1991), other companies have explicit or implicit policies against employing nonheterosexuals (Hays, 1991).

Two earlier studies reported that discrimination in the workplace against gay men (Levine, 1979) and lesbians (Levine & Leonard, 1984) was a widespread problem. Paralleling the changing social attitudes in general, progress has been made toward greater acceptance of gays and lesbians in the corporate world. Since 1970, many private companies, professional organizations, and unions have adopted policies prohibiting discrimination based on sexual orientation (Hedgpeth, 1979/1980). Gays and lesbians must rely on these corporate policies and local ordinances for protection against discrimination, given the absence of federal protection.

A list of 238 corporations with their policies regarding discrimination based on sexual orientation was published in 1981 by the National Gay Task Force, which has since changed its name to the National Gay and Lesbian Task Force (NGLTF). The list was a result of the NGLTF's survey conducted between 1976 and 1981 of over 850 corporations, including the Fortune 500 corporations and over 300 leading nonindustrial corporations (e.g., finance, insurance, and retail sales). Self-selection undoubtedly contributed to the obtained results. The results do indicate that many major corporations across various industries are adopting specific policies against discrimination based on sexual orientation. Of the 238 respondents, 143 explicitly stated that they did not discriminate on the basis of sexual orientation.

What may be even more important to a given employee than a companywide policy is how the policy is implemented and the attitudes of his or her immediate supervisor and coworkers. During the first author's research for this chapter, she discovered that a major national media corporation has a policy against discrimination based on sexual orientation. Interestingly, a subsidiary company has no such policy. The author interviewed a gay male employee of the subsidiary, who has revealed his sexual orientation to his manager and coworkers, to learn of his personal experiences. Despite the absence of a written policy, the employee stated that he believes he is treated very fairly in the workplace. He attributed his comfortable working conditions to the value systems of those in his specific department and the organization's employees in general. He added that he believes his situation is rare among the gay community. According to him, he knows several gays employed by other organizations who fear they will be fired or harassed if they are discovered by their respective employers and/or coworkers.

## CURRENT FORCES AFFECTING PERSONNEL ACTIONS

The authors speculate that several forces may contribute to the personnel actions made in the private sector regarding gays and lesbians: the AIDS (acquired immune deficiency syndrome) crisis, the increasing diversity of the workforce, the anticipated shortage of entry-level skilled workers, the trend of corporate restructuring of the past decade, and the recent wave of negative sentiment among the public against minority groups. Most of the same forces, excluding corporate restructuring, may also affect personnel decisions in the public sector.

## The AIDS Crisis

The impact of the AIDS crisis may be mixed. In one way, the AIDS crisis has forced employers to discuss the issue with their employees. To combat the fear of AIDS in the workplace, some companies are developing and implementing special educational programs about the disease, what it is and how it is contracted (Krugel, 1990). Such training programs about AIDS may include sections on homosexuality, given gay men have been identified as a high-risk group for the disease. The training programs and the enhanced education of the public in general may be succeeding. The 1989 Gallup Poll indicates that the general public is becoming more sophisticated about the disease and aware of the behaviors that increase a person's chances of contracting AIDS.

On the other hand, the fear of getting AIDS may have raised the level of discomfort about being around gays for some heterosexuals. Although health officials have argued to the contrary, 7% of respondents thought that "working alongside or in close proximity to someone with AIDS" is "a way for people to catch AIDS" (Gallup Poll, 1989b). This belief, which has been discredited by health officials, has received varied public support, with an endorsement rate of 11% in 1987 decreasing to 5% in 1988 and increasing to 7% in 1989.

## Workforce Diversity

*Workforce 2000,* the well-known publication by Johnston and Packer (1987), reports that the American workforce of the year 2000 will look very different than the workforce before the 1970s. Since the 1970s, a number of trends have affected the complexion of the workforce. More women have entered the workforce; the median age of our society in general has been increasing; the ethnic diversity of the workforce is increasing; more persons with physical and mental disabilities are entering the workforce; our country is producing many young adults who cannot read, write, or work simple math problems; people's values are changing, with a greater emphasis on personal fulfillment. To manage the increasing diversity of the workforce, some companies are developing and implementing training programs designed to improve employees' and managers' sensitivity to the diversity. Many of the companies with such diversity training programs are incorporating sexual orientation into their programs. Kronenberger (1991) and Jamieson and O'Mara (1991) describe some specific cases.

### Shortage of Entry-Level Skilled Workers

The anticipated shortage of young entry-level workers with needed skills (Carnevale, 1991) is closely tied to the increasing diversity of the workforce. Both originate from the changing demographics of the United States. The changing demographics have their roots in the aging of the Baby Boomers (those born between 1946 and 1964) and the low birth rate during the 1960s and 1970s. As a result of the low birth rate of the 1960s and 1970s, the number of young workers between 16 and 24 years of age will decline by almost 8% by the year 2000 (Johnston & Packer, 1987). Consequently, employers will be competing for a limited number of entry-level workers with the necessary skills. Employers may then focus on applicants' knowledges, skills, and abilities, and less on personal characteristics, such as sexual orientation.

### Corporate Restructuring

It is uncertain how the declining number of young workers entering the workforce over the next decade will interface with the past decade of corporate restructuring. The trend in corporate restructuring has been the result of a decade of materialism, a desire to maximize profits, and increasing competition with other industrialized countries. The corporate world has been reshaped by a proliferation of mergers, acquisitions, leveraged buyouts, and downsizing. These actions have left millions of Americans without work.

One possible outcome of the increasingly fierce competition is that more employers may tend to focus on skills and the flexibility of employees rather than personal characteristics. An alternative outcome is the shortage of jobs may lead employers to take the opportunity to be very selective, rejecting or firing those who do not fit the corporate image.

One perhaps lasting change in the American workforce will be a larger proportion of contingent workers, comprised of temporaries, part-timers, and consultants on contract. Many employers have increased their use of contingent workers to cut costs of benefits. This author speculates that the job seekers with the desired skills who are willing to be flexible in mobility, task assignments, and conditions of employment will be the most successful in securing jobs. The days of lifetime employment with one company are gone, and the reciprocal loyalty between employer and employee has withered (Carnevale, 1991; Hallet, 1989).

### Negative Sentiment Against Minorities

The recent recession, which began at the end of 1990, has brought human survival instincts to the fore, resulting in aggressive acts of self-preservation. As thousands compete for a limited number of jobs, people from all walks of life are fighting to put food on the table. Many who did not do so before are beginning to consider principles of affirmative action to be anachronistic.

The economic problems our country is experiencing, however, is only one force contributing to the evident hostility toward minorities and women (Youngstrom, 1991). The lack of leadership to bring our country together and the dismantling of civil rights programs by the Reagan and Bush administrations have exacerbated the "me and now" mentality. The social conscience of our citizenry seems to have faded. Our society has witnessed an increase in hate crimes against various minority groups, gays and lesbians as well as racial, ethnic, and religious groups (Herek, 1989; Youngstrom, 1991). Increased public awareness of the hate crimes against gays and lesbians compelled the U.S. Congress to pass the Hate Crimes Statistics Act of 1990, which recognized lesbians and gay men as having special status needing protection from hate-motivated crimes.

Although there is evidence (Morin & Rothblum, 1991) that the attitudes toward gays and lesbians have become more favorable over the past 15 years, the recent hate acts indicate that much more progress is needed before the stigma against gays and lesbians is completely removed.

## RECOMMENDATIONS

The increasing diversity of the workforce has been noted elsewhere (Jamieson & O'Mara, 1991; Johnston & Packer, 1987). Given the changing complexion of the general workforce, with more minorities, women, and older workers as well as more known gays and lesbians, the authors offer some recommendations for managing such diversity. Some of the recommendations are borrowed from Munyard (1988). The position from which these recommendations are offered is that personnel actions should be based only on job-related dimensions and all employees should be treated fairly.

1. *Develop an explicit policy prohibiting discrimination based on sexual orientation.* Such a policy proclaims top management's intolerance of discriminatory personnel actions and sets the atmosphere of the organizational climate toward same-gender activities. Top management's support is usually necessary for any organization-wide policy to succeed. Similar policies have been suggested for the prevention of sexual harassment (Ledvinka & Scarpello, 1991) and discrimination against AIDS victims (Krugel, 1990). The policy should leave no question about the behaviors prohibited, and it should specify the consequences for exercising discriminatory behavior.

2. *Educate all employees about the policy.* It is not sufficient to have a policy without publicizing it and teaching employees what it is. Written literature or training programs should be used to educate employees about the specifics of the policy.

3. *Implement diversity training.* Employees may intellectually understand an organization's antidiscrimination policy, but may not emotionally appreciate it. Sensitize employees to others' perspectives and lifestyles. Role playing and

videos have been found to be two of the more successful training techniques for changing attitudes.

4. *Document performance appraisal information and employees' job-related activities.* Supervisors and/or managers may need to reprimand, fire, demote, or transfer an employee justifiably for job-related reasons. If the person is practicing same-gender sexual behavior, the question of discrimination based on sexual orientation may arise. Documentation of employees' past job performance is needed to determine the fairness and accuracy of personnel actions. Similarly, a manager's or supervisor's rationale for certain personnel actions may emerge by perusing records and documents of similar past cases.

5. *Sanction support groups for gays and lesbians.* Management's open approval of support groups is a public declaration of the organization's acceptance of gays and lesbians in their workforce. In addition, support groups may help gays and lesbians come to accept themselves if they have not yet done so. Management need not initiate the formation of such groups. However, management's permission to advertise openly meetings and to circulate information about such groups would indicate management's support. Hundreds of support groups currently exist for employees of specific companies and for professional groups.

## REFERENCES

Adam, B. D. (1987). *The rise of the gay and lesbian movement.* Boston: Twayne.

Adler, T. (1991a, November). Hypothalamus study stirs social questions. *The APA Monitor, 22,* 8–9.

Adler, T. (1991b, November). Study may affect attitudes toward gays. *The APA Monitor, 22,* 8.

Bersoff, D. N., & Ogden, D. W. (1991). APA amicus curiae briefs: Furthering lesbian and gay male civil rights. *American Psychologist, 46,* 950–956.

Carnevale, A. P. (1991). *America and the new economy.* Washington, DC: Department of Labor.

Committee on Lesbian and Gay Concerns. (1991). Avoiding heterosexual bias in language. *American Psychologist, 46,* 973–974.

Conger, J. (1975). Proceedings of the American Psychological Association, for the year 1974: Minutes of the annual meeting of Council of Representatives. *American Psychologist, 30,* 620–651.

Decker, P. J. (1980). Homosexuality and employment: A case law review. *Personnel Journal, 59,* 756–760.

Gallup Poll. (1989a, October). Homosexuality. *Gallup Report* (Report No. 289), 11–15.

Gallup Poll. (1989b, November). AIDS. *Gallup Report* (Report No. 290), 11–16.

Gorman, C. (1991, September). Are gay men born that way? *Time,* 60–61.

Hallet, J. J. (1989). Work and business in a new economy. In Employment Benefit Research Institute (Ed.), *Business, work, and benefits: Adjusting to change* (pp. 27–40). Washington, DC: Employment Benfit Research Institute.

Harvard University. (1989). Developments in the law—Sexual orientation and the law. *Harvard Law Review, 102,* 1508–1593.

Hays, J. (1991). Cracker Barrel comes under fire for ousting gays. *Nation's Restaurant News, 25,* 1ff.

Hedgpeth, J. M. (1979/1980). Employment discrimination law and the rights of gay persons. *Journal of Homosexuality, 5,* 67–78.

Herek, G. M. (1989). Hate crimes against lesbians and gay men. *American Psychologist, 44,* 948–955.

Herek, G. M. (1990). Gay people and government security clearances: A social science perspective. *American Psychologist, 45,* 1035–1042.

Herek, G. M., Kimmel, D. C., Amaro, H., & Melton, G. B. (1991). Avoiding heterosexist bias in psychological research. *American Psychologist, 46,* 957–963.

Jamieson, D., & O'Mara, J. (1991). *Managing workforce 2000: Gaining the diversity advantage.* San Francisco: Jossey-Bass.

Johnston, W. B., & Packer, A. E. (1987). *Workforce 2000: Work and workers for the 21st century.* Indianapolis, IN: The Hudson Institute.

Kronenberger, G. K. (1991). Out of the closet. *Personnel Journal, 70,* 40–44.

Krugel, C. (1990). AIDS and employment discrimination: What court decisions have prescribed for employers (unpublished dissertation).

Lamal, P. A., & Greenspoon, J. (1991, May). *Into the wider world.* Paper presented at the meeting of the Association for Behavior Analysis, Atlanta, GA.

Ledvinka, J., & Scarpello, V. G. (1991). *Federal regulation of personnel and human resource management.* Boston: PWS-Kent.

Levine, M. P. (1979). Employment discrimination against gay men. *International Review of Modern Sociology, 9,* 151–163.

Levine, M. P., & Leonard, R. (1984). Discrimination against lesbians in the work force. *Signs: Journal of Women in Culture and Society, 9,* 700–710.

LeVay, S. (1991). A difference in hypothalamic structure between heterosexual and homosexual men. *Science, 253,* 1034–1037.

Melton, G. B. (1989). Public policy and private prejudice: Psychology and law on gay rights. *American Psychologist, 44,* 933–940.

Morin, S. F., & Garfinkle, E. M. (1978). Male homophobia. *Journal of Social Issues, 34,* 29–47.

Morin, S. F., & Rothblum, E. D. (1991). Removing the stigma: Fifteen years of progress. *American Psychologist, 46,* 947–949.

Munyard, T. (1988). Homophobia at work and how to manage it. *Personnel Management, 20,* 46–50.

National Gay and Lesbian Task Force Policy Institute. (1991, November). *Lesbian and gay civil rights in America.* Washington, DC: Author.

National Gay Task Force. (1981). *The NGTF corporate survey.* New York: Author.

Riley, M. (1991, November). The no-win election. *Time,* 43.

Rivera, R. R. (1991). Sexual orientation and the law. In J. C. Gonsiorek & J. D. Weinrich (Eds.), *Homosexuality: Research implications for public policy* (pp. 81–100). Newbury Park, CA: Sage.

Youngstrom, N. (1991, November). Campus life polluted for many by hate acts. *The APA Monitor, 22,* 38.

## LIST OF CASES

*Adams v. Laird,* 420 F.2d 230 (D.C. Cir., 1969)
*Bowers v. Hardwick,* 478 U.S. 186 (1986)
*Craig v. Boren,* 429 U.S. 190 (1976)
*High Tech Gays v. Defense Industrial Security Clearance Office,* 668 F.Supp. 361 (N.D. Cal., 1987)
*Jantz v. Muci,* 759 F.Supp. 1543 (D. Kansas, 1991)
*Kadrmas v. Dickinson Public Schools,* 108 S.Ct. 2481 (1988)
*McKeand v. Laird,* 490 F.2d 1262 (9th Cir., 1973)
*Norton v. Macy,* 417 F.2d 1161 (D.C. Cir., 1969)
*Padula v. Webster,* 822 F.2d 97, 104 (D.C. Cir., 1987)
*Palmore v. Sidoti,* 466 U.S. 429 (1984)
*Singer v. United States Civil Service Commission,* 530 F.2d 247 (9th Cir., 1976)
*Soroka v. Dayton Hudson Corp.,* 6 IER 1491 (1st App. Dist., Div. 4, Cal., 1991)
*Watkins v. United States Army,* 847 F.2d 1329 (1988)
*Watkins v. United States Army (rehearing en banc)* 847 F.2d 1362 (9th Cir., 1988)

## APPENDIX

### Lesbian and Gay Civil Rights in America

| | Public employment | Public accommodations | Private employment | Education | Housing | Credit | Union practices | 1990 Census *Population* |
|---|---|---|---|---|---|---|---|---|
| Arizona | | | | | | | | |
| Tucson | x | | | | | | | |
| California | x | | | x | x | | | |
| Berkeley | x | | x | x | x | x | x | 102,724 |
| Cathedral City | x | | | | | | | |
| Cupertino | x | | | | | | | |
| Davis | x | x | x | | x | x | x | |
| Hayward | x | | x | x | x | | | 111,498 |
| Laguna Beach | x | x | x | x | x | x | x | |
| Long Beach | x | | x | | | | | 423,433 |
| Los Angeles | x | x | x | x | x | x | x | 3,485,398 |
| Mountain View | x | | | | | | | |
| Oakland | x | x | x | | x | x | x | 372,242 |
| Palo Alto | | | | x | | | | |
| Riverside | x | | | | | | | 226,505 |
| Sacramento | x | x | x | x | x | x | x | 369,365 |
| San Diego | x | x | x | x | x | x | x | 1,110,549 |
| San Francisco | x | x | x | x | x | x | x | 723,959 |
| San Jose | x | | | | | | | |
| Santa Barbara | x | | | x | | | | |
| Santa Cruz | x | | | | | | | |

| | Public employment | Public accommodations | Private employment | Education | Housing | Credit | Union practices | 1990 Census *Population* |
|---|---|---|---|---|---|---|---|---|
| Santa Monica | x | x | x | x | x | x | x | |
| West Hollywood | x | x | x | x | x | x | x | |
| Alameda County | | | | | | | | 1,279,182 |
| San Mateo County | x | | x | | x | | | 649,623 |
| Santa Barbara County | x | | | | | | | 369,608 |
| Santa Cruz County | x | | | | | | | 229,734 |
| Colorado | x | | | | | | | |
| Aspen | x | x | x | | x | | | |
| Boulder | x | x | x | | | | | |
| Denver | x | x | x | x | x | | x | 467,610 |
| Connecticut | x | x | x | x | x | x | x | |
| Hartford | x | x | x | x | x | x | x | 139,739 |
| New Haven | x | x | x | x | x | x | x | 130,474 |
| Stamford | x | x | x | x | x | x | x | |
| District of Columbia | | | | | | | | |
| Washington | x | x | x | x | x | x | x | |
| Florida | | | | | | | | |
| Key West | x | x | x | | x | x | x | |
| Tampa | x | x | x | | x | | | |
| Hillsborough County | | | | | x | | | 834,054 |
| Palm Beach County | x | | | | | | | 863,518 |
| Georgia | | | | | | | | |
| Atlanta | x | | | | | | | 394,017 |
| Hawaii | x | | x | | | | | |
| Honolulu | x | | | | | | | 365,272 |
| Illinois | x | | | | | | | |
| Champaign | x | x | x | | x | x | x | |
| Chicago | x | x | x | | | x | | 2,783,726 |
| Evanston | x | | | | | x | | |
| Oak Park | | x | | | x | | | |
| Urbana | x | x | x | | x | x | | |
| Cook County | x | | | | | | | 5,105,067 |
| Iowa | | | | | | | | |
| Ames | x | x | x | x | x | x | x | |
| Iowa City | x | x | x | | | x | x | |
| Maryland | | | | | | | | |
| Baltimore | x | x | x | x | x | | | 736,014 |
| Gaithersberg | x | | x | | x | x | x | |
| Rockville | x | x | x | x | x | x | x | |
| Howard County | x | x | x | x | x | x | x | 187,328 |
| Montgomery County | x | | x | | x | x | x | 757,027 |
| Massachusetts | x | x | x | x | x | x | x | |
| Amherst | x | x | x | x | x | x | x | |
| Boston | x | x | x | x | | x | x | 574,283 |

| | Public employment | Public accommodations | Private employment | Education | Housing | Credit | Union practices | 1990 Census *Population* |
|---|---|---|---|---|---|---|---|---|
| Cambridge | x | x | x | x | x | x | x | |
| Malden | x | x | x | x | x | x | | |
| Worcester | x | x | x | x | x | x | | |
| Michigan | x | | | | | | | |
| Ann Arbor | x | x | x | | x | x | x | 109,392 |
| Detroit | x | x | x | x | x | x | x | 1,027,974 |
| East Lansing | x | x | x | | x | x | x | |
| Flint | x | x | x | x | x | | x | 140,762 |
| Saginaw | | | | x | x | | | |
| Ingham County | x | | | | | | | 282,912 |
| Minnesota | x | | | | | | | |
| Marshall | x | x | x | | x | x | | |
| Minneapolis | x | x | x | x | x | x | x | 368,383 |
| St. Paul | x | x | x | x | x | | x | |
| Hennepin County | x | | | | | | | 1,032,431 |
| New Jersey | x | | | | | | | |
| Essex County | x | | | | | | | 778,204 |
| New Mexico | x | | | | | | | |
| New York | x | | | | | | | |
| Alfred | x | x | x | x | x | x | x | |
| Brighton | x | | | | | | | |
| Buffalo | x | | | | | | | 328,123 |
| East Hampton | x | x | x | | | | | |
| Ithaca | x | x | x | x | x | x | x | |
| New York | x | x | x | x | x | | x | 7,322,564 |
| Rochester | x | | | | | | | 231,636 |
| Syracuse | x | x | x | x | x | | | |
| Troy | x | | | | | | | |
| Watertown | x | | | | | | | |
| Suffolk County | x | | | | | | | 1,321,264 |
| North Carolina | | | | | | | | |
| Chapel Hill | x | | | | | | | |
| Raleigh | x | | | | | | | 207,952 |
| Ohio | x | | | | | | | |
| Columbus | x | x | x | x | x | x | | 632,910 |
| Cincinnati | x | | | | | | | 364,040 |
| Dayton | x | | | | | | | 182,044 |
| Yellow Springs | x | x | x | | x | x | x | |
| Cayahoga County | x | | | | | | | |
| Oregon | x | | | | | | | |
| Portland | x | | | | | | | 437,319 |
| Pennsylvania | x | | | | | | | |
| Harrisburg | x | x | x | x | x | x | x | |
| Lancaster | x | x | x | x | x | x | x | |

| | Public employment | Public accommodations | Private employment | Education | Housing | Credit | Union practices | 1990 Census *Population* |
|---|---|---|---|---|---|---|---|---|
| Philadelphia | x | x | x | | x | x | x | 1,585,577 |
| Pittsburgh | x | x | x | | x | x | x | 369,879 |
| Northampton County | x | | | | | | | 247,305 |
| Rhode Island | x | | | | | | | |
| South Dakota | | | | | | | | |
| Minnehaha County | x | | | | | | | 123,509 |
| Texas | | | | | | | | |
| Austin | x | x | x | | x | x | x | 465,622 |
| Houston | x | | | | | | | 1,630,553 |
| Vermont | | | | | | | | |
| Burlington | x | | x | | | | | |
| Virginia | | | | | | | | |
| Alexandria | x | x | x | x | x | x | | 111,283 |
| Arlington County | x | | | | | | | 170,936 |
| Washington | x | | | | | | | |
| Olympia | x | | | | | | | |
| Pullman | x | | | | x | x | | |
| Seattle | x | | x | | x | x | x | |
| Clallam County | x | | | | | | | |
| King County | | | | | x | x | | 1,507,319 |
| Wisconsin | x | x | x | x | x | x | x | |
| Madison | x | x | x | | x | x | x | 191,262 |
| Milwaukee | x | | | | | | | 628,088 |
| Dane County | x | | | | | | | 367,085 |

*Source:* National Gay and Lesbian Task Force Policy Institute, 1991.

Part Three

# Special Places, Special Roles

Chapter 4

# Stigma and Honor: Gay, Lesbian, and Bisexual People in the U.S. Military

**Clinton W. Anderson**
**H. Ron Smith**

*"They gave me a medal for killing two men*
*And they discharged me for loving one."*

—Tombstone Epitaph of Leonard Matlovich

Many gay, lesbian, and bisexual people have served honorably in the U.S. military (Berube, 1990; Gibson, 1978; Harry, 1984; Hippler, 1989; Humphrey, 1990; Livingood, 1969; Murphy, 1988; Williams & Weinberg, 1971), and a majority of U.S. residents approve (Colasanto, 1989; Penn & Schoen, 1991).

We thank the veterans who shared their experiences with us, particularly Tanya Domi and Alan Stephens, who read and commented on the chapter. We also thank John Anderson, Ph.D., and Gregory M. Herek, Ph.D., who also read the chapter and gave us comments, and Craig Waldo and Mike Jenkins for typing and word processing. Without their contributions, the chapter could not have been completed. In writing this chapter we have drawn extensively on the work of Gregory M. Herek, Ph.D., and the *amicus curiae* briefs of the American Psychological Association, whose principal authors were Donald Bersoff, Ph.D., and David Ogden. For additional information or comments, contact the first author at the American Psychological Association, 750 First Street, NE, Washington, DC 20002-4242.

Yet, the U.S. military continues to defend (e.g., U.S. General Accounting Office, 1992; Gellman, 1991) and enforce (e.g., Keen, 1992) a policy that gay, lesbian, or bisexual people cannot serve. Although gay, lesbian, or bisexual people are members of this major social institution from which they are officially banned, the experiences and concerns of these members of the U.S. armed forces are largely unknown.

At the time of this writing in February 1993, the President of the United States has stated that he will rescind the military ban on gay, lesbian, and bisexual people by executive order in July. The issue of whether the ban should be lifted, how to do so over what time period, and whether Congress should intervene in the President's intentions will be actively debated for some time. Congressional hearings will take place over the next months. This chapter has been written in the context of the policy, but a rescission of the policy will not render it obsolete. First, Congress may intervene to institute the ban in statute. Second, the problems faced by gay, lesbian, and bisexual people in the military derive from the military's actions and attitudes, as much as from the ban per se. Attitudes and actions will continue for some time to reflect the policy after the policy itself has been rescinded. It must be remembered that racial segregation in the military was ended by executive order in 1948, but the military did not proactively address race relations until the Vietnam War. Thus, we can expect that much of the experience of gay, lesbian, and bisexual people in the military will not change rapidly regardless of the status of the policy against them.

In this chapter, we discuss how the policy actually works in practice; how gay, lesbian, and bisexual people cope; how identification as a homosexual occurs, and how these people's lives are affected. We first present an overview of the U.S. military as an institution in order to provide a context for the reader. Second, we discuss the history of the military policy on homosexuality and consider its rationale and empirical basis. Third, we present the results of a small set of interviews with veterans and active duty personnel in which the actual experience of serving in the military is described. We conclude with our recommendations for policy change and for counseling and advising gay, lesbian, and bisexual people.

## THE U.S. MILITARY: CONTEXT AND BACKGROUND

Although the U.S. military is conservative, oriented toward tradition, and resistant to change, it has a long history of successfully implementing change and thereby functioning as an agent of social change. However, the military cannot afford uncalculated risk. That change which it has undertaken has been accomplished with the support of hard scientific evidence, a cadre of professional experts and consultants to guide the process, and a serious commitment to learn from its mistakes. Examples of broad social changes that the U.S. military has systematically accomplished include the integration of African Americans since

1948 (Binkin, Eitelberg, Schnexnider, & Smith, 1982; Karst, 1991; MacGregor, 1981) and the inclusion of women in all noncombatant occupational fields since 1973 (Karst, 1991; Schneider & Schneider, 1988; Steihm, 1989). The military also implemented policies to accommodate single-parent families and dual-career couples in the 1970s and early 1980s as these types of families increased among the all volunteer force (U.S. Air Force Academy, 1984). Thus, the military, since World War II, has become a model for equal access to personal development and upward mobility (Janowitz & Little, 1965) for such groups as ethnic minorities, women, single parents, and dual-career couples.

In considering the U.S. military as an agent of change, it is important to understand that the military has the power of a total institution (Goffman, 1961). It provides its personnel with transportation, housing, food, clothing, medical services, education (both for military personnel and their dependents), and much more. Thus, perhaps more so than any other social institution in our society, the U.S. military has the power for implementing social change. Furthermore, the military is a model of U.S. society. Although its composition does not exactly mirror the U.S. population in terms of socioeconomic status, age, and racial composition (Congressional Budget Office, 1989), it does draw its members from all segments of U.S. society. Thus, it has a powerful role to play as a social leader.

The U.S. military provides opportunities for personal development, exposure, and upward mobility for young men and women from socially and economically isolated or disadvantaged segments of the U.S. population (Janowitz & Little, 1965). For this reason, it has increasingly drawn its members from minority groups (racial/ethnic, gender, single parents) and lower socioeconomic strata (Congressional Budget Office, 1989), since World War II when educational and housing programs became part of the discharged veteran's benefits package. This trend has increased with the institution of an all volunteer force and as pay, benefits, and status of career military personnel increased during the 1980s (U.S. Air Force Academy, 1984).

The military has also played an important role in broadening the sociocultural perspectives of the U.S. population. By deploying men, women, and their families throughout the world, it has exposed millions of U.S. citizens to diverse cultures with varied mores, belief systems, diets, and political systems. It has played a critical role in modeling for U.S. society the integration of African Americans, the broadening of occupational roles for women, and the expansion of gender and familial roles for both men and women. Military personnel have had a long history of interracial and intercultural marriages. Indirectly it facilitated the increase in civil liberties and responsibility of U.S. youth with the decrease in the voting age from 21 to 18 during the Vietnam era. Although the institution is conservative, its personnel have often been socially nontraditional (Janowitz & Little, 1965).

Furthermore, the U.S. military has funded research and development of many psychological technologies; for example, intelligence testing during World War I, the study of social psychology during World War II, and racial prejudice reduction in the 1960s and 1970s.

## THE U.S. MILITARY AND HOMOSEXUAL ORIENTATION

> Homosexuality is incompatible with military service. The presence in the military environment of persons who engage in homosexual conduct or who, by their statements, demonstrate a propensity to engage in homosexual conduct, seriously impairs the accomplishment of the military mission. The presence of such members adversely affects the ability of the Military Services to maintain discipline, good order, and morale; to foster mutual trust and confidence among service members; to ensure the integrity of the system of rank and command; to facilitate assignment and worldwide deployment of service members who frequently must live and work under close conditions affording minimal privacy; to recruit and retain members of the Military Services; to maintain the public acceptability of military service; and to prevent breaches of security. (U.S. Department of Defense Directive 1332.14, January 28, 1982)

The Department of Defense (DoD) policy on homosexuality has its historical source in an obsolete and antiquated psychiatric understanding of same-gender sexual orientation* adopted during World War II that has since been rejected by psychiatry and the other mental health professions (American Psychiatric Association, 1973; Conger, 1975; National Association of Social Workers, 1988). Although the language and administration of the current DoD policy on homosexuality have changed since 1941, the policy is a direct descendant of Army and Selective Service policies adopted for the large-scale mobilization for World War II (Berube, 1990). Prior to World War II, homosexuality was viewed by the military as criminal behavior prohibited by the sodomy law in the Uniform Code of Military Justice. At the beginning of World War II, the military adopted new administrative policies on homosexuality. The original rationale was that to define homosexuality as a mental disorder, instead of a criminal act, was a more humane basis for screening out recruits and separating persons already on active duty, than charging them under sodomy statutes. This new approach was also thought to be less costly to the government and identification during induction physicals was seen as a psychiatric contribution to the U.S. war effort that could benefit the profession's prestige (Berube, 1990).

*In this chapter we use gay, lesbian, and bisexual people as a collective term to refer to the population on which our chapter focuses. It is not merely the population of all people who engage in same-gender sexual behavior; rather it is the population of those persons who have a same-gender sexual orientation. By same-gender sexual orientation we refer to the aspect of identity that emerges from and underlies patterns of sexual behavior and desire. Because of the history of the terms in a psychiatric context, we do not use "homosexual" and "homosexuality" except when we are specifically referring to the military policy and the military system of enforcing it. For a recent discussion of language issues, see Committee on Lesbian and Gay Concerns (1991).

In 1973, homosexuality was declassified as a mental disorder by the American Psychiatric Association (1987) and the other major mental health professions have supported the declassification (Conger, 1975; National Association of Social Workers, 1988). The removal of homosexuality from the list of disorders was the result of a reevaluation of the "illness model" of same-gender sexual orientation based on extensive scientific findings by a large number of researchers. This body of psychological research, conducted over almost three decades, has conclusively established that same-gender sexual orientation is not related to psychological adjustment or maladjustment (Gonsiorek, 1991).

The research literature has also demonstrated that, in civilian settings, gay, lesbian, and bisexual people have an overall potential to contribute to society, including the workplace, that is the same as that of heterosexual people (Bell & Weinberg, 1978; Herek, 1991a; Snyder & Nyberg, 1980). In the United States today, an increasing number of gay, lesbian, and bisexual people are identified as such to at least some of their coworkers, and the sexual orientation of employees is decreasing as a factor in employment decisions (Herek, 1991a; Stewart, 1991). A national poll conducted for the *San Francisco Examiner* found that 54% of the respondents had revealed their sexual orientation to their coworkers (Hatfield, 1989). Many large organizations have adopted policies of nondiscrimination on the basis of sexual orientation (Human Rights Foundation, 1984; National Gay Task Force, n.d.). For example, USWest, one of the regional phone companies created from the breakup of AT&T, provides employee support groups for its gay, lesbian, and bisexual employees as part of its affirmative action program (Duke, 1991). One of the authors' employers, the American Psychological Association, sponsored educational meetings for its staff during Lesbian and Gay Pride Week.

Although the mental health basis of the policy has been rejected, the military has been unwilling to reconsider its policy, unlike civilian professions and corporations as well as quasi-military organizations (e.g., law enforcement agencies). The military claims that the ultimate criterion for the military policy on homosexuality is combat effectiveness, a criterion that renders the military unique. On the basis of DoD's criterion, some groups of people may be excluded from military service or from combat—those groups that in the professional judgment of military commanders are considered to be harmful to combat effectiveness. It is DoD's position that scientific data are not necessary to justify excluding these groups; professional military judgment is sufficient.

Although the policy on homosexuality originated in a psychiatric context, DoD does not claim a mental health basis for the policy now. It does not claim that lesbian, gay, and bisexual people are unfit for service because of their mental health. Furthermore, although the policy as written specifies security concerns, the military no longer claims that homosexuality is a serious security issue. Rather the military's current position is that homosexuality—defined as sexual desire or behavior directed toward a member of one's own sex—harms the combat effectiveness of military units. The causal pathways for this effect are as follows:

• social attitudes toward homosexuality are negative (i.e., homosexual desire and behavior are not socially approved);
• the social disapproval of homosexuality has been internalized in the negative attitudes of service members toward homosexual desire and behavior;

Pathway 1

• proper emotional bonding among service members in combat units is necessary to morale, discipline, and good order;
• the negative attitudes of service members toward homosexual desire and behavior prevents proper emotional bonding of military personnel in combat units;

Pathway 2

• the military environment provides no privacy or choice of living situation;
• in the military environment, service members have no way to maintain distance between themselves and the homosexual desire or behavior that they disapprove;
• the forced contact of service members with homosexual desire and behavior that they do not approve frustrates privacy needs of heterosexual service members;
• the frustration of needs disrupts morale, discipline, and good order;

The Two Pathways Come Together

• combat effectiveness is harmed when morale, discipline, and good order are disrupted;
• homosexual desire and behavior must be excluded from the military because of their effect on combat effectiveness (U.S. General Accounting Office, 1992).

Given the prejudicial attitudes toward, stereotyping of, and discrimination against same-gender sexual orientation that exist in the United States, the rationale for the military policy has to be assumed to be prejudice implemented via regulation until the military can provide contrary evidence. We do not accept subjective military judgment as sufficient justification. The military has demonstrated neither a rational nor empirical basis for its policy of excluding persons of same-gender sexual orientation. Rather, it simply asserts that such a basis exists. In fact, studies commissioned by DoD to consider the basis of the policy have been consistently rejected when the conclusions did not match the prior expectations of the policymakers (e.g., Dyer, 1990).

Empirical research confirms that those holding negative attitudes about same-gender sexual orientation are more likely than those with positive attitudes to believe in false stereotypes about gay, lesbian, and sexual people. Studies have also shown that people holding negative attitudes "are less likely to have had personal contact with lesbians and gay men," and, hence, are not basing their attitudes on accurate information or personal experience (Herek, 1984, 1991a). Similarly, several studies indicate that exposure to truthful information about gay, lesbian, and bisexual persons often leads to a reduction in prejudice and stereotyping (Herek, 1984). Public opinion research demonstrates that people who are acquainted with someone who does not conceal his or her same-gender sexual orientation have, in general, significantly more favorable attitudes toward gay, lesbian, and bisexual people (Schneider & Lewis, 1984).

One leading researcher has summarized the nature of negative stereotypes toward homosexuals in the following way:

> Most common stereotypes are related to cross-sex characteristics. Additionally, significant numbers of individuals characterize male homosexuals as mentally ill, promiscuous, lonely, insecure, and likely to be child molesters, while lesbians have been described as aggressive and hostile toward men. (Herek, 1984, p. 9, citations omitted)

The same researcher explains that "labeling itself can lead people to perceive stereotypical behaviors, whether or not they occur," and that stereotypes can be so influential that those gay, lesbian, and bisexual people "who violate stereotypical expectations (e.g., masculine gay men and feminine lesbians) may actually be disliked" for that reason (Herek, 1984, p. 9; also see Herek, 1991a).

The evidence thus supports the conclusion reached by the principal social science studies analyzing military policies regarding gay, lesbian, and bisexual persons—these policies reflect stereotypical beliefs about nonheterosexual orientations that have been rejected by scientific research (Dyer, 1990; Herek, 1991b; Kauth, 1991; Steihm, 1991; Williams & Weinberg, 1971).

Psychologists have found that anti-gay prejudice can be conceptualized as manifesting the same psychological dynamics as racial and other ethnic prejudice (Herek, 1991a). Herek summarized the literature on intergroup contact and prejudice in the following way:

> Empirical research with other minority groups has shown that intergroup contact often reduces prejudice in the majority group when the contact meets several conditions: when it is encouraged by the institution in which it occurs, makes shared goals salient, and fosters inter-group cooperation; when the contact is ongoing and intimate rather than brief and superficial; and when members of the two groups are of equal status and share important values (Allport, 1954; Amir, 1969). (Herek, 1991c, p. 171, citations in original; see also Brewer & Kramer, 1985)

Several studies of prejudice against gay, lesbian, and bisexual people suggest that intergroup contact may reduce prejudice based on sexual orientation.

Exposure to information about gay, lesbian, and bisexual people often leads to a reduction in anti-gay prejudice (Herek, 1984, 1991a). Similarly, people who know someone who is openly gay have more favorable attitudes toward gay people than people who do not (Gentry, 1987; Hatfield, 1989; Herek, 1984, 1988; Schneider & Lewis, 1984). Another study suggests that contact not only lessens heterosexuals' negative *attitudes* toward gay men and lesbians, but also significantly improves the ability of heterosexuals to *work* effectively with them (Rudolph, 1989).

One important factor that influences the effect of contact or attitudes is "institutional support" (Allport et al., 1953; Amir, 1976; Ashmore & Del Boca, 1976; Stephan, 1985), or the attitude of those in authority toward the stigmatized group and discrimination against it. If the military chooses to oppose prejudice, prejudice will recede; if the military continues to endorse prejudice through the exclusionary policy, prejudice will continue.

## GAY, LESBIAN, AND BISEXUAL EXPERIENCE IN THE MILITARY*

Why do gay, lesbian, and bisexual persons join the military in the first place? First, many are highly supportive of the military and hold strong patriotic beliefs, notwithstanding their opposition to the military policy on homosexuality. No one we interviewed saw same-gender sexual orientation as disqualifying a person from military service.

The motivation to join the military includes desires for economic betterment, educational opportunities (in the military or after separation), getting ahead in life, getting away from home, and traveling. It also includes attraction to particular professions, particularly more skilled professions in which special education is required (e.g., linguistics), and awareness that the military provides excellent training and experience in those fields. The military is also a way to change the course of lives and careers going in unwanted directions. Additional reasons given for joining the military include membership in military families, a general admiration of the military by families, a sense of duty to country, and a deep personal wish to be in the military. In other words, many of the reasons our interviewees cited for joining the military were straightforward responses to the military marketing and advertising messages and not different

*This section is based on interviews of 18 veterans: 12 gay men, four lesbians, one bisexual woman, and one heterosexual man. Most interviewees were Caucasian, never married, and college educated. Most had been enlisted (three had been officers and four had both enlisted and commissioned service). All had been honorably discharged. Their current average age was 35, with an average induction age of 20 and separation age of 26. The average years of military service was nine (ranging from one to 20). Ten questions were used in the interview. Nine subjects were interviewed as individuals with the remainder in two groups (one group of gay men and one group of lesbians). The questions paralleled the topics in the section.

from what one would expect any sample of veterans might cite as their reasons for choosing military enlistment.

These gay, lesbian, and bisexual people also cited in some cases a wish to disprove stereotypes, to prove to others what one believed about oneself—that being gay or lesbian was not a barrier to successful service in the military. The attraction to the masculine image of the military for some gay men may be related to conflict they feel between their own emerging sexual orientation and society's feminine stereotypes of gay men. They may join the military in hopes of reducing or eliminating the conflict.

### Tolerance of Homosexual Orientation among Military Personnel

Despite regulations making homosexual behavior and same-gender sexual orientation grounds for less than honorable discharge, the large majority of gay, lesbian, and bisexual people who have served in the military have received honorable discharges (Harry, 1984; Livingood, 1972). The published literature about gay, lesbian, and bisexual persons serving in the military, as well as personal communication from military psychologists and psychiatrists, indicates that a limited form of openness is common in the military, particularly within professional settings. One well-known example is the case of Sergeant Perry J. Watkins (Bersoff & Ogden, 1988) in which his same-gender sexual orientation was known from his initial enlistment. Such evidence clearly contradicts the government's claim that the presence of gay, lesbian, and bisexual persons is necessarily disruptive to the U.S. military. Openly gay, lesbian, and bisexual persons are accepted for military service in other countries (U.S. General Accounting Office, 1992; Tielman & de Jonge, 1988).

The enforcement of the DoD policy has waxed and waned since World War II (Berube, 1990; Dyer, 1990; Karst, 1991). Our interviewees (both men and women) reported that the policy was not as severely enforced in the period at the end of the Vietnam conflict when an all volunteer force was being adopted. This was also the case during the recent Desert Storm/Shield operation in the Middle East. During the mobilization period, all discharges were suspended. As soon as the need for armed forces personnel decreased, discharges for gay, lesbian, and bisexual persons were among the first processed for separation (Shilts, 1991). Consequently, it appears that the enforcement of the policy is directly related to DoD personnel needs. When personnel needs are high and personnel resources limited, enforcing the policy is suspended. As soon as the personnel resources available exceed the needs, enforcing the policy is reinstated.

Many of the veterans we interviewed told stories in which they indicated that they tried to be honest about their sexuality in their induction interviews and examinations, but the signals or cues they gave out were ignored. Thus, our impression is that from the very beginning gay or lesbian persons in the military receive confusing and mixed signals—from the official policy that they are not wanted, but from the behavior of other personnel that they will be accepted as long as the information that they are gay or lesbian is not explicitly known.

The attitudes toward same-gender sexual behavior among military service members probably mirrors that of the population at large. Interviewees reported a wide range of reactions by other military personnel and leaders to gay, lesbian, and bisexual military personnel. These reactions ranged from extreme hostility and punishment through benign neglect or denial to acceptance and support. The actual tolerance of gay, lesbian, and bisexual military service members varies by the mission, the commander, the local investigative services, and period of service. Consequently, interviewees' perceptions of protection and risk were variable and situation based.

**Mission, Occupation, and Type of Unit** In terms of mission, personnel in combat units were perceived as less tolerant than those in support units. The interviewees felt this was because of the inconsistency between the stereotypical perceptions of male homosexuality as associated with effeminacy, mental illness, promiscuity, loneliness, and insecurity, and of the combatant as associated with toughness, masculinity, and team orientation in combat units. Some saw military occupation or type of unit as making a difference; those in highly specialized occupations (linguists) or units (medics) were seen as being less likely to be eliminated from service because of greater tolerance, because the organization had invested so much in their training, or because the military would have difficulty obtaining replacement personnel with the same skills. By all accounts, those interviewees assigned to the medical departments of the various services perceived a higher toleration for gay, lesbian, and bisexual people. Likewise, intelligence personnel, for example linguists, were perceived to be very tolerant. However, discharge rates do not always confirm these perceptions (U.S. General Accounting Office, 1992).

Some interviewees believed life for gay, lesbian, or bisexual people in the military was easier overseas, while others believed life was easier in the United States. Those interviewed believed that overseas, the job took precedence, whereas in the United States, rules and regulations were more stringently followed because overseas there was a "real" or important job to do, whereas in the United States the jobs were less "important" militarily. Others saw overseas military communities as smaller than U.S. military communities and therefore gay, lesbian, and bisexual people were more at risk for having their daily activities observed and monitored. Likewise, interviewees who were assigned to military installations in large U.S. cities (such as Los Angeles, CA, or Washington, DC) saw living a gay life as easier and less risky. Also, interviewees who did not reside in military housing saw being gay as easier and less risky.

The bottom line appears to be that the mission and commander are what make the difference between some safety and little safety for gay, lesbian, and bisexual service members. Most commanders appear to "not want to know" or "not care" as long as the person does a good job and keeps her or his sexual activities from becoming public knowledge or openly suspected. Unfortunately, because an allegation is all that is needed (no evidence required) for the organization to invoke its power and punitive systems against gay, lesbian, and bisexual persons, safety is an illusion and risk is ever present. Various strategies are adopted to decrease the risk, but that risk can never be totally eliminated.

**Discharge Rates*** Our interviewees perceived the Air Force as more tolerant and officers to be at greater risk than enlisted personnel, while perceptions about differences between men and women were mixed. Women reported that the Women's Army Corps (WAC) infrastructure protected lesbians, a protection that was lost when the WAC's personnel were fully integrated into the Army. Dyer (1990) provides data that give some objective picture of how discharges for homosexuality vary by branch, gender, and rank. The data indicate that the Navy has the highest discharge rate (0.13% of total military personnel), whereas the other three branches have the same discharge rates (0.05%). Enlisted personnel and female personnel have higher discharge rates (enlisted, 0.08% versus officers, 0.01%; females, 0.16% versus males, 0.06%). The Navy has a higher rate for enlisted personnel (0.14% versus 0.06% for the other three services), while the Army has a lower rate for officers (0.004% versus 0.02% for the Navy and 0.01% for the Marines and the Air Force). For males, the Navy has a higher rate (0.11% versus 0.04% for the other three branches). Among females, the discharge rates vary across the four branches, but appear to be more similar for the Marines and Navy versus the Army and the Air Force (Marines 0.30%, Navy 0.24%, Army 0.15%, and Air Force 0.10%). There is no difference between the genders among officers (0.01%), but enlisted women are discharged at a notably higher rate (females 0.19%, males 0.07%). Based on these data, enlisted women bear the brunt of homophobia in the U.S. military. We interpret this effect as being largely composed of the two factors of homophobia and sexism. Sexism appears greatest in the Marines because enlisted men in the Marines are not discharged at a higher rate than enlisted men in the Air Force and Army are but enlisted women in the Marines are discharged at the highest rate of all four branches. Homophobia appears to play a greater role in the Navy where discharges for homosexuality are considerably elevated for both enlisted men and women. While, overall, enlisted personnel are more affected by the military policy on homosexuality, Army officers appear to be considerably less subjected to discharge for homosexuality. This interpretation is offered, with caution, because the four branches have many administrative discharge routes. For instance, gay, lesbian, and bi-

*The discharge rates presented in this chapter reflect averages over the three-year period of 1985–1987. The rates cited in the text are a secondary analysis of data presented in Dyer (1990).

sexual officers may be more frequently discharged for "conduct unbecoming an officer" rather than for "homosexuality."

### The Military as a Teacher of Homophobic Attitudes

Use of undesirable homosexual stereotypes by military drill instructors in basic training has been reported in the scholarly literature (Arkin & Dobrofsky, 1978; Eisenhart, 1975; Karst, 1991). We asked whether our interviewees perceived the military as teaching anti-gay attitudes. Most reported little or no homophobic teachings initially. Even so, they indicated that homophobia is so pervasive in society that gay, lesbian, and bisexual people in the military saw homophobic acts and statements by military personnel (such as drill instructors, sergeants, and officers) as part of being gay and did not always register them as slurs. They reported that in basic training recruits are referred to as "ladies," "latrine queens," "cunt-caps," "punk panties," and "lace on your drawers." People not performing to a drill instructor's liking might be asked "are you gay or something?" Although some of these examples indicate that sexism is alive and well within the military, our interviewees perceived that the military tolerates derogatory comments related to sexual orientation to an extent no longer tolerated for race and gender. Our interviewees concluded the military policy and practice reinforced the stereotypes and anti-gay attitudes that exist in the United States culture at large. The policy institutionalizes a form of prejudice—just as policies on women and blacks did at one time—and thus legitimizes it.

### Coping Strategies

Among the interviewees, some knew of their gayness or saw themselves as bisexual before induction. Others "came out" on active duty. Some had sexual experiences with other military personnel, while some only had sexual experiences with civilians. Others had a combination of civilian-military sexual partners whereas others were celibate. Gay, lesbian, and bisexual people told us stories about their attempts to be honest about their sexuality in induction interviews and entrance examinations. Of course, in most cases this did not mean an open admission of homosexuality or they would not have made it through the induction. Rather, it seemed to mean that they tried to be themselves, to give out the cues that they would normally in situations in which open admission is not appropriate, but subtle cues are given to people who know how to interpret the cues. But our interviewees found these cues were ignored. This epitomizes the dilemma of gay and lesbian people in the military. They try to be honest in the face of risk of exposure, but become trapped when others do not acknowledge the existence of gay people.

**Social Networks and Social Support** Some interviewees sought out other gay, lesbian, and bisexual people for support and social contact. Others avoided gay networks. Some sought to align themselves with more powerful individuals who were willing to serve as a protector against the system if and when needed. Others sought isolation, anesthetized their feelings with alcohol, only masturbated, dated heterosexually, formed marriages of convenience, etc. Others avoided close or intimate heterosexual relationships because those individuals wanted more commitment than the interviewee was comfortable making. Some believed that as they advanced in rank (whether officer or enlisted), the ability to maintain social networks, relationships (both friends and lovers), and personal integrity got harder.

Celibacy and avoiding contact with other gay, lesbian, and bisexual people provided the greatest protection from identification and investigation. For example, one of our interviewees reported that before he enlisted he received very strong advice about how to succeed in the military. The advice was to be discreet, to avoid other gay people, and to absolutely avoid any sexual or romantic involvements with other military personnel. He followed that advice, lived a relatively open gay life outside of his military service, and was not negatively affected by the military policy in any way that he understood. However, he left after only one term of enlistment because he was unwilling to continue to maintain the strict separation between his work life and his personal life. Other interviewees adopted the strategy of avoiding openly gay people, for example, "flamboyant queens." An officer we interviewed indicated that the gay or lesbian person in the military must realize that he or she must confide in no one, that anyone else knowing about one's sexual orientation puts one at risk. A lesbian officer indicated that officers must be very careful.

For many of the people we interviewed, this pattern of keeping themselves celibate and separate from other gay and lesbian people was present. Most of the people we interviewed had limited sexual experience and little lesbian or gay identity prior to induction. For this category, identifying other gay and lesbian members of the military and developing social networks or sexual contacts take a long time, and for a number of our interviewees, who only remained in the military for one term, they never really developed either social networks or any way of regularly making sexual contacts.

**Indispensability** One strategy offered by interviewees was to perform well, to prove oneself, to rise above the stigma of being gay or lesbian. A related strategy was to perform well so as to be left alone, above suspicion. It appears that some people go into the military and "try to be the best little boy in the world." Another strategy was an association with a powerful person who would recognize and value the gay, lesbian, and bisexual person's skills and provide protection of that gay, lesbian, and bisexual person in order to maintain access to his or her skills and abilities.

**Denial** Some of our interviewees indicated that they used the military service as a way to psychologically deny their sexual orientation. For example, one person we interviewed was in the Navy Reserve Officer Training Corps (ROTC) in college. He reported that he knew of his same-gender sexual orientation, but said to himself, "Since I am in Navy ROTC, I can't be gay." Many expressed feelings of low self-esteem and self-rejection wherein they desired to be "normal" but could not find a way to be so and therefore adopted negative self-images. Some convinced themselves they had created a strong heterosexual outer image as a way of protecting themselves from the constant fear of identification. These people had a split experience; a perception of protection combined with an inner vulnerability.

**Invisibility** Some people dealt with being gay in the military by "playing the game." By this people meant keeping personal life off-base, off-ship, out of the workplace, and maintaining the expected decorum. These people experienced a strong separation between gay nonmilitary social networks and straight military relationships. Others coped by sneaking around, by pretending to be heterosexual and changing names and pronouns when speaking of one's lovers and friends, and by not sharing personal life with others in the military. However, avoiding talking about one's personal life is not effective forever because eventually others begin to notice that one does not share one's personal life with them.

**Marriage** Some people engaged in marriages of convenience. These were perceived to be more common among enlisted service members than officers. They provided privacy because married people could move off base and out of the barracks. They also provided economic benefits because of the added living allowances for married people. They have their disadvantages, as well. Over time people reported that guilt and feelings of regret developed. Also, the spouse can become a potential liability, or a potential blackmailer.

**Functional Coping** While the military experience appeared to create considerable conflict for many of our interviewees, one group—those who were not investigated but who did have sexual involvements while on active duty—appeared largely to escape conflict. These people were enlisted, first-termers, served during the 1960s or early 1970s, and felt they could control what happened to them but did not attempt to create a false heterosexual image. Instead they tried to perform well, conformed to all military demands made of them, such as maintaining their uniforms, being dependable, performing their duties well, and saw the military as intolerant of many things (dress, appearance, etc.) not just their sexual orientation. They had a solid sense of self-esteem and general day-to-day competence, saw their role as making the most of whatever situation was at hand, were not confrontational about their sexual orientation but were not self-denying either, and did not engage in sexual behavior until they had gained insight into the rules of the organization (both formal and informal). Likewise, they found ways of making themselves indispensable to their boss, recognized the military's emphasis on team vs. individual needs, and did well in physical training, marksmanship, and other basic military skills. These people also viewed poorly performing gay, lesbian, and bisexual people as offensive and people who gave gay, lesbian, and bisexual people a "bad name." Likewise, these individuals did not seem to feel any more oppressed in the military than they did in the civilian world and at the same time recognized what the dos and don'ts were in both the civilian and military environments. They did not seem to feel a need to apologize for being gay but did not impose gayness on those who could not accept it.

### Military Identification and Investigation

Not all gay, lesbian, and bisexual people in the military are identified (Berube, 1990; Harry, 1984; Humphrey, 1990; Williams & Weinberg, 1971). For those people who are officially identified as homosexual, the identification occurs in a number of ways.

Some gay, lesbian, and bisexual people identify themselves for the purpose of getting out of the military or because they can no longer accept the closet. One interviewee, a medical corpsman, identified himself to his commander. Within two weeks he was quickly and honorably discharged.

Another way for someone to be officially identified or come under suspicion of being a gay, lesbian, or bisexual person is through being identified by others. When the military's investigative services interrogate someone accused of being gay or lesbian, it was consistently reported by interviewees that the person conducting the interrogation always tried to get the person under investigation to name others. This is one way that witchhunts get initiated. Our interviewees told us of witchhunts they experienced in several places: one in Korea focused on lesbians, and another in Monterey, California, focused on gay men. Retaliation by third parties can also lead to identification. One female interviewee reported that she was turned in by the civilian boyfriend of her civilian lover.

In addition to self-identification and identification by other individuals, the military also uses many of the same techniques for identifying gay, lesbian, and bisexual people as do civilian law enforcement organizations, such as surveillance and entrapment in places where people meet, and raiding bars. One interviewee reported that she had experienced surveillance of bars in San Antonio, Texas, and Naples, Italy. In addition, people are sometimes caught in sexual acts. For example, we were told of a Navy man and a Marine who were caught in oral sex. The "giver" was discharged but the "receiver" was not.

Once an allegation is made, military policy states that the case has to be investigated. There have even been cases of nonhomosexuals being investigated and discharged for homosexuality. Investigations initiated at one location can and do follow the individual to another location. Some of those investigated endured more than one investigation. Some of these investigations resulted in discharge while others resulted in exoneration. However, even when exonerated, the investigation sometimes resulted in other forms of more subtle punitive actions such as poor efficiency reports, reassignment, etc. Investigations can also leave internal scars from knowing one has falsified official records when signing statements that one is not gay, lesbian, or bisexual. Some people decide to leave the military before an investigation results in a negative outcome.

Our interviewees displayed a high level of cynicism about investigations and investigative personnel and their tactics. They perceived a high level of injustice and incompetence in the system. Other information supports this perception. For example, the explosion of a gun on the USS Iowa was initially attributed by the Naval Investigative Service (NIS) to a sailor who was distressed over an unrequited homosexual relationship. Subsequent Congressional hearings resulted in the repudiation of the NIS explanation and cast doubt on the professionalism and competence of its investigation.

One of our interviewees told us that the military called him in and told him they had irrefutable evidence that he had had sex with a particular man. He asked if he could have a lawyer. They told him they would only infer from his asking for a lawyer that he was guilty. Typically a person accused of homosexuality is threatened—"come clean and we will be easy on you, but if you don't we'll come down really hard." One person reported the following circumstances. He was read his rights and given formal papers to sign. The investigation went on for seven months. Although the investigators found no evidence, he was yanked from his position, marched to his desk in front of his coworkers, and ordered to clean out his desk. The interviewee asserted, "as soon as you are accused, you are in limbo, you can't be deployed, you can't have a weapon. Questions are raised about your performance."

Even if there is no proof and no court-martial, but there is an absence of a direct refusal or proof of heterosexual lifestyle (most often being married), doubts remain in supervisors' thoughts that can result in poor efficiency reports, job reassignments, etc. Likewise, there is the aspect of falsifying official records—signing statements that the individual is not a homosexual. Fear, paranoia, self-rejection, self-denial, etc., were reported.

The women we interviewed felt that women were abused more in investigations and that witchhunts more often involved women. Several possibilities for this suspicion were suggested. First, women may react differently to interrogation, perhaps more compliantly, and thus give out names more than men do, leading to investigations of other women. Alternatively, women may know more sexual partners by name, because men may be more likely to engage in anonymous sexual activities. Also, the military may harass women more because of sexism. Whatever the reasons, discharge statistics bear out that enlisted women are discharged for homosexuality at a rate greatly disproportionate to their numbers in the military (Benecke & Dodge, 1992; Dyer, 1990; U.S. General Accounting Office, 1992).

Every one of our interviewees who was identified reported that the experience was horrible, regardless of the outcome. Some interviewees expressed resentment that gays and lesbians are required to do things that criminals are not asked to do. Alleged gays are asked to sign statements they are not homosexuals; alleged thieves are not asked to sign statements they are not thieves.

A complete description of investigative techniques, the types of administrative boards and discharges, conditions under which court-martial and imprisonment occur, and the effect on individuals is beyond the scope of this chapter. Even so, we wanted to include some information on this topic and report some of the interviewees' comments. For more detailed and current information, a list of resources for a military service member accused of being homosexual is included in Appendix A.

### The Effect on Gay and Lesbian People of Being in the Military

Most of the interviewees indicated their military experience was very positive, except for the homophobia they encountered and their own fear of being identified and punished by the military. Some indicated they grew a lot personally through their military experience, gained self-respect, and some even indicated that they grew from the negative experiences. Others indicated being in the military helped them to form a positive image of themselves—an image of gay and lesbian people doing well even in a homophobic system.

On the other hand, our interviewees indicated that the military experience is not positive for many gay people because of the "direct experience of homophobia," "the isolation, keeping separate, not being able to share, lying." The policy is experienced as a "sword of Damocles—no matter what you do you can get fucked; they don't need evidence to screw your career even though you aren't discharged." "There is a constant state of fear." Many interviewees left because they thought their luck was eventually going to run out and they would be investigated and discharged. People may also leave because of a glass ceiling that functions in one of two ways: (1) Qualitative Management Programs (QMPs) offer ways to separate gay, lesbian, and bisexual people from military service without citing homosexuality; and (2) gay, lesbian, and bisexual persons place limits on their own career opportunities by separating before retirement eligibility.

There appears to be some degree of damage to every gay, lesbian, and bisexual person who enters the military, whether officially identified or not. Gay, lesbian, and bisexual people in the military are reluctant to accept themselves, and are apprehensive about entering into relationships, be they social, sexual, or romantic. Women reported that as they got older and more senior, trust between them and younger, more junior women began to break down. Women reported that internalized homophobia (Malyon, 1982) is very common and severe among higher ranking lesbians in the military. The manifestations include alcohol problems, a high level of personal toughness, and "maliciously going out of their way to hurt other lesbians." These constant threats lead to stress and illness in some persons. Among officers, same-gender sexual orientation is contrary to the honor code and therefore creates internal conflict. For women, being accused of being a lesbian is used as a form of sexist harassment (Benecke & Dodge, 1992).

The effect of being identified, investigated, and discharged is clearly negative. An allegation of being homosexual, regardless of any proof, can result in the revocation of a security clearance or the end of a career. Being investigated had a tremendous impact on the interviewees. Many indicated both internal changes and behavioral changes as a result. At the individual level, investigations invoke tremendous inner conflicts, most regarding the differences between inner knowledge of one's self and an outer image. Attitude changes were also reported. Some became more closeted or more conscious of their behavior. Others became personally and/or politically radicalized. One woman reported that an investigation led to her becoming paranoid. She lost all trust in her fellow officers. Another reported that she turned away from lesbian relationships, although the investigation was the reason for her becoming aware of her sexual orientation.

One unexpected aspect of our interviews is extremely noteworthy. Almost uniformly, interviewees expressed a sense of relief or catharsis from the interview, particularly when they were interviewed in groups. Such a result is very much in line with an understanding of the military experience for gay, lesbian, and bisexual persons as being traumatic and stressful. Helping professionals should assume in their work with gay, lesbian, and bisexual people with military experience that there has been traumatic stress that the person needs to talk out (Ochberg, 1988).

### Impact of the Policy on the Military

Among the interviewees, none perceived that the policy has a positive effect on the military. The commonly held view was that the policy has multiple negative effects. One officer (who was not gay, lesbian, or bisexual) believed the policy served no purpose. Furthermore, he asserted that it is out-of-date and does not reflect current social thinking. He concluded that "The military led the way regarding social progress for racial minorities and women, but it is behind on the gay issue." The policy deflects the energy of gay, lesbian, and bisexual persons from their duties to the risk of identification and discharge and it also deflects the energies of commanders and investigative services from other legitimate concerns. Team building is harmed because people have to conceal themselves and have to seek out support and personal bonds outside of the primary military work unit. The military is deprived of talent, wastes money, and causes real psychological and economic harm to individuals. Just as the presence of racism and sexism harms the military, the military's reinforcement of homophobia is a reinforcement of interpersonal divisions that undermine the development of the group cohesion that sustains the fighting spirit. Many interviewees expressed the strong sentiment that the focus on homosexuality in the evaluation of persons for security clearances was a diversion from the real issues that indicated a weakness in security priorities.

The policy also creates a dilemma for commanders. Commanders' performances are judged by the quality of their units' performances. Bad conduct of individuals in their units is a cause of negative judgments of the commanders' leadership abilities. Thus it is best for a commander to have no homosexuality identified in his or her unit. Because gay, lesbian, and bisexual people are likely to be present in most units, the policy sets up a lose-lose situation for commanders. Commanders with gay, lesbian, and bisexual people in their units fear losing good performers and having a conduct problem that would reflect poorly on their leadership. This may be one of the key reasons that military personnel choose to deny the existence of gay, lesbian, and bisexual service members.

The DoD policy also raises troubling conflicts with professional standards for psychologists and other professionals. The policy places mental health professionals employed by the military in ethical dilemmas between the expectations of the military and the expectations of the professions. For example, a clinical psychologist in the military is bound to inform his or her superiors if a condition that indicates a client is unfit comes to his or her attention. For the military, homosexual orientation indicates unfitness, but for the psychological profession it does not.

## CONCLUSION

Although national defense is a social and political necessity, the U.S. military is fully equipped to integrate gay, lesbian, and bisexual people, thereby providing a social model for reducing or ameliorating homophobia and stereotypical beliefs, and still maintain the integrity of its mission. Resistance to the integration of openly gay, lesbian, and bisexual service members will certainly be a problem for the military among those military members with anti-gay prejudices. However, the military has available to it a long history of dealing with similar problems, with regard to African Americans (Binkin et al., 1982; MacGregor, 1981) and women (Stiehm, 1989). The Defense Equal Opportunity Management Institute (formerly the Defense Race Relations Institute) is devoted to the task. A DoD-commissioned study offered the recommendation that "it would be wise to consider applying the experience of the past 40 years to the integration of homosexuals'' (Dyer, 1990, p. 25).

The U.S. military policies and regulations against same-gender sexual orientation do not merely reflect society. They go beyond the current level of discrimination prevalent in civilian society. The U.S. military actively seeks to identify gay, lesbian, and bisexual people, to investigate their lives using degrading and stressful techniques that include intimidation, and to actually brand them as inadequate and unacceptable. The active hunting out, intense investigation and interrogation, and the discharge with a stigma branded on an official document leave gay, lesbian, and bisexual veterans with psychological damage of varying levels of severity. Particularly vulnerable are young people recruited by military advertising prior to the emergence of their same-gender sexual orientation. These young people are submitted to trauma and stress at a crucial phase in the natural development of their personal identity. The DoD policy causes real harm to individuals.

The great majority of gay, lesbian, and bisexual people adjust to the stigma, prejudice, and discrimination associated with their sexual orientation. Studies demonstrate that these people are psychologically well-adjusted, but the small group who fail to do so are troubled and dysfunctional (Bell & Weinberg, 1978; Hammersmith & Weinberg, 1973; Weinberg & Williams, 1974). Clinicians writing about those clients who have great difficulties with the stigma and prejudice against their homosexual orientation have referred to the condition as ''internalized homophobia'' (Malyon, 1982). By stigmatizing gay, lesbian, and bisexual people, the U.S. military policy fosters internalized homophobia and its self-destructive effects, and thereby does additional psychological harm.

Even for those persons who successfully adjust to stigma without serious psychological difficulties, the DoD policy and the services' regulations give reason for concealing or denying their sexual orientation, an obstacle to their achieving optimal psychological development (Gonsiorek & Rudolph, 1991). This concealment also introduces a degree of alienation between military personnel and the institution.

For these reasons—the military's capacity to change, the lack of any demonstrated impact of the change on national security, and the real harm caused by the policy—we strongly support rescission. We believe the benefits are clear: the elimination of a harmful and useless policy and the provision of an extremely influential model of integration and nondiscrimination. The latter will be a major step toward honor without stigma for all lesbian, gay, and bisexual persons in the United States.

## REFERENCES

Allport, F. H., et al. (1953). The effects of segregation and the consequences of desegregation: A social science statement. *Minnesota Law Review, 37,* 429–440.

American Psychiatric Association. (1973). Position statement on homosexuality and civil rights. *American Journal of Psychiatry, 131*(4), 497.

American Psychiatric Association. (1987). *Diagnostic and statistical manual of mental disorders* (3rd ed. rev.). Washington, DC: Author.

Amir, Y. (1976). The role of intergroup contact in change of prejudice and ethnic relations. In P. A. Katz (Ed.), *Towards the elimination of racism.* New York: Pergamon.

Arkin, W., & Dobrofsky, L. R. (1978). Military socialization and masculinity. *Journal of Social Issues, 34*(1), 151–168.

Ashmore, R. D., & Del Boca, F. K. (1976). Psychological approaches to understanding inter-group conflicts. In P. A. Katz (Ed.), *Towards the elimination of racism.* New York: Pergamon.

Bell, A. P., & Weinberg, M. S. (1978). *Homosexualities: A study of diversity among men and women.* New York: Simon & Schuster.

Benecke, M. M., & Dodge, K. S. (1992). Lesbian baiting as sexual harassment: Women in the military. In W. Blumenfeld (Ed.), *Homophobia: How we all pay the price.* Boston: Beacon.

Bersoff, D. N., & Ogden, D. W. (1988). Brief of *amicus curiae* American Psychological Association in support of plaintiff-appellant: The U.S. Court of Appeals for the ninth circuit (No. 85-4006): Sergeant Perry J. Watkins, Plaintiff-Appellant, v. United States Army, et al., Defendants-Appellees. [Available from the American Psychological Association, 750 First Street, NE, Washington, DC 20002-4242]

Berube, A. (1990). *Coming out under fire: The history of gay men and women in World War Two.* New York: The Free Press.

Binkin, M., Eitelberg, M. J., Schexnider, A. J., & Smith, M. M. (1982). *Blacks and the military.* Washington, DC: Brookings Institution.

Brewer, M. B., & Kramer, R. M. (1985). The psychology of intergroup attitudes and behavior. *Annual Review of Psychology, 36,* 219–243.

Colasanto, D. (1989). Tolerance of homosexuality on rise among public. *Gallup News Service, 54*(24), 1–3.

Committee on Lesbian and Gay Concerns. (1991). Avoiding heterosexist bias in language. *American Psychologist, 48,* 973–974.

Congressional Budget Office. (1989). *Social representation in the U.S. military.* Washington, DC: Author.

Conger, J. J. (1975). Proceedings of the American Psychological Association for the year 1974: Minutes of the Annual Meeting of the Council of Representatives. *American Psychologist, 30,* 620–651.

Duke, L. (1991, August 4). Employer puts pluralism first. *Washington Post,* A1, A22–A23.

Dyer, K. (Ed.). (1990). *Gays in uniform: The Pentagon's secret reports.* Boston: Alyson.

Eisenhart, R. W. (1975). You can't hack it little girl? A discussion of the covert psychological agenda of modern combat training. *Journal of Social Issues, 31*(4), 13–23.

Gellman, B. (1991, August 1). Cheney rejects idea that gays are security risks. *Washington Post,* p. A33.

Gentry, C. S. (1987). Social distance regarding male and female homosexuals. *Journal of Social Psychology, 127,* 199–208.

Gibson, E. L. (1978). *Get off my ship: Ensign Berg vs. the U.S. Navy.* New York: Avon.

Goffman, E. (1961). *Asylums: Essays on the social situation of mental patients and other immates.* New York: Doubleday.

Gonsiorek, J. C. (1991). The empirical basis for the demise of the illness model of homosexuality. In J. C. Gonsiorek & J. D. Weinrich (Eds.), *Homosexuality: Research implications for public policy* (pp. 115–136). Newbury Park, CA: Sage.

Gonsiorek, J. C., & Rudolph, J. R. (1991). Homosexual identity: Coming out and other developmental events. In J. C. Gonsiorek & J. D. Weinrich (Eds.), *Homosexuality: Research implications for public policy* (pp. 161–176). Newbury Park, CA: Sage.

Hammersmith, S. K., & Weinberg, M. S. (1973). Homosexual identity: Commitment, adjustment, and significant others. *Sociometry, 36,* 56–79.

Harry, J. (1984). Homosexual men & woman who served their country. *Journal of Homosexuality, 10*(1/2), 117–125.

Hatfield, L. D. (1989, June 30). Gays say life getting better. *San Francisco Examiner,* A15.

Herek, G. M. (1984). Beyond "homophobia": A social psychological perspective on attitudes toward lesbians and gay men. *Journal of Homosexuality, 10,* 1–21.

Herek, G. M. (1988). Homosexuals' attitudes toward lesbians and gay men: Correlates and gender differences. *Journal of Sex Research, 25*(4), 451–477.

Herek, G. M. (1991a). Stigma, prejudice, and violence against lesbians and gay men. In J. C. Gonsiorek & J. D. Weinrich (Eds.), *Homosexuality: Research implications for public policy* (pp. 60–80). Newbury Park, CA: Sage.

Herek, G. M. (1991b, August). *Is homosexuality compatible with military service? A review of the social science data.* Symposium conducted at the meeting of the American Psychological Association, San Francisco.

Herek, G. M. (1991c). Myths about sexual orientation: A lawyer's guide to social science research. *Law & Sexuality, 1,* 133–172.

Hippler, M. (1989). *Matlovich: The good soldier.* Boston: Alyson.

Human Rights Foundation. (1984). *Demystifying homosexuality: A teaching guide about lesbians and gay men.* New York: Irvington.

Humphrey, M. A. (1990). *My country, my right to serve: Experiences of gay men and women in the military, World War II to the present.* New York: Harper Collins.

Janowitz, M. F., & Little, R. D. (1965). *Sociology and the military establishment.* New York: Russell Sage Foundation.

Karst, K. L. (1991). The pursuit of manhood and the desegregation of the armed forces. *UCLA Law Review, 38,* 499–581.

Kauth, Michael R. (1991, August). *Ethnic minority and gender integration: Lessons to be learned.* Symposium conducted at the meeting of the American Psychological Association, San Francisco.

Keen, L. M. (1992, May 29). DoD policy rings hollow in face of Pentagon studies, assaults. *Washington Blade, 23*(22), 1, 15.

Livingood, J. M. (Ed.). (1972). *National Institute of Mental Health Task Force on Homosexuality: Final report and background papers.* (DHEW Publication No. (HSM) 72-9116). Washington, DC: U.S. Government Printing Office.

MacGregor, M. J., Jr. (1981). *Integration of the armed forces 1940–1965* (CMH Pub. 50-1). Washington, DC: United States Army, Center of Military History.

Malyon, A. (1982). Psychotherapeutic implications of internalized homophobia in gay men. In J. Gonsiorek (Ed.), *Homosexuality and psychotherapy: Practitioners' handbook of affirmative models.* New York: Haworth.

Murphy, L. R. (1988). *Perverts by official order: The campaign against homosexuals by the United States Navy.* New York: Haworth.

National Association of Social Workers. (1988). Lesbian and gay issues. In *Social work speaks: NASW policy statements* (pp. 92–93). Silver Spring, MD: Author.

National Gay Task Force. (n.d.). *NGTF corporate survey.* Washington, DC: Author.

Ochberg, F. M. (Ed.). (1988). *Post-traumatic therapy and victims of violence.* New York: Brunner Mazel.

Penn & Schoen Associates, Inc. (1991). *A report to the Human Rights Campaign Fund on public attitudes toward homosexuals and their place in the military.* (Available from Human Rights Campaign Fund, 1012 14th St., NW, Washington, DC 20005).

Rudolph, J. (1989). Effects of a workshop on mental health practitioners' attitudes toward homosexuality and counseling effectiveness. *Journal of Counseling and Development, 68*(1), 81–85.

Schneider, D., & Schneider, C. J. (1988). *Sound off! American military women speak out.* New York: Paragon House Publishers.

Schneider, W., & Lewis, I. A. (1984, February/March). The straight story on homosexuality and gay rights. *Public Opinion, 7,* 16–20, 59–60.

Shilts, R. (1991, August 5). In wake of war military again targets gays. *San Francisco Chronicle,* A1.

Snyder, W., & Nyberg, K. L. (1980). Gays and the military: An emerging policy issue. *Journal of Political and Military Sociology, 8,* 71–84.

Steihm, J. (1989). *Arms and the enlisted woman.* Philadelphia: Temple University Press.

Steihm, J. (1991, August). *Problems in managing the military's exclusion policy.* Symposium conducted at the meeting of the American Psychological Association, San Francisco.

Stephan, W. G. (1985). Intergroup relations. In G. Gardner & E. Aronson (Eds.), *Handbook of social psychology: Volume 2* (3rd ed.), 693.

Stewart, A. (1991, December 16). Gay in corporate America. *Fortune, 124,* 42–48.

Tielman, R., & de Jonge, T. (1988). Country-by-country survey: A worldwide inventory of discrimination and liberation of lesbians and gay men. In Pink Book Editing Team (Eds.), *Second ILGA pink book* (pp. 185–242). Utrecht, Netherlands: International Lesbian & Gay Association.

U.S. Air Force Academy. (1984). The military family. In *Proceedings* of the Ninth Biennial Psychology in the Department of Defense Symposium. Colorado Springs, CO: Author.

U.S. Department of Defense. (1982). DoD Directive 1332.14, January 28, 1982, Enlisted administrative separations.

U.S. General Accounting Office. (1992). Defense force management: DoD's policy on homosexuality. (Report to Congressional Requesters #GAO/NSIAD-92-98). Washington, DC: Author.

Weinberg, M. S., & Williams, C. J. (1974). *Male homosexuals: Their problems and adaptations.* New York: Oxford University Press.

Williams, C. J., & Weinberg, M. S. (1971). *Homosexuals and the military: A study of less than honorable discharge.* New York: Harper & Row.

## APPENDIX: RESOURCES

For professionals working with veterans, we strongly suggest referrals to gay, lesbian, and bisexual veteran support organizations or groups. For information, contact the Gay, Lesbian, and Bisexual Veterans of America at 1350 North 37th Place, Milwaukee, Wisconsin 53208; (414) 342-6543.

For clients currently in service or considering service, we recommend that the clients seek counselors with experience in military issues. For this reason, the following list is provided for referral purposes.

American Civil Liberties Union Lesbian and Gay Rights Project
132 West 43rd Street
New York, NY 10036
(212) 944-9800, Ext. 545

CCCO
2208 South Street
Philadelphia, PA 19146
(215) 454-4626

Citizen Soldier
Todd Ensign, Esq.
175 5th Avenue #808
New York, NY 10010
(212) 777-3470

Human Rights Campaign Fund
1012 14th Street, NW
Washington, DC 20005
(202) 628-4160

Lambda Legal Defense and Education Fund
666 Broadway
New York, NY 10012
(212) 995-8585

Midwest Committee for Military Counseling
Ray Parrish
343 S. Dearborn #1113
Chicago, IL 60604
(312) 939-3349

Military Law Panel
Kathy Gilberd and Bridget Wilson
1168 Union #201
San Diego, CA 92101
(619) 233-1701

National Gay and Lesbian Task Force
1734 14th Street, NW
Washington, DC 20009
(202) 332-6483

Chapter 5

# Homosexuality and the Church

**J. R. McSpadden, Jr.**

Only recently has the question of ordaining a homosexual to the Christian ministry in the United States been a problem. Heretofore, homosexuality was almost universally condemned in churches as immoral, contrary to the Bible, and incompatible with Christian faith and life. The negative attitudes toward homosexuality found in churches reflect those prevalent in the larger society.

Probably there have always been homosexual persons among the clergy, but open avowal of their orientation would have been professional suicide. Today, the approval of openly gay or lesbian persons for ordination is still rare, but there is more diversity of opinion on the subject. As homosexuality has become a matter of public debate, some Christians have felt compelled to reexamine the nature of the homosexual condition. This reconsideration has resulted in heated debate and bitter controversy in local churches and denominations.

To understand the situation of lesbians and gay men in the churches, it is important to recognize the diversity in beliefs and practices among Christians. Persons unfamiliar with churches may assume that the Christian church in the United States is monolithic. They mistakenly assume that only minor differences in observable rituals such as weddings and funerals distinguish Protestants from Roman Catholics or Protestant groups from one another. Actually, Christian churches vary greatly in patterns of governance, sources of authority, views of Scripture, and requirements for ordination to the ministry or priesthood.

A church with a congregational form of government (e.g., independent Baptist) recognizes no authority beyond itself as to whom it can ordain as a minister. In the Roman Catholic Church, which is hierarchical in its governance, ordination and the appointment of a parish pastor are controlled by bishops and ultimately the papal office. A Southern Baptist congregation can unilaterally hire and fire its ministers, but in a United Methodist Church such decisions are made by an area conference and bishop. The Church of Christ is literalistic in interpreting the Bible; whereas the Presbyterian Church USA has more flexibility in interpreting Scripture and is not bound by a belief that the Bible is inerrant.

Moreover, Christian denominations vary greatly in their requirements for men and women seeking ordination to the ministry or priesthood. In some fundamentalist congregations, it is possible for someone to announce that God has called him to enter the ministry, whereupon the congregation votes immediately to confirm his ordination. On the other hand most mainline churches require four years of college and three of seminary education of candidates for ordination. The norm for ordination to the priesthood in the Roman Catholic Church is three-and-a-half years of seminary after college. It is still true, however, that in many Protestant bodies in the United States it is possible to become ordained with little or no formal education.

It should be pointed out, however, that these differences among denominations mean that there are some churches in which the potential for change in attitudes toward lesbian and gay clergy is greater than in others. Actually, very few Protestant bodies have taken national and denominational positions that permit a lower church court (e.g., a presbytery or a conference) to ordain an avowed homosexual to the office of minister, priest, deacon, or bishop. Many of the mainline Protestant denominations are currently grappling with this issue and that struggle has similarities to the debates in the late 1960s and early 1970s over the ordination of women.

This chapter will survey: (1) the current positions several denominations have taken regarding the ordination of gay men and lesbians to offices of leadership; (2) some of the Biblical material that Protestant and Roman Catholic churches have used to refuse ordination to homosexual men and women; and (3) several personal issues facing gay and lesbian religious leaders in the practice of ministry.

## CURRENT ECCLESIASTICAL POSITIONS

The *Yearbook of American and Canadian Churches 1991* includes data from 219 religious bodies in the United States. This is not an exact number of religious denominations or ecclesiastical communions; but of those religious bodies responding, there is a reported total membership of 147.6 million Americans who have been or are currently involved in religious institutions (National Council of Churches of Christ in the United States of America, 1991). Within each of the religious bodies reporting, there will be some spread of political and theological beliefs within the membership. It is harder to see those differences in smaller communions of less than 50,000 members; but in the larger mainline denominations, there are serious political tensions around the acceptance of gay and lesbian church leaders and clergy.

James B. Nelson has attempted to organize the various theological and ecclesiastical positions of Christian churches in terms of their willingness to accept homosexual men and women as leaders (Nelson, 1978). The first grouping is those denominations with a *rejecting-punitive* orientation in which homogenital behavior is condemned without exception by local and/or national governing bodies. This is the position of most fundamentalist denominations, evangelical movements, and independent Bible congregations that tend to be authoritarian and theological purists. The two largest bodies in the United States that have taken this position are the Church of Jesus Christ Latter Day Saints (Mormon) and the Southern Baptist Convention.

The Southern Baptist Convention has engaged in a 13-year contest for control of the convention boards and institutions. The party that favors more rigid doctrinal standards for seminaries, publications, and missionaries now dominates the convention. The moderates who favor greater freedom and acceptance of diversity have been virtually deprived of a voice in making policies and decisions. Hence the condemnation of the convention was predictable, when in 1992, a congregation in Chapel Hill, North Carolina, granted a license to preach (a preliminary step toward ordination) to a gay divinity school student. At about the same time, another congregation in Raleigh, North Carolina, blessed the union of two gay men.

Historically, Southern Baptists have treasured and protected the autonomy of local congregations to make their own decisions. They have also condemned homosexuality on biblical and theological grounds. For example, at the 1988 Southern Baptist Convention, the issue of homosexuality was debated for 10 minutes and the "messengers" voted their disapproval of homosexuality "as an abomination in the eyes of God, a perversion of divine standards, and a violation of nature" (Nugent & Gramick, 1989, p. 25).

When a choice was faced between recognizing the autonomy of churches and opposition to homosexuality, the longstanding tradition of autonomy was ignored. In 1992, the annual meeting of the Southern Baptist Convention voted to amend its constitution, so that no congregation could be in "friendly cooperation" with the convention if it acts to "affirm, approve, or endorse homosexual behavior." Because for nearly 150 years the only requirement to be a cooperating church of the Southern Baptist Convention had been a financial obligation, this was a radical departure from tradition and signified the intensity of the leaders' feelings against homosexuality.

It is not uncommon in other fundamentalist and independent congregations to hear their clergy interpret the AIDS epidemic as an act of God to punish and eliminate homosexuals. Many spokespersons in this camp think that homosexuality is solely a matter of will and that one can decide to change sexual orientation as readily as a decision to change one's clothes. The rejecting-punitive view also incorporates societal stereotypes about male homosexuals being effeminate child molesters, "over-sexed," and promiscuous. Regrettably, this may be the most popular view among U.S. Christians and the one that is often held (albeit privately) even within the mainline denominations that are becoming more tolerant of gays and lesbians in their stated ecclesiastical positions.

The second cluster of churches includes those with a *rejecting-nonpunitive* view. This category represents most of the mainline denominations (not in terms of numbers of members, but numbers of denominations) that have policy statements that reject homogenital sex but accept homosexual persons. The most recent teachings of the magisterium of the Roman Catholic Church represent this view, arguing that genital sex is ordained by God for the purpose of procreation and that homogenital sex is condemned as an object disorder and is therefore "intrinsically evil" (Nugent & Gramick, 1989, p. 33). One of the best resources for understanding the current position of the Catholic Church and related theological and polity issues is Robert Nugent and Jeannine Gramick's *Building Bridges: Gay and Lesbian Reality and the Catholic Church* (1992).

In 1992 the United Methodist Church, while continuing to encourage ministries with the homosexual community and to provide pastoral and congregational care for gays and lesbians, voted not to change the phrase "that homosexuality is incompatible with Christian teaching" in *The Book of Discipline of the United Methodist Church.* After years of study by a special committee, the social principles statement remains: "Although we do not condone the practice of homosexuality and consider this practice incompatible with Christian teaching, we affirm that God's grace is available to all" (*The Book of Discipline of the United Methodist Church,* 1988, p. 96). The United Methodists concluded at the end of the 1992 report that they "had been unable to arrive at a common mind on the issue" and asked the church to continue its study of the compatibility of homosexuality with the Christian faith.

The American Baptist Church, USA, at its 1991 biennial meeting, took actions that reflect its disunity on this issue. On one day the delegates voted to ask their general board to appoint a task force to make a study to help guide the denomination to a Christian perspective on sexuality. The next day, however, they voted a statement flatly rejecting the practice of homosexuality. They followed that by defeating a statement that appealed for openness and dialogue in "learning more about our sexuality, its responsible expression, and God's gift of sexuality in others." A year later the general board rejected an urgent appeal from the churches of one of the regions to condemn homosexual behavior as outside the Christian lifestyle, but the vote, after three hours of debate, was close—91 to 88. The general secretary made it clear later that the vote "does not imply an endorsement of the other side of the issue." No action was taken with respect to the two North Carolina congregations cited above, which were dually aligned with both the American Baptist Churches and the Southern Baptist Convention.

The Episcopal Church, at its triennial General Convention in 1991, decided, after creating an ecclesiastical double-bind that stated that individual dioceses (a particular governing area) could ordain homosexual men and women to the priesthood and also had a resolution that no one engaging in genital relations outside of marriage could be ordained, to study the subjects of ordination and human sexuality (Radner & Sumner, 1991).

The final Protestant denomination in the rejecting-nonpunitive group that has made a major study and decision on homosexuality and the ordination of gays and lesbians in recent years is the Presbyterian Church USA. This church had taken positions in the late seventies against the ordination of self-acknowledged and active homosexuals; but the general assembly was asked again in 1987 to form a special committee on human sexuality to report to the 1991 general assembly. In the spring of 1991 an explosion occurred within the Presbyterian Church when drafts of the study entitled "Keeping Body and Soul Together: Sexuality, Spirituality, and Social Justice" were dropped initially into the church press and later the national media. Before the material in the report and in the subsequent minority report were studied and considered by the various governing levels or judicatories of the church, stories were being carried in the *New York Times* and *NBC Nightly News* that stirred up individual members, church bureaucrats, seminary professors, and local pastors.

There are several reasons why the Presbyterian Church eventually rejected this report, which would have allowed homosexuals to serve as ministers and officers. The report not only brought homosexuality "out of the closet" and into the consciousness of the church, but it also brought discussions of the actual sexual behavior of Americans living in the late 20th century into the consciousness of Presbyterians who wish they could return to 19th century morality. The report took a long look at the contemporary sexual behavior of single persons—before marriage, between marriages, widowed, and widowers. It further attempted to help the church develop an ethic that linked a healthy spirituality with an emotionally healthy sexuality. And the report challenged those literalistic biblical readers who feel that any right-thinking Presbyterian can draw a line straight *from* the patriarchal Biblical narrative that was written 2,500 years ago *to* an issue like the sinfulness of consenting and responsible unmarried elderly adults having intercourse in the late 20th century.

Since the decision not to ordain Presbyterian homosexual men and women to the ministry within the church, test cases are beginning to emerge throughout the country challenging the 1991 general assembly position. One such challenge to the Presbyterian Church's denominational position is by a Presbyterian lesbian who was ordained prior to her public declaration that she was a lesbian. She has been offered a position on the staff of a congregation in Rochester, New York, but the judicatory that is responsible for allowing her to accept the position is currently debating the issue. A summary of the issues in this case can be found in "Gay Issues Kept Alive for Presbyterians" (Aquino, 1992).

A few smaller religious bodies have been able to move to a full acceptance position of gay and lesbian clergy. Developing Nelson's typology, this position "holds that homosexuality is part of the divine plan of creation, and that homosexual people are present as a sign of the rich diversity of creation, and that homosexual expression is as natural and good in every way as heterosexuality" (Nugent & Gramick, 1989, p. 39). Religious groups falling into this cluster are the United Church of Christ, Quakers (Friends), Disciples of Christ, Unitarian Universalists, and the Metropolitan Community Church. The Metropolitan Community Church was founded for gay men and lesbians by the Rev. Troy Perry in the mid-1960s.

## BIBLICAL MATERIAL

The majority of Protestant denominations and the Roman Catholic Church justify their refusal to ordain self-affirming homosexual men and women by citing several passages of Scripture (both the Old and New Testaments). Although the Bible does not have to be the sole source for making decisions about Christian morality, it is the starting point in discussions of ethical issues facing the church. Biblical passages commonly appealed to in this debate may be classified as follows: (a) homosexual behavior between consenting adults Lev. 18:22, Lev. 20:13, and Rom. 1:26–27; (b) homosexual rape Gen. 19:1–29; and (c) homosexual behavior in general I Cor. 6:9–10 and I Tim. 1:9–10. All of the references are found in the *New Revised Standard Version Bible.*

### Homosexual Behavior Between Consenting Adults

Leviticus 18:22 reads "You shall not lie with a male as with a woman; it is an abomination." Within the Levitical Holiness Code (ceremonial and moral laws found in Leviticus chapters 17–26) there are other abominations that are repugnant to God and the norms of society. For example, diseased or disabled men could not serve as priests, sexual intercourse during the seven days of a female's menstrual period was forbidden, nudity was outlawed as was incest, child sacrifice, and bestiality. Violations of the code meant death: ". . . whoever commits any of these abominations shall be cut off from their people" (Lev. 18:29). As the Israelites settled in Canaan, there was considerable contact with other religious groups that used fertility rituals in temple worship (Deuteronomy 23:17).

"Since the [Canaanite] gods were understood as sexual they were to be worshipped in overt sexual acts. Whenever homosexual activity is mentioned in the Old Testament, the author usually has in mind the use male worshippers made of male prostitutes provided by the temple authorities" (McNeill, 1988, p. 57). The Israelite leaders wanted to clearly differentiate themselves and their people from what was idolatrous, so we have a linkage in the Holiness Code between homosexual behavior and idolatry.

But the writers of Scripture did not understand homosexuality as a sexual orientation (a psycho-social condition that affects the way one thinks and feels about others of the same sex) but rather their focus was on homosexual acts that defile cultic ritual practices. McNeill states: "It is important to understand that the genuine homosexual condition—or inversion, as it is often termed—is something for which the subject can in no way be held responsible. In itself it is morally neutral. Like the condition of heterosexuality, however, it tends to find expression in specific sexual acts; and such acts are subject to moral judgement" (McNeill, 1988, p. 41).

Leviticus 20:13: "If a man lies with a male as with a woman, both of them have committed an abomination; they shall be put to death; their blood is upon them." Within the priestly tradition that was evolving through the time of the monarchy, homosexual behavior was viewed as a capital crime. McNeill reminds the contemporary reader of Leviticus that we are reading a passage that looked only at the behavior (specific homosexual acts) and viewed it as what we might call a perversion. The writers of Leviticus did not have our contemporary lenses to distinguish between inversion and perversion (McNeill, 1988).

Romans 1:26–27 on the surface is a forceful denunciation by Paul of male and female homosexual behavior. "For this reason God gave them up to degrading passions. Their women exchanged natural intercourse for unnatural, and in the same way also the men, giving up natural intercourse with women, were consumed with passion for one another. Men committed shameless acts with men and received in their own persons the due penalty for their error." Paul seems to be saying that erotic and sexual attraction between same-sex partners is a "degrading passion" and that homosexual activity is "unnatural" (*para physin*). Scholars are not sure what Paul means by "unnatural." Does he mean what is customary (what is taught within one's culture), what is referred to today as "natural law," or what is normative within a specific community's value structure? McNeill and others feel that the weight of the contextual evidence is against the more popularly held position that homosexuality is intrinsically sinful or wrong and subscribe instead to the view that because homosexuality is a condition (inversion) both heterosexuals and homosexuals are capable of alienation from God (being consumed by passion or compulsion) that would in effect be viewed as idolatrous (McNeill, 1988).

## Homosexual Rape

Genesis 19:1–29. The Old Testament passage that has been a cornerstone in the church's criticism of homosexuality is the story of Sodom and Gomorrah. The account begins in chapter 18 as Abraham and his wife Sarah go out of their way to welcome three visitors into their camp near Mamre. As the story unfolds we learn that the three guests are actually God and two angels. God wants to go to Sodom and punish the people for some unspecified sin (we are only told that some people have behaved "wickedly"). After Abraham greets the guests and orders that a meal be prepared for them, he and Sarah (who are both elderly) are told that she will have a son. In the next paragraph, Abraham is told of God's plan to destroy Sodom and he tries to strike a deal with God that would protect any innocent people from being destroyed. He bargains with God down from a position of finding 50 to just 10 righteous men. If Abraham can find them, the city will be spared, according to the biblical writer. The angels are mistaken by the townsfolk of Sodom to be ordinary men; and while they are visiting Lot, the men of the town surround the house and demand that the guests come out of the house so that the males of Sodom "may know them" (19:5). While "to know" (*yadha*) has been translated "to engage in coitus" (homosexual coitus), the Hebrew word that is normally used in the Old Testament for both homosexual coitus and bestiality is *shakkabh* (Bailey, 1955, p. 10). G. A. Barton, in an article on "sodomy," has written that because of the variations in meaning and that the account focuses on the angels as foreigners that *yadha* could be translated as "to get acquainted with" (Barton, 1921).

If, however, one decides on the more traditional interpretation of the men having homosexual coitus with God's messengers then the event would be viewed as gang rape. Such a violent assault of males by males in the Ancient Near East was not uncommon behavior among warriors who wanted to humiliate their victims.

For centuries this story has been interpreted to mean a blanket condemnation of homosexual behavior. The early church (II Peter 2:6–10 and Jude 7), in its references to the Sodom and Gomorrah account, does not suggest that the sin or event that led to the destruction of the cities was homosexual behavior as much as it was a more general sexual misconduct. The inhospitality of the people of Sodom and the threatened sexual assault of God's messengers were the principal issues that lead to the city's judgment and destruction. When the behavior of the Sodomites is placed beside Sarah and Abraham's warm reception of the angelic guests, the preoccupation of the biblical writers with offering hospitality to the stranger is a far more convincing position than the one taken by most Christian denominations who use the story to condemn all homosexual persons (Edwards, 1989, p. 25).

It is also important to note that in the Old Testament book of Ezekiel the interpretation given to the events in Sodom was that God destroyed the city because of its inhospitality to those who were poor and needy (Ezekiel 16:49).

### Homosexual Behavior in General

I Corinthians 6:9–10. Paul is also the author of I Cor. 6:9–10. Of all the communities around the Mediterranean Sea, where he helped to establish Christian churches, Corinth was probably the most cosmopolitan. Corinth had a sizable Jewish population of merchants and craftsmen. The local synagogue was usually the starting place for the formation of any congregation of believers Paul might be able to assemble. It was to this new congregation that he wrote: "Do you not know that wrongdoers will not inherit the kingdom of God? Fornicators, idolators, adulterers, male prostitutes, sodomites, thieves, the greedy, drunkards, revilers, robbers—none of these will inherit the kingdom of God."

Once again there is a discussion within the community of biblical scholars as to the meaning Paul was giving to "male prostitutes." Was he suggesting "all homosexual persons, homosexual perverts, homosexual prostitutes, sodomites, promiscuous homosexual persons, anyone (whether heterosexual or homosexual) who engages in any form of homosexual behavior, all of the above, or none of the above? At this distance in both time and culture, we cannot answer such a question with confidence" (United Presbyterian Church, 1978, p. 28).

I Timothy 1:9–10. The preoccupation of the writer of First Timothy seems to be the order and survival of his first century believing community. "This means understanding that the law is laid down not for the innocent but for the lawless and disobedient, for the godless and sinful, for the unholy and profane, for those who kill their father or mother, for murderers, fornicators, sodomites, slave traders, liars, perjurers, and whatever else is contrary to the sound teaching. . ." (I Tim. 1:9–10). The writer of this passage has placed homosexual acts as one of a number of behaviors that violates God's will for humanity.

If a jury was handed all of the biblical passages mentioned above and was asked to judge whether or not the Bible taken at face value condemns homosexual sex, the verdict would be that the Bible views homosexual behavior as sinful. From the Levitical code it is clear that the writers reflect the desire of the Israelite community to preserve the tribe, prevent cultic defilement, resist idolatry, and populate the region. In his summary analysis of the Old Testament, James Nelson writes: "There is no general condemnation of same sex *orientation* (a notion foreign to the writers), nor is there any reference to genital *love* between gay persons who are committed to each other.'' What is clear is that sacral male prostitution is anathematized, for it involves cultic worship of foreign gods and denies Yahweh's exclusive claim—Deuteronomy 23:17; I Kings 14:24, 15:12, 22:46 (Nelson, 1978, pp. 184–185).

The New Testament writings reflect less of a concern for the survival of an ethnic or religious group and more of a need for orderly behavior (''the purity of the church'') in a politically and religiously pluralistic environment. While John Boswell concludes in his book, *Christianity, Social Tolerance and Homosexuality,* that there is no single clear ethic emerging from the New Testament that forbids homosexual acts, most Protestant and Roman Catholic Christians in the United States do view homosexuality as sinful and support that conclusion in part on the biblical material (Boswell, 1980). The question that these Christian believers fail to ask themselves is whether or not their biblical judgment against homosexuality is the correct one. The Bible also suggests that believers should not accumulate wealth and property (Mark 10:25), that owning slaves is acceptable (Exodus 21:1–11), that Christians should not marry (I Corinthians 7:1, 8), and that women are inferior to men (I Corinthians 14:13b–36 and I Timothy 2:11–15).

Many Christians do not understand or accept that the scriptures of the Old and New Testaments are culturally relative, historically conditioned, or that they may be ethically unjust. George Edwards challenges the biblical reader to remember that ''Biblical theology and biblical ethics are many-faceted, and in many instances plainly heterogeneous. The truth at which one seeks to arrive in the study of scripture is not found by facile compilation of prooftexts that sweeps counterbalancing evidence under the rug. The reappropriation of biblical guidance required by the moral and theological needs of succeeding generations means that evidence subdued or disregarded in the time-worn generalizations about a consistent body of doctrine may become decisive in the epochal shifts history imposes upon human responsibility'' (Edwards, 1989, p. 101).

''Prooftexting'' is used in fundamentalist faith communities to support theological and ethical claims within their congregations and denominations. The process begins with the assumption that every word in Scripture is historically true and without error. This closed hermenutic process will not allow scientific, historical, psychological, linguistic, and philosophical material to challenge its process. Literalistic Christians, however, will allow material from other disciplines that support their truth claims. If evangelical Christians really lived a biblically based life, they would have to reinstitutionalize slavery and follow strict dietary laws; and because they are unwilling to ''practice what they preach,'' one must assume that beneath all of the prooftexting are some a priori sociological, political, and psychological assumptions. Those unspoken assumptions among U.S. Christians are basically racist, sexist, nationalistic, and homophobic; and until those assumptions are exposed, challenged, and changed, the anti-gay sentiment will remain operative within the church.

## GAY AND LESBIAN RELIGIOUS LEADERS

Because most Protestant communions and the Roman Catholic Church refuse to ordain practicing homosexuals, most gays and lesbians stay "in the closet" with respect to members of their congregations and their ecclesiastical authorities. They run the risk of being fired (divested from office) if they do "come out," and it may be difficult for them to find a congregation or a bishop to call (hire) them in a new work setting.

One gay Presbyterian minister told no church officials or authorities that he had AIDS for fear that he would be divested of office and lose his insurance. Before his death, he became increasingly paranoid that someone would discover his medical condition. At the end of his life he was essentially alone and separated from his colleagues in ministry because of his denomination's inability to accept homosexual clergy.

Other gay clergy report feeling tired of the duplicity and partial truths they are forced to tell officials, governing boards, and members of their congregations. One way of managing the stress is in the development of support groups with friends and colleagues who are comfortable with their sexual orientation. One gay pastor in a denomination that refuses to ordain homosexuals wrote in a letter:

> My support group of good friends have spent many hours together, sometimes over Bibles, at other times over beers, and sometimes both. And when the subject (arises) of coming out to supervisors and higher-ups in the governing body their answer to me has always been "no." The "no" came from an honest healthy need to protect me, and my position. Their "no" was never condescending. They would say in all love and candor that it would be professional suicide. I am just as much as a pastor, just as capable and dependable as the next guy. What mattered to them (my friends) was not so much my sexual orientation, but my commitment to the church and a professional ministry. A result of coming out with good friends is that it creates advocacy. Now they push the issue where and when it is appropriate. They see the stupidity of people's fears about gay clergy. We are not any more likely to commit an indiscretion than straight clergy. In fact we are probably safer.

Those clergy who do "come out" within rejecting-punitive and rejecting-nonpunitive denominations currently pay a high professional and emotional price. One gay clergyman who recently came out, ended a marriage of 23 years, had to find a secular job, and had to move away from his children wrote: "I'm angry that the church, by its hostile attitude toward lesbians and gay men, has intercepted God's freeflowing grace and withheld it from a whole category of 'little ones' who miss the message that Jesus loves them, too, just as they are. I'm angry because the fallacious and unloving use of a few, isolated, overemphasized Bible passages taken out of context has perpetuated a form of institutionalized child abuse against young people struggling with their sexual identity.'' And he concluded: ''I'm angry that the church, by failing to recognize, sanction, and even bless committed, loving, same-sex relationships has played a part in driving people into the far country of secrecy and promiscuity, which in turn, has contributed to the spread of AIDS'' (Carroll, 1991, p. 256).

Chris Glaser is a gay Presbyterian who met all the educational requirements for ordination in his denomination but was refused because of his sexual orientation. After years of working in the church and fighting for acceptance within local and national judicatories, he left his work in the church to write. In his book, *Uncommon Calling,* he expressed what is probably the biggest obstacle to the acceptance of homosexuals within the life of the church. ''I believe accepting another's sexual orientation may be dependent on first accepting one's own. Outside of socially induced homophobia, I believe that most Christians have difficulty accepting homosexuality in the church because they are unable to accept *any* sexuality as a means of God's grace'' (Glaser, 1988, pp. 211–212).

Until Christians become more comfortable accepting and understanding their own sexuality, members of mainline denominations will continue to have disagreements over the issue of ordaining homosexuals. Glaser has suggested that the struggle over homosexuality is really a struggle about sexuality; and within Christian denominations that struggle is manifested in national debates about abortion, teenage pregnancy, sex outside of marriage, and the ordination of gays and lesbians. Presently, that debate is being avoided or sidestepped in most local congregations; but the AIDS epidemic is slowly tearing down ecclesiastical defenses that Christians use to hide behind in order to avoid controversy.

Despite the ambivalent or rejecting position held by most denominations and despite those evangelical fundamentalists who presently exclude oppressed minorities, the acceptance of gays and lesbians within every facet of the church will likely follow the same historical route as did the matters of slavery, ordination of women, and racial desegregation. Churches may not change their institutional positions quickly; but there are enough individual Christians, who are able to face both the power and vulnerability associated with human sexuality, who will continue to tear down the barriers erected by others whose unconscious fears have displaced their Christian compassion.

## REFERENCES

Aquino, J. (1992). Gay issues kept alive for Presbyterians. *The Christian Century, 109*(5), 118–119.

Bailey, D. (1955). *Homosexuality and the western christian tradition.* New York: Longmans.

Barton, G. A. (1921). *Sodomy. Encyclopedia of religion and ethics, 11*(67a).

Boswell, J. (1980). *Christianity, social tolerance and homosexuality.* Chicago: University of Chicago Press.

Carroll, W. (1991). God as unloving father. *The Christian Century, 108*(8), 255–256.

Edwards, G. (1989). A critique of creationist homophobia. In Richard Hasbany (Ed.), *Journal of Homosexuality, 18*(3/4), 95–118.

General Assembly Special Committee on Human Sexuality, Presbyterian Church (USA). (1991). *Keeping body and soul together: Sexuality, spirituality and social justice.* Louisville: General Assembly of the Presbyterian Church (USA).

Glaser, C. (1988). *Uncommon calling.* New York: Harper & Row.

McNeill, J. (1988). *The church and the homosexual.* Boston: Beacon Press.

National Council of Churches of Christ in the United States of America. (1991). *Yearbook of American and Canadian churches 1991.* New York: National Council of Churches of Christ in the United States of America.

Nelson, J. (1978). *Embodiment: An approach to sexuality and christian theology.* Minneapolis: Augsburg Publishing House.

Nugent, R., & Gramick, J. (1989). Homosexuality: Protestant, catholic and jewish issues: A fishbone tale. In Richard Hasbany (Ed.), *Journal of Homosexuality, 18*(3/4), 7–46.

Nugent, R., & Gramick, J. (1992). *Building bridges: Gay & lesbian reality and the catholic church.* Mystic, CT: Twenty-Third Publications.

Patterson, Ronald P. (Ed.). (1988). *Book of discipline of the United Methodist Church.* Nashville: United Methodist Publishing House.

Radner, E., & Sumner, G. (1991). Waiting on the spirit: Episcopalians and homosexuality. *The Christian Century, 108*(28), 910–913.

United Presbyterian Church. (1978). *The Church and homosexuality.* San Diego: The General Assembly of the United Presbyterian Church in the United States of America.

Chapter 6

# The Helping Professions: Attitudes Toward Homosexuality

**Richard D. McAnulty**

> I will use my power to help the sick to the best of my ability and judgement; I will abstain from harming or wrongdoing any man by it (excerpt from Hippocratic oath).
>
> Psychologists respect the dignity and worth of the individual and strive for the preservation and protection of fundamental human rights (American Psychological Association, 1990, p. 390).
>
> [Physicians] must provide high-quality non-judgmental care without regard to their own personal risk, real or perceived. Physicians and nurses alike are charged by the ethics of their healing profession to treat patients with all forms of sickness and disease [including AIDS]. (American College of Physicians, 1988, p. 462)

Few topics have elicited more controversy among health care professionals than homosexuality. Throughout the history of medicine and related health professions, homosexuality has remained a perplexing subject. Current evidence reveals that the controversy is not near resolution. Professionals in the "helping

Robyn Fishel and Garrett Wilhelm assisted with the preparation of this chapter.

professions" continue to debate whether homosexuality is a vice, a disorder, or merely a variant in sexual orientation, and whether it merits modification and treatment, punishment, or just acceptance. The goal of this discussion is to offer a review of the research findings on the attitudes and practices of health professionals toward homosexuality. Implications for the quality of care provided to homosexual patients are also discussed, along with suggestions for amelioration. For purposes of this discussion, the health professions include medicine (physicians, nurses, and hospital staff), and all of the mental health fields (psychology, psychiatry, and social work).

## HISTORICAL PERSPECTIVES

In the course of history homosexuality has been alternately conceptualized and treated as a moral weakness or sin, a crime, an illness, and a sexual perversion. The official classification scheme of the American Psychiatric Association (APA), the Diagnostic and Statistical Manual of Mental Disorders (DSM), provides an illustration of the trends in professional attitudes toward homosexuality. In the first version of the official psychiatric nosology, DSM-I (1952), homosexuality was classified as a sexual disorder alongside other mental disorders. In 1973, the APA removed homosexuality as a separate diagnostic category, retaining instead a category of "ego-dystonic homosexuality." The latter label was reserved for homosexual individuals who are dissatisfied with their sexual orientation.

Homosexuality per se was not deemed a mental disorder unless the individual is distressed by his or her sexual orientation (APA, 1980). In the latest, revised version of DSM (1987), the ego-dystonic category has been dropped.

The changes in the psychiatric nosology resulted from a vote of the membership of the APA. The ensuing decision to delete homosexuality as an official mental disorder appears to have been highly influenced by sociopolitical factors rather than a medical action. A subsequent survey of a representative sample of APA members revealed that more than two-thirds of psychiatrists continued to view homosexuality as a mental disorder (Lief, 1977).

The American Psychological Association adopted the official statement that "homosexuality per se implies no impairment in judgement, stability, reliability, or general social or vocational capabilities" (Conger, 1975, p. 633). However, here also it is clear that the official position does not necessarily represent the beliefs of individual members. In a frequently cited article, Davison (1976) argued that most therapists of varying persuasions view homosexuality as "undesirable, sometimes pathological, and at any rate in need of change toward a heterosexual orientation" (p. 158). Davison further commented that therapists who attempt to modify sexual orientation are implicitly reinforcing socio-legal prejudices toward homosexuals and, thus, engaging in ethically questionable practices. On the other hand, Halleck (1976) replied to these concerns by noting that "accepting homosexuality is after all as much a value judgment as condemning it" (p. 168). This controversy illustrates the lack of consensus among experts with respect to homosexuality. All diagnostic labels reflect some degree of value judgment (Wakefield, 1992), but homosexuality seems to elicit more debate and disagreement than most topics among health care professionals.

Thus, although several professional health care organizations have officially endorsed efforts to reduce prejudices against homosexuality, some controversy continues. The consistent impression from the official statements is that several health care organizations advocate tolerance and impartial care. However, the official statements are not necessarily representative of the attitudes of many individual providers, or even a significant minority in some cases.

Several important questions are raised by this controversy. Of paramount concern is the question of the quality of care provided homosexual patients by health care professionals. Are individuals who are homosexual, or even suspected of homosexuality, receiving optimal care from health care professionals? Related to the latter question is the concern with quality of care for patients who are HIV-infected. If predictions about the prevalence of HIV disease in our society are accurate, the answers to the previous questions may have a dramatic impact on a significant percentage of the population. Finally, there is the question of how professionals respond to colleagues who are gay.

## PHYSICIANS' ATTITUDES

In a recent study of a national random sample, Gerber, Maguire, Bleecker, Coates, and McPhee (1991) examined attitudes and actual experiences of 1,121 physicians in treating patients with AIDS. Approximately 75% of respondents had treated at least one patient with HIV disease and 23% had seen more than 10. Sixty-eight percent of physicians felt a responsibility to treat people with AIDS, however, 50% reported that they would not treat these patients if they could avoid it. Only 42% of physicians reportedly welcomed patients with HIV disease in their practices; 32% did not want persons at high risk for AIDS as patients. In the study, the authors evaluated physician attitudes that might affect their practices toward AIDS. More than one-third of respondents viewed homosexuality as a threat to basic social institutions and one-third reported feeling uncomfortable among homosexual persons. Perhaps most important was the finding that 83% of physicians felt the need for more knowledge about HIV disease.

Rizzo, Marder, and Willke (1990) conducted a survey of a nationally representative sample of physicians. Of the 2,884 participants, 49% reported having treated at least one patient with HIV disease. Similar to the findings of Gerber et al. (1991), the majority of physicians (75.3%) felt an obligation to treat HIV-seropositive patients. Of interest was the observation that perceived ethical responsibility to treat patients with HIV disease varied as a function of area of specialization. Among practitioners in general internal medicine, 85% felt such an obligation as did 82% of psychiatrists. In contrast, only 59% of physicians in specialized surgery reported such a perceived responsibility. A plausible explanation for this variability is the physicians' perceived risks of exposure to HIV. Surgeons are more vulnerable to contact with patients' blood than physicians in the other specialities, thus, their greater reluctance to treat AIDS patients may stem from a greater fear of contagion (Rizzo et al., 1990).

In a survey of medical residents in internal and family medicine, Hayward and Shapiro (1991) examined amount of reported experience treating AIDS patients as well as attitudes toward AIDS. Of the 1,745 participants in the cross-sectional survey, 73% felt competent to treat patients with AIDS. In contrast to the study by Gerber et al. (1991), 23% (vs. 50% in Gerber et al., 1991) reported that they would *not* treat patients with AIDS if given a choice. In responding to questions about interest in avoiding specific types of patients, the highest percentage (42%) was reported for intravenous (IV) drug users with AIDS, followed by IV drug users (41%) whose HIV antibody status is unspecified. A total of 23% of respondents would have preferred not to care for gay patients with AIDS and 11% would have preferred not to treat homosexual men.

Similarly, Pritchard et al. (1988) examined attitudes toward homosexuality among 117 family practice residents. Sixty-nine percent of males and 90% of females had treated at least one patient with AIDS. A significant effect of gender was noted in attitudes toward homosexual persons. A total of 12.8% of respondents reported feeling uncomfortable with homosexual individuals; however, nearly 10 times more males than females admitted to such discomfort (19.7% vs. 2.5%). In terms of attitudes toward homosexuality within the medical profession, 89.2% believed that a qualified homosexual applicant should be admitted to medical school. In spite of this reported acceptance, up to one-third of respondents stated that they would not refer patients to a homosexual colleague. Again some variability was associated with area of specialization of the hypothetical "colleague." The respondents in the survey were most reluctant to refer patients to a gay pediatrician (29.7% would not refer to a homosexual pediatrician) and family practitioner (25.3%) and the least reluctance was noted in referral to a radiologist who is homosexual (15.3%).

In their study of 157 physicians from cities with moderate AIDS prevalence, Kelly, St. Lawrence, Smith, Hood, and Cook (1987) asked subjects to read four vignettes describing hypothetical patients. All vignettes were identical with the exception of the patient's illness (AIDS vs. leukemia) and patient's sexual orientation (homo- vs. heterosexual). The physicians considered the AIDS patient responsible for his illness, deserving of his disease and suffering, more dangerous, and deserving quarantine. Furthermore, the physicians described themselves as less willing to engage in conversation with an AIDS patient than with a leukemia patient. Respondents were also less willing to attend a party where a patient with AIDS was present or had prepared food. They also reported more reluctance to renew a past friendship and were less willing to allow children to visit a patient with AIDS. In sum, physicians held rather punitive and fearful attitudes toward the AIDS patient in comparison to the leukemia patient.

Richardson, Lochner, McGuigan, and Levine (1987) used a different approach in studying this issue by comparing attitudes and experiences of heterosexual and homosexual physicians in the Los Angeles area. A total of 115 male physicians who belonged to a predominantly gay professional organization were compared to 199 predominantly heterosexual physicians. The homosexual physicians reported treating more gay patients but no differences were noted in the number of AIDS patients for whom the two samples provided care. The physicians generally agreed that community physicians were typically unprepared to treat AIDS patients and more than 80% favored the creation of specialized AIDS treatment clinics. More than 65% of respondents agreed that health care professionals seemed unwilling to care for AIDS patients; homosexual and heterosexual physicians were in agreement in noting this reluctance to treat AIDS patients within their profession. Significant differences were found in attitudes toward homosexuality as the heterosexual physicians held more negative and punitive attitudes. The heterosexual physicians were more prone to blaming the gay community for AIDS, felt more anger and less sympathy toward homosexual persons, and were more likely to believe that their staff would object to their accepting AIDS patients into their practice. These negative responses were endorsed by approximately one-third of the sample. Approximately 21% of participants feared that their office staff would resign if they were to accept AIDS patients in their practice. Risk of contagion was a moderate to major deterrent for more than 23% of physicians; current evidence from more than 1,400 health care professionals who have treated AIDS patients reveals that these concerns are inflated (Centers for Disease Control, 1985). As with previous studies, a large percentage of respondents felt the need for more education on the medical management of patients with AIDS.

Most recently, Weinberger, Conover, Samsa, and Greenberg (1992) conducted a statewide, random survey stratified by medical specialty. A total of 156 primary care physicians, 104 surgeons, and 67 physicians in emergency medicine responded to the survey. Forty percent of the physicians reported either refusing or referring HIV-infected patients. A large percentage (60%) of physicians expressed concerns with risk of personal infection from AIDS-patient care; a slightly higher percentage expressed similar concerns on behalf of their staff. When adjusting for specialty, surgeons were the most concerned with exposure to HIV from patients (87%), followed by practitioners of emergency medicine (64%), and those in primary care (46%) were the least concerned. More than half the physicians expressed concerns with insufficient medical training in the care of HIV disease. Finally, approximately one-third of physicians feared that caring for AIDS patients would drive away other patients; thus, a significant number of physicians were also concerned for financial reasons.

These studies confirm the findings of other studies showing that a sizable percentage of physicians hold prejudiced attitudes toward homosexual persons and patients with HIV disease. This bias is extended to colleagues who are gay. Although a majority of physicians and residents feels a responsibility to provide care to this patient group, many (up to 50% of respondents) would avoid treating AIDS patients if possible. This is a clear violation of medical ethics. As the American Medical Association's Council on Ethical and Judicial Affairs stated, "a physician may not ethically refuse to treat a patient whose condition is within the physician's current realm of competence solely because the patient is seropositive [for human immunodeficiency virus]" (1988, p. 1360). In an editorial statement, Clarke and Conley (1991), of the American Medical Association, reiterated the longheld mission of the medical profession. In the spirit of the Hippocratic oath, Clarke and Conley (1991) noted that the "profession's defining mission is to care for the sick; practitioners are not free to ignore that objective simply because it entails a small degree of personal risk or because they harbor negative attitudes toward the patients who are stricken by illness" (p. 2876). The authors finally caution that disciplinary action by medical licensure boards against physicians who refuse to treat HIV-infected patients is warranted.

Several important issues are raised by findings such as those reported by Gerber et al. (1991). First and foremost is the concern that these prejudicial attitudes may detract from optimal medical care for patients with HIV disease. Given recent epidemiological projections, it is expected that a proportionately greater number of patients will be adversely affected by this prejudice. Finally, the burden of caring for AIDS patients will be unevenly borne by those physicians who practice ethically. Thus, professionals who refuse to treat HIV-afflicted patients are committing a disservice not only to the sick, but also to their colleagues and to the profession as a whole.

The reluctance of some health care professionals to provide services to patients infected with a dreaded disease is not a recent phenomenon. As Zuger and Miles (1987) described, the bubonic plague ("Black Death") is estimated to have devastated Europe during the 14th century, killing up to one-fourth of the population. Numerous physicians fled areas of infestation or refused to treat patients who were contagious. Similar scenarios were documented in the 17th century during the Great Plague of London and during the outbreak of Yellow Fever in Philadelphia in the 18th century. The ambivalence exhibited by some health care professionals in treating HIV-infected persons is reminiscent of other epidemics in history. Zuger and Miles (1987) observed that as in the past, there is much variability in how medical professionals react to patients infected with dreaded diseases. During these epidemics, countless physicians were reported to flee areas of pestilence or to sequester themselves in order to avoid exposure. In fact, several cities, such as Venice and Cologne, passed laws prohibiting physicians from attempting to escape the plague through flight (Zuger & Miles, 1987).

However, AIDS bears little resemblance to past epidemics in terms of threat to health providers. Unlike the bubonic plague, risks of contagion from treating AIDS patients are extremely small and largely preventable. Nevertheless, some element of personal risk is inherent in the practice of medicine (Emanuel, 1988).

The obligation to provide medical services to patients with AIDS requires a recognition of medicine as a profession rather than solely as a financial enterprise (Emanuel, 1988). It also assumes a recognition that some risk is inherent in providing services to those who are ill. Finally, physicians hold a responsibility to their colleagues and to the profession in bearing some of the burden and risks in caring for AIDS patients.

## ATTITUDES AMONG NURSES AND HOSPITAL STAFF

As might be expected, there is some similarity between the attitudes toward homosexuality and AIDS among other medical professions. In an investigation of 581 registered nurses (RNs), Scherer, Wu, and Haughey (1991) examined AIDS knowledge and attitudes toward homosexuality, terminal illness, and caring for AIDS patients. Twenty-five percent of RNs admitted that their attitudes toward homosexual persons had become more negative since the AIDS crisis. Almost 60% reported feeling more sympathy for an AIDS patient who had contracted HIV through a blood transfusion than one who had been exposed through homosexual practices. In all, 25% of RNs claimed that they would feel uncomfortable in a professional relationship with a homosexual patient; another 20% were undecided.

Similar findings were reported by Kelly, St. Lawrence, Hood, Smith, and Cook (1988). Using a similar methodology to that in their study of physicians (Kelly et al., 1987), nurses were asked to compare a patient with AIDS to a leukemia patient. The subjects were consistently more negative in their ratings of the patients with AIDS. Furthermore, the nurses were more negative toward homosexual patients regardless of their diagnosis, suggesting that sexual orientation was an important factor in their prejudice independent of HIV antibody status.

In a large-scale study of RNs, Marram van Servellen, Lewis, and Leake (1988) examined attitudes among 1,019 subjects. More than one-third (39%) admitted to experiencing a moderate-to-high level of discomfort in caring for male homosexual patients.

Pleck, O'Donnell, O'Donnell, and Snarey (1988) conducted a survey of 237 hospital workers at a major AIDS inpatient-care facility. The sample was comprised of nurses (48%), medical technicians (19%), house officers (14%), LPNs and aides (11%), and social workers (8%). A small minority of respondents held extremely negative views toward AIDS: 5% believed the disease to be a punishment from God for immorality and the same proportion disagreed that AIDS patients were entitled to the same quality in medical care as other patients. A larger percentage of the hospital workers endorsed items suggesting a more moderate level of prejudice: 16% were morally offended by AIDS patients, 17% would terminate a relationship with a friend who contracted AIDS, and almost 20% felt less tolerant of homosexuality because of the AIDS crisis. As with the physicians, a large percentage (42%) felt that they should not be required to work with AIDS patients. Nearly 60% believed that a person with AIDS should not be permitted to work in a hospital. As expected, amount of professional contact with AIDS patients was higher than for most medical professionals (currently spending an average of 3.5 hours per week working with AIDS patients). The majority of subjects felt unprepared for dealing with the emotional needs of patients with AIDS and their families. The strongest predictors of negative attitudes toward AIDS were age, staff position, and amount of contact with patients with HIV disease. Negative attitudes were associated with being older and having less contact with this patient group. Being a social worker was predictive of acceptance in contrast to other groups. As expected, the strongest predictor of AIDS-phobia was homophobia.

The study by Pleck et al. (1988) is of interest because it addresses AIDS attitudes among several health care groups in a specialty hospital with an AIDS treatment program. Even in this setting, some prejudice is noted though it appears that increased amount of contact with AIDS patients tends to lead to more empathy and less punitive attitudes. Of course, a selection bias is possible because those employees who object most to working with this population probably request a transfer to other medical services or may even resign. Nevertheless, it seems likely that having professional contact with AIDS patients may help the professional realize that, with the exception of the diagnosis, these patients are like any other patient group. All are cases of human beings suffering from an illness; in the case of AIDS, the disease carries a profound stigma in our society (Herek & Glunt, 1988).

## MENTAL HEALTH PROFESSIONALS

The training of mental health professionals is designed to foster empathy, unconditional positive regard, and respect for the individual. Consequently, it might be expected that these professionals should be more compassionate and less judgmental and biased than some of the other helping professions. Results of studies suggest that many therapists are critical and judgmental in their attitudes toward homosexuality and patients with HIV disease.

Thompson and Fishburn (1977) examined attitudes toward homosexuality among graduate students in a counselor training program. Of the 64 respondents, 86% felt that most mental health professionals were inadequately prepared for dealing with homosexual clients. A breakdown by gender revealed that 96% of males felt ill-equipped for treating gay clients compared to 76% of females. Nearly one-third of students believed that homosexual persons were far more likely to need counseling than heterosexuals would.

Garfinkle and Morin (1978) studied a similar sample of 80 practicing psychotherapists. They were asked to rate a healthy person versus hypothetical clients using semantic differential scales. The case histories provided to the subjects described the client as heterosexual male, homosexual male, heterosexual female, or homosexual female. The ratings of the client adjustment varied as a function of client sexual orientation and therapist gender. The therapists rated the homosexual clients as more stereotypically feminine than the psychologically healthy person. This trend was especially true for male therapists. This finding replicates previous studies that showed that males were more critical and prejudiced than females in attitudes toward homosexual persons.

Under the auspices of the journal *Medical Aspects of Human Sexuality,* Lief (1977) described the results of a survey of 2,500 psychiatrists' attitudes toward homosexuality. A total of 69% viewed homosexuality as a psychiatric disturbance, and 73% agreed that homosexual males were generally more unhappy than heterosexual counterparts. Interestingly, respondents appeared somewhat more tolerant of lesbians as only 55% believed them less capable of a mature loving relationship. Finally, almost half of subjects (43%) believed homosexuality to be a risk when holding positions of responsibility. Similar findings were reported by Fort, Steiner, and Conrad (1971) who surveyed 163 psychotherapists (63 social workers, 50 psychologists, and 50 psychiatrists). Eighty-three percent of the sample labeled homosexuality a "sexual deviation," consistent with official psychiatric nomenclature of the time (DSM-II; APA, 1968). Furthermore, 35% asserted that homosexuality was a disorder in the same category as pedophilia. Homosexuality was not officially removed from the classification system until two years later, and thus, their judgments were representative of the official view of homosexuality. Consistent with the results discussed by Lief (1977), almost one-third (27%) favored restricting homosexual applicants from security-sensitive government positions.

Behavior therapy has been stereotyped as a form of "mind control," which borders on brainwashing. Practitioners of behavior therapy have been described as rigid, inflexible, and intolerant. Davison and Wilson (1973) found that 87% of the 86 behavior therapists they surveyed disagreed that homosexuality was "prima facie" evidence of maladjustment and 91% believed it was possible for homosexual persons to achieve happiness and stability. Nevertheless, 43% of respondents employed aversion therapy in an effort to reorient homosexual clients to a heterosexual orientation. Most commonly, these treatments were reserved for cases of ego-dystonic homosexuality. Finally, the behavior therapists viewed homosexual clients as less good, less masculine, and less rational than heterosexuals.

In a large-scale survey of members of the American Psychological Association, Garnets, Hancock, Cochran, Goodchilds, and Peplau (1991) obtained responses from 2,544 licensed psychologists. Overall, 58% of the respondents identified specific incidents of bias in the provision of psychotherapeutic services to homosexual clients. The reported incidents included instances of insensitivity, prejudice, and incompetence, often in the form of lack of appreciation for the unique problems faced by homosexual clients. No information pertaining to attitudes toward persons with AIDS was solicited from the subjects in this study.

Virtually all studies of the attitudes of mental health professionals toward homosexuality have been conducted prior to the increased awareness of the AIDS epidemic. There have been no surveys of the magnitude of those conducted with physicians to assess how mental health professionals view and manage clients with HIV disease. Thus, it is impossible to gauge whether the increased awareness of AIDS has affected attitudes and practices among these professionals. If the trends evident among other health care professions apply to this group, then it would follow that prejudice is also a problem among some mental health professions.

Several reasons may account for the relative absence of studies on how mental health professionals view AIDS-afflicted individuals. The predominant focus on physicians may relate to the fact that they are the primary care providers for most patients with HIV disease. Furthermore, concerns for personal risks in caring for AIDS patients are most salient among medical professionals because they are more likely to be exposed to patient bodily fluids (although perceived risks are generally exaggerated in view of current knowledge on transmission of HIV). Finally, the failure to provide adequate medical care may appear to be a more serious and life-threatening violation than the provision of inadequate psychotherapy.

A growing literature on psychotherapy with homosexual clients (e.g., Barrows & Halgin, 1988) and patients with HIV disease exists (e.g., Kelly & St. Lawrence, 1988a, 1988b). Unfortunately, without surveys of actual practices of mental health professionals it is impossible to determine if these treatments are widely accepted and implemented.

## RECOMMENDATIONS

The purpose of this discussion is not to modify health professionals' attitudes toward homosexual persons and patients with HIV disease. Personal beliefs and attitudes are resistant to change as studies summarized in this section have illustrated. However, it is imperative that the current practices of some professionals be modified. There is no justification for prejudicial and unethical practices in patient/client care. Even those professionals who believe that homosexuality is a disorder will not argue that only the psychologically and physically healthy are entitled to health care services. There is a flagrant contradiction and injustice in claiming that all individuals merit health care services unless they are homosexual and/or suffer from AIDS. Yet, surveys of practices among health care professionals suggest that prejudice against homosexuality is common. The absurdity of this position should be recognized and challenged *regardless* of one's personal and moral beliefs about homosexuality.

As the ethical principles listed in the preface specify, health care professionals are not free to choose arbitrarily and with prejudice to discriminate against certain patient groups. Unfortunately, surveys suggest that up to half of them actually do or would under certain conditions. Even more alarming is the belief by a small minority of professionals that AIDS patients do not merit quality medical care.

Several problems are at the root of the bias against homosexual persons and patients with AIDS. First, ignorance is a problem and education is the necessary remedy. Some individuals exhibit homophobia, the irrational fear of homosexual persons. Many professionals grossly overestimate their risks of contracting HIV from patients; this misinformation should be addressed with education efforts. The provision of factual information in combination with reassurance should help alleviate irrational fears and concerns, especially if the information is provided by a credible and respected source. Surveys have shown that a significant percentage of health professionals desire more information and training in the management of HIV disease.

A second problem pertains to the motives of some health care professionals. Those who view their professions exclusively as a financial enterprise appear most susceptible to biases. Only when professionals recognize that their primary mission is the delivery of services will they achieve objectivity. Furthermore, such a humanitarian attitude will enhance the public's trust in the helping professions. Thus, an altruistic approach to health care provision will ultimately benefit the individual providers and their professions.

Finally, these problems need to be systematically addressed and emphasized in the training of professionals. Studies reveal that many professionals in training are receptive to relevant information. Courses on ethics should stress the fact that ethical principles apply to *all* patients.

A number of empirical questions are also raised by results of these studies. First, the attitudes and practices of mental health professionals toward clients with AIDS should be investigated. While several surveys of medical professionals have been conducted, mental health professionals have been largely ignored. Epidemiological predictions of HIV disease suggest that an increasing number of professionals from all health related disciplines will be needed for service delivery. Second, the effectiveness of efforts to modify prejudice toward homosexual patients should be empirically tested. Finally, more research is necessary to identify predictors of prejudice among professionals. This would facilitate the identification of targets for attitude change efforts. Only then will health care professionals fulfill their ethical guidelines to "strive for the preservation and protection of fundamental human rights" and to "provide high-quality non-judgmental care without regard to their own personal risk, real or perceived."

## REFERENCES

American College of Physicians. (1988). The acquired immunodeficiency syndrome (AIDS) and infection with the human immunodeficiency virus (HIV). *Annals of Internal Medicine, 108,* 460–469.

American Psychiatric Association. (1952). *Diagnostic and statistical manual of mental disorders.* Washington, DC: Author.

American Psychiatric Association. (1968). *Diagnostic and statistical manual of mental disorders* (2nd ed.). Washington, DC: Author.

American Psychiatric Association. (1980). *Diagnostic and statistical manual of mental disorders* (3rd ed.). Washington, DC: Author.

American Psychiatric Association. (1987). *Diagnostic and statistical manual of mental disorders* (3rd ed. rev.). Washington, DC: Author.

American Psychological Association. (1990). Ethical principles of psychologists. *American Psychologist, 45,* 390–395.

Barrows, P. A., & Halgin, R. P. (1988). Current issues in psychotherapy with gay men: Impact of the AIDS phenomenon. *Professional Psychology: Research and Practice, 4,* 395–402.

Centers for Disease Control. (1985). Recommendations for preventing transmission of infection with HTLV-III/LAV in the workplace. *Morbidity and Mortality Weekly Report, 34,* 682–695.

Clarke, O. W., & Conley, R. B. (1991). The duty to "attend upon the sick." *Journal of the American Medical Association, 266,* 2876–2877.

Conger, J. (1975). Proceedings of the American Psychological Association, for the year 1974: Minutes of the annual meeting of Council of Representatives. *American Psychologist, 30,* 620–651.

Council on Ethical and Judicial Affairs. (1988). Ethical issues in the growing AIDS crisis. *Journal of the American Medical Association, 259,* 1360–1361.

Davison, G. C. (1976). Homosexuality: The ethical challenge. *Journal of Consulting and Clinical Psychology, 44,* 157–162.

Davison, G., & Wilson, T. G. (1973). Attitudes of behavior therapists toward homosexuality. *Behavior Therapy, 4,* 686–696.

Emanuel, E. J. (1988). Do physicians have an obligation to treat patients with AIDS? *The New England Journal of Medicine, 318,* 1686–1690.

Fort, J., Steiner, C. M., & Conrad, F. (1971). Attitudes of mental health professionals toward homosexuality and its treatment. *Psychological Reports, 29,* 347–350.

Garfinkle, E. M., & Morin, S. F. (1978). Psychologists' attitudes toward homosexual psychotherapy clients. *Journal of Social Issues, 34,* 101–111.

Garnets, L., Hancock, K. A., Cochran, S. D., Goodchilds, J., & Peplau, L. A. (1991). Issues in psychotherapy with lesbians and gay men. *American Psychologist, 46,* 964–972.

Gerber, B., Maguire, B. T., Bleecker, T., Coates, T. J., & McPhee, S. J. (1991). Primary care physicians and AIDS: Attitudinal and structural barriers to care. *Journal of the American Medical Association, 266,* 2837–2842.

Halleck, S. L. (1976). Another response to "Homosexuality: The ethical challenge." *Journal of Consulting and Clinical Psychology, 44,* 167–170.

Hayward, R. A., & Shapiro, M. F. (1991). A national study of AIDS and residency training: Experiences, concerns, and consequences. *Annals of Internal Medicine, 114,* 23–32.

Herek, G. M., & Glunt, E. K. (1988). An epidemic of stigma: Public reactions to AIDS. *American Psychologist, 43,* 886–891.

Kelly, J. A., & St. Lawrence, J. S. (1988a). AIDS prevention and treatment: Psychology's role in the health crisis. *Clinical Psychology Review, 8,* 255–284.

Kelly, J. A., & St. Lawrence, J. S. (1988b). *The AIDS health crisis: Psychological and social interventions.* New York: Plenum.

Kelly, J. A., St. Lawrence, J., Hood, H., Smith, S., & Cook, D. (1988). Nurses' attitudes toward AIDS. *The Journal of Continuing Education, 19,* 78–83.

Kelly, J. A., St. Lawrence, J., Smith, S., Hood, H., & Cook, D. (1987). Stigmatization of AIDS patients by physicians. *American Journal of Public Health, 77,* 789–791.

Lief, H. (1977). Sexual survey #4: Current thinking on homosexuality. *Medical Aspects of Human Sexuality, 11,* 110–111.

Marram van Servellen, G., Lewis, C., & Leake, B. (1988). Nurses' responses to the AIDS crisis: Implications for continuing education programs. *The Journal of Continuing Education in Nursing, 10,* 4–8.

Pleck, J. H., O'Donnell, L., O'Donnell, C., & Snarey, J. (1988). AIDS-phobia, contact with AIDS, and AIDS-related job stress in hospital workers. *Journal of Homosexuality, 15,* 41–55.

Pritchard, J. G., Dial, L. K., Holloway, R. L., Mosley, M., Bale, R. M., & Kaplowitz, H. J. (1988). Attitudes of family medicine residents toward homosexuality. *Journal of Family Practice, 27,* 637–639.

Richardson, J. L., Lochner, T., McGuigan, K., & Levine, A. M. (1987). Physician attitudes and experience regarding the care of patients with acquired immunodeficiency syndrome (AIDS) and related disorders (ARC). *Medical Care, 25,* 675–685.

Rizzo, J. A., Marder, W. D., & Willke, R. J. (1990). Physician contact with and attitudes toward HIV-seropositive patients: Results from a national survey. *Medical Care, 28,* 251–260.

Scherer, Y. K., Wu, Y. B., & Haughey, B. P. (1991). AIDS and homophobia among nurses. *Journal of Homosexuality, 21,* 17–27.

Thompson, G. H., & Fishburn, W. R. (1977). Attitudes toward homosexuality among graduate counseling students. *Counselor Education and Supervision, 17,* 121–130.

Wakefield, J. C. (1992). The concept of mental disorder: On the boundary between biological fact and social values. *American Psychologist, 47,* 373–388.

Weinberger, M., Conover, C. J., Samsa, G. P., & Greenberg, S. M. (1992). Physicians' attitudes and practices regarding treatment of HIV-infected patients. *Southern Medical Journal, 85,* 683–686.

Wisniewsky, J. J., & Toomey, B. G. (1987). Are social workers homophobic? *Social Work, 32,* 454–455.

Zuger, A., & Miles, S. M. (1987). Physicians, AIDS, and occupational risk: Historic traditions and ethical obligations. *Journal of the American Medical Association, 258,* 1924–1928.

Chapter 7

# And Gladly Teach: Lesbian and Gay Issues in Education

**Ruth E. Fassinger**

The education of society's young has long constituted a zealously monitored profession. Schools—public and private, elementary, secondary, and postsecondary—historically have served as vehicles for the inculcation of both knowledge and prevailing social values. Due to societal expectations and the high visibility inherent in teaching, educators have traditionally been held to more stringent moral and legal standards than in most other occupations, forced to serve as paragons of law-abiding citizenship and moral virtue, the "determinate role model[s] of the parents' moral values" (Dressler, 1979b, p. 315). Historically, for example, teachers could be fired from their positions for smoking, drinking, dancing, cursing, theater-going, divorce, breaking the Sabbath, or (for women) staying out after dark. It is hardly surprising, then, that homosexual orientation and gay/lesbian lifestyles, recently more visible but regarded by much of society as deviant and immoral, have become a battleground within the nation's schools (Dressler, 1985; Newton & Risch, 1981; Schneider-Vogel, 1986), creating a controversy that is "one of the most publicly volatile and personally threatening debates in our national history" (Harbeck, 1992, p. 1).

Longstanding patterns of societal homophobia are very much present and especially strong in regard to teaching; indeed, Dressler (1979b) asserted that gay and lesbian educators are victims of more substantial employment discrimination than in any other occupation. A recent extensive national poll (see Fassinger, 1991) indicated that although a majority (81%) of the American public opposed discrimination based on sexual orientation, 57% disapproved of lesbian/gay people living together as married couples, and almost one-fifth believed homosexuality should be illegal. In addition, a 1987 Gallup poll (cited in Parmeter & Reti, 1988) revealed that 60% of the public objected less to gay priests and doctors than to gay educators, and attempts (some successful, as in Oklahoma) have occurred in several states to legally bar gay teachers from the educational system.

Despite these conflicting public images of teachers and of homosexuality, it is clear that gay and lesbian people historically have been and currently are in education in large numbers (e.g., Faderman, 1991; Harbeck, 1992; Rubinstein & Fry, 1981). From early times, when Sappho and Socrates educated youth in ancient Greece, to the present day, lesbian women and gay men have chosen teaching as a profession, and there are hundreds of thousands of gay educators (most of them closeted and invisible) in our nation's schools and universities. The commonly cited 10% gay population figure translates into at least two lesbian/gay educators in each school (based on the national average of 24.8 teachers per school), probably an extremely conservative estimate, because teaching traditionally has attracted single women and nontraditional men (Harbeck, 1992); also, these figures do not include colleges and universities, which tend to be more hospitable places for lesbian and gay professionals, and where demographic estimates often place them at one-third of the population. Of course, there are many more thousands of young people who are gay or struggling with same-sex feelings who are being educated in the schools, and even more people throughout the educational system whose lives will be affected by homosexuality in some direct or indirect way. As Newton and Risch (1981) assert, "[w]e can hardly expect that schools will hide much longer from an issue that is so profoundly significant for so many educators" (p. 191).

This chapter presents an overview of the issues surrounding the presence of lesbian women and gay men in the field of education. First, general information regarding the extent and effects of occupational discrimination is presented, followed by a discussion of the relevant legal issues and court cases. Next, professional and educational issues are reviewed, and the chapter concludes with recommendations regarding individual, systemic, and societal action and changes that must occur in order to address the difficulties encountered by lesbian/gay educators.

## OCCUPATIONAL DISCRIMINATION

General occupational discrimination against gay and lesbian people has been documented by several researchers (Bradford & Ryan, 1987; Hall, 1989; Levine, 1979; Levine & Leonard, 1984; Olson, 1987; Schneider, 1987). Because these studies survey a largely invisible population, samples are not representative and data probably underestimate the problems that exist. Despite their methodological limitations, however, these studies indicate widespread difficulties for lesbians and gays in the workforce, whether they disclose their homosexuality or remain hidden.

Levine (1979), Levine and Leonard (1984), and Garnets and Kimmel (1992) summarized results of several studies of job discrimination, and noted estimates of occupational difficulties related to sexual orientation ranging from 20% to 35%. Levine (1979) reported, for example, that 29% of the gay male population had their careers negatively influenced by homosexuality, and 17% lost or were denied employment because of sexual orientation. In the lesbian population, an average of 13% had experienced job discrimination (8% having lost their jobs because of lesbianism), and 31% anticipated discrimination due to sexual orientation (Levine & Leonard, 1984). A recent national poll (cf. Fassinger, 1991) indicated that only half of the gay sample surveyed had disclosed identity to coworkers (one-third of the lesbians), and 16% reported that sexual orientation was a factor in their choice of a job. Schneider (1987) noted the double jeopardy faced by lesbians, who suffer discrimination based on both gender and sexual orientation, and identified working with children as a particular risk factor in decisions to disclose identity in the workplace; such difficulties may, in part, explain the lower numbers of women who are "out" at work, because many women are concentrated in the field of teaching. Discrimination problems that have been documented in the literature include disclosure issues in hiring, legal prohibitions, dual public-private identities and the pain of remaining invisible, loss of collegial support, retention and promotion problems, surveillance, bias in classroom and job assignments, harassment and abuse, poor evaluations, job tracking and underutilization of abilities, hate crimes and incidents of violence, limitation of future options, and negative work climate (Bradford & Ryan, 1987; Hall, 1989; Harbeck, 1992; Levine, 1989; Levine & Leonard, 1984; Olson, 1987; Schneider, 1987).

Although both the National Education Association and the American Federation of Teachers have expressed union commitment to nondiscrimination based on sexual orientation, and despite the existence of employment protection for gay people in a number of states, counties, and cities, the widespread discrimination in hiring, tenure/promotion, and general work climate in education cannot be denied. Dressler (1979a, p. 23) explains:

> When a gay person chooses to be a teacher, he or she has struck at the public's emotional jugular vein. Parents . . . guard their children zealously as the most vital

> national resource. They expect teachers to indoctrinate their children in all those values—including, of course, heterosexuality—which the nation holds sacred and also to serve as a role model for . . . youths. Because of the accepted stereotypes of a homosexual, parents fear that the gay teacher will exhibit improper sex roles and may even seduce their youth.

Such attitudes have enormous impact on whether an openly gay individual could be hired in even the most liberal of schools. Hiring double binds is particularly troublesome, because immediate dismissal and conviction of fraud are possible consequences of misrepresentation on application forms; thus, one can disclose identity (which probably precludes being hired), or one can maintain secrecy in order to obtain a position, but risk termination and legal action if identity later becomes known. In addition, because homosexual acts (e.g., sodomy) are currently illegal in most places, admissions of homosexuality are assumed to represent ipso facto violations of the law, and elementary/secondary gay and lesbian educators can be fired, disciplined, or transferred to positions of noncontact with students if their homosexual identity becomes suspect or known (Levine, 1979). In higher education, discrimination is usually more subtle; Newton (1987) observed that homophobia "strikes in closed-door meetings of tenure-review and promotion committees and in secret letters of recommendation. Rejection and denial are almost always attributed to the victim's alleged personal and intellectual shortcomings" (p. 104). Preserving one's privacy often involves elaborate and exhausting identity and information management strategies: "passing" as heterosexual (including implicit or explicit pretense of opposite-sex lovers); distancing oneself from coworkers; avoidance of homosexual issues in and out of the classroom; highly selective disclosure to colleagues; rigorous separation of work and private lives into dual identities (including long commutes in order to maintain residence far from school); and leaving the teaching profession altogether (Garnets & Kimmel, 1992; Griffin, 1992; Woods & Harbeck, 1992). One study (Olson, 1987) found that 25% of a sample of 97 gay and lesbian teachers had left the profession, and half of them claimed sexual orientation as a reason.

Such profound loss of personnel and compromised professional effectiveness in our nation's already besieged schools is an important resource problem, and one with which school administrators ought to be concerned. One study (Dressler, 1985) surveyed a national sample of secondary (junior high and high school) principals to determine opinions regarding the legal rights of gay teachers to practice their profession, as well as actual experiences of the respondents in dealing with teachers whom they knew or thought to be homosexual. Four schools were selected randomly from each of 50 states, and a little over half of the original 200 questionnaires were completed. Respondents were asked to give their opinions regarding the revocation of the license of a "previously exemplary" gay male teacher with six years of experience across 10 hypothetical circumstances, from discharge of the teacher according to mere status, to alleged sexual conduct by the teacher with a child. Results of the study indicated that a significant minority of principals (8%) believed that the homosexual teacher should lose his license solely due to status. The criminality of homosexuality seemed to be particularly salient to this sample, because two-thirds favored dismissal of the teacher for conviction of a private, consensual, adult homosexual act. A substantial minority of this sample also favored revocation of the teacher's license simply if the teacher was active in gay rights activities (24%), spoke of homosexuality in the classroom in a nonjudgmental manner (42%), or disclosed sexual orientation to students (46%).

Interestingly, however, the actual treatment of gay teachers by this sample of principals was more lenient than their attitudes would suggest. According to self-reporting of the respondents, teachers who disclosed their sexual orientation, against whom there were no claims of misconduct, were rarely subjected to any kind of administrative discipline. Even in cases of arrest or sexual advances in the classroom, warning was a more common response than formal discipline. However, it is worth noting that principals frequently concluded that a teacher was gay based on rumor, stereotypes, or association, and a sizeable number of cases (19%) were reported in which teachers thought to be gay were warned or disciplined in the absence of claims of misconduct or admissions of homosexuality. It is also notable that teachers with poor teaching records were subjected to discipline far more often in this sample than teachers with good records, even where sexual misconduct occurred. And, finally, results of this study indicated that retention of a teacher whose (alleged) homosexuality became public rarely created long-term problems for a school in the disruption of activities or her/his teaching effectiveness, a legal argument frequently advanced by school boards as grounds for dismissing homosexual teachers. Overall, the preoccupation of subjects in this study with the criminal implications of homosexuality suggests that legal issues are inseparable from discrimination practices; thus, relevant legal issues are briefly reviewed in the following section.

## LEGAL ACTIONS AND ISSUES

It has been noted (e.g., Rubinstein & Fry, 1981) that the position of gay and lesbian people in our society is comparable to that of the Jews in Nazi Germany, in that they are a minority group against whose very existence laws exist. In addition, all states have codes and certification requirements that set qualifications for teachers, with exacting standards for their moral and professional conduct at the cornerstone of concern in most of these codes (Schneider-Vogel, 1986). Most states, for example, have statutes permitting the revocation of teaching credentials or dismissal of teachers for immorality, moral turpitude, unprofessionalism, or unfitness to teach (cause). Historically, gay and lesbian teachers have been dismissed or sanctioned for a range of behavior related to sexual orientation, such as conviction under sodomy or solicitation statutes, public homosexual displays, classroom comments regarding homosexuality, and private declarations of homosexual orientation (Harbeck, 1992; Harvard Law Review, 1990).

Most of the judicial activity to date has taken place in appellate and lower courts, and Harbeck (1992) noted that the courts have thus far avoided direct declarations regarding lesbian and gay educators' constitutional right to teach. However, the Supreme Court in related cases has asserted a dual purpose of public schools: to serve as a forum for free speech by teachers and students, and to serve as a tool for the inculcation of norms and duties imposed by society. These two conflicting interests create a unique setting in which greater restrictions on First Amendment rights are permissible than in other public institutions (Harvard Law Review, 1990). Two broad classes of disputes commonly brought to the courts have involved discrimination claims by gay/lesbian students regarding restrictions on their freedoms of speech and association, and conflicts between school administrators and faculty members involving the views or sexual orientation of faculty members. Recognizing different standards for mandatory school attendance versus public employment, the courts have generally supported a student's right to express his/her sexual orientation, but they have largely determined that the unique position of those in the teaching profession gives educators little discretion to discuss homosexuality or reveal homosexual orientation (Harvard Law Review, 1990).

Two issues seem to be at the heart of much of the legal argument regarding lesbian/gay teachers: fitness to teach and disruption of the educational environment (Dressler, 1979b). Fitness questions revolve around the assumption that a lesbian/gay teacher will seduce or molest children, or will provide an undesirable role model, leading children into a deviant way of life (Dressler, 1979b). In *Sarac v. State Board of Education* (1967), the California Supreme Court held that homosexuality was abhorrent and immoral, and in itself constituted unfitness to teach. In *Morrison v. State Board of Education* (1969), however, the California Court articulated the requirement that a nexus must exist between a teacher's homosexual conduct and the teacher's effectiveness in the classroom (the Morrison "nexus" or "fitness" test), and Harbeck (1992) noted that this decision established one of the strongest statements in favor of an individual's right to retain employment despite a variety of personal indiscretions. Specifically, in determining fitness, precedent was set for school boards to consider such issues as: the likelihood that the conduct may have adversely affected students or other teachers; the recency of the conduct; the type of teaching certificate held (related to age and maturity of students); the motives resulting in the conduct; the likelihood of recurrence; and the extent to which disciplinary action might have adverse impact or a "chilling" effect on the constitutional rights of this or other teacher(s). Effectively, the Morrison decision places a high burden of proof on boards of education, and prevents school systems from sanctioning or dismissing teachers for unfitness on grounds of status (i.e., sexual orientation) alone. As Harbeck (1992) concludes, "credential revocation on the basis of homosexuality is a thing of the past" (p. 132).

However, if homosexuality per se cannot be used to challenge a teacher's fitness, then potential disruption of the academic environment becomes the issue: that is, whether the school's mission and activities and/or the effectiveness of the teacher in question will be compromised by public reaction to the presence of that teacher. In the case of *Gaylord v. Tacoma School District No. 10* (1977), the Washington Supreme Court upheld the dismissal of a gay teacher with 12 years of exemplary service preceding the disclosure of his homosexuality. The court concluded that Gaylord's acknowledgment of his sexual orientation implied homosexual (and therefore illegal) conduct, but, more importantly, accepted the lower court opinion that public knowledge of Gaylord's homosexuality and the resultant disruption would impair his teaching effectiveness and injure the school. Particularly disturbing about this decision is that support for the contention of impaired performance due to public knowledge consisted of the testimony of a small handful of teachers and administrators who objected to Gaylord's presence. The implication, of course, is that even though school systems are legally compelled to establish a nexus between homosexuality and teaching effectiveness, the negative attitudes of only a few people can generate enough "disruption" to "impair" the effectiveness of a gay/lesbian teacher (Dressler, 1979a; Schneider-Vogel, 1986).

## LEGAL PRINCIPLES

Several legal principles are commonly invoked in conflicts about gay and lesbian people in education. The two main principles are the right to privacy and equal protection of the laws (grounded in the Fifth and Fourteenth Amendments to the U.S. Constitution), and there are also relevant implications in due process and free speech and association rights (Bersoff & Ogden, 1991; Dressler, 1979b; Harbeck, 1992; Harvard Law Review, 1990; Rubinstein & Fry, 1981; Schneider-Vogel, 1986).

The right to privacy is not explicitly guaranteed in the Bill of Rights but is considered an "unenumerated right," and although there is a lack of consensus on exactly where the right is implied in the text, the majority view holds that privacy is an essential part of the protection of liberty; it is thus protected by due process rights ensuring that governmental procedural action is neither capricious nor arbitrary (Bersoff & Ogden, 1991). The U.S. Supreme Court has identified two related interests encompassed by the right to privacy: the right to make certain decisions without government intrusion, and the right to nondisclosure of personal matters.

The Court has been inconsistent in the application of these principles, however (Bersoff & Ogden, 1991). In fact, in *Bowers v. Hardwick* (1986), the U.S.

Supreme Court's first major ruling on a gay rights issue, the Court refused to extend constitutional protection to private homosexual acts between consenting adults, essentially supporting the constitutionality of the sodomy laws. Because these laws, by their very existence, make the private activities of many gay people illegal, the denial of the right to privacy in the Bowers case sets a dangerous precedent for continuing legalized occupational discrimination against lesbians and gay men based on their personal lives. As the Court has clearly and deliberately protected the rights of heterosexuals in similar cases (Bersoff & Ogden, 1991), the issue of inequality in the application of the law becomes salient.

Conflicts regarding the principle of equal protection of the law arise when an alleged inequality is the result of governmental actions (laws, regulations, or practices) that create discriminatory classifications. Certain standards are used by the courts in determining whether equal protection has been violated, based on "rational basis" and "strict scrutiny tests." In the rational basis test, differentiation among persons must bear some rational relationship to a legitimate government purpose; in the strict scrutiny test, on the other hand, the government must show a compelling reason for its classificatory practice, and demonstrate that no other alternative is viable. Strict scrutiny is particularly required when dealing with "suspect" classifications, those groups that require extraordinary legal protection because of historical subjection to unequal treatment, political powerlessness, victimization by legislative prejudice, and powerlessness to control the trait on which the classification is based (Bersoff & Ogden, 1991; Dressler, 1979a). The courts are required to use strict scrutiny standards in cases where fundamental rights are violated or suspect classifications are involved; thus, many of the legal attempts to protect gay people are based on ensuring fundamental rights (e.g., privacy) or designating them as a suspect class and thus entitled to more careful scrutiny of potential rights violations.

Other constitutional principles that have been implicated in legal cases regarding lesbian/gay educators are the rights of due process and freedom of speech and association. Due process rights, which are designed to ensure that actions taken against an individual are not capricious and have followed careful procedures, entitle teachers to notice of reasons for a proposed termination and an opportunity for a hearing on the disputed issues. It has been noted (Harbeck, 1992; Schneider-Vogel, 1986) that increased litigation in procedural due process since the McCarthy era has resulted in most educational systems' incorporation of due process guarantees into contracts and administrative policies, so that teacher termination cases that reach the courts are typically related to immorality, unprofessional conduct, and unfitness (cause), rather than to due process violations.

The right of free speech and association (commonly argued in gay student rights issues) has been implicated both directly and indirectly in cases related to gay educators. Legal precedent has established that although teachers and other public employees are not denied constitutionally mandated rights (e.g., speech) simply by accepting public employment, these rights are protected only when exercised in a manner that does not interfere with the efficient operation of the work setting, and considerable latitude may be allowed in determining the extent to which the work setting has been disrupted (Schneider-Vogel, 1986). Generally, courts do not interfere with school systems that sanction teachers for "inappropriate" discussion in the classroom, but are less likely to allow school systems to sanction teachers for activities in their lives as private citizens (Harvard Law Review, 1990). However, for speech occurring in the workplace but outside regular teaching activities, the courts have tended to defer to local school systems, even where such extracurricular speech has limited effect on the efficiency of the workplace (Harvard Law Review, 1990); also, it cannot be denied that even speech and association occurring completely outside of the school setting are often sanctioned.

In *Rowland v. Mad River Local School District* (1985), for example, a court held that a school district could transfer a guidance counselor to a position of noncontact with students simply because she revealed her bisexuality to a colleague. In *Acanfora v. Board of Education of Montgomery County* (1974), the courts held that a gay teacher's failure to include his former membership in a college gay organization on his employment application constituted misrepresentation and adequate grounds for dismissal (not surprisingly, school officials admitted that they would not have hired him if he had included these activities); particularly disturbing in the Acanfora case is that the negative verdict occurred against a backdrop of favorable judicial comment regarding the fundamental rights of gay teachers and acceptance of the establishment of sexual orientation by age six (thereby undermining judicial attack based on the "harmful" effects of homosexual role models). In *Gish v. Paramus Board of Education* (1977), the court upheld a school board's order requiring a gay activist teacher to submit to a psychiatric exam. Finally, in the Gaylord case, where a teacher was dismissed because of the anticipated disturbance in the workplace caused by publicity surrounding his homosexuality, the teacher's sexual orientation was originally suspected simply because of his membership in a gay organization; further, the court rejected Gaylord's contention that it was the school board (not he) that had publicized his homosexuality, asserting that by associating with homosexuals, he took the risk that his sexual orientation would be discovered. Clearly, legal precedent suggests that exercising the right to freely associate gives gay educators the untenable choice between honest disclosure resulting in (probable) unemployment, or (likely) subsequent dismissal for misrepresentation and fraud (Rubinstein & Fry, 1981). Even gay and lesbian students who exercise their speech and association rights are at risk, because present involvement in gay organizations may harm their chances for future employment, particularly in the public sector (Harvard Law Review, 1990). Rubinstein and Fry (1981, p. 43) conclude:

> Homosexual teachers will remain beyond the pale of constitutional protections until the Supreme Court rules that these educators are constitutionally protected by the right of privacy or equal protection. Additionally, the homosexual teacher's freedom of association and speech will be chilled by his [sic] fear that the free exercise of those rights can be employed as evidence of his [sic] status or adverse public reactions. . . . Irrational fears of homosexual teachers will undeniably persist as long as concealment is judicially encouraged.

One final issue related to the legal rights of lesbian and gay educators that must be addressed is that of pervasive judicial ignorance and homophobia (Dressler, 1979a). Given that law involves personal and collective *interpretations* of definitions and rights, the knowledge, attitudes, and beliefs of the judiciary are crucial determinants of the outcome of individual cases. Harbeck (1992) found that an assessment of contemporary educational law and policy textbooks revealed an "astounding lack of even the smallest references to homosexual educators" (p. 136), suggesting that knowledge of relevant case law is nonexistent for most of the judiciary. Because members of the judiciary are conditioned by the same homophobia that operates in society, lack of knowledge severely compromises their presumed impartiality and confounds legal analysis of the issues:

> Although judges usually pride themselves on writing scholarly, objective opinions, the form of many gay rights opinions is largely emotional. Judges have gratuitously described homosexual behavior as bizarre, repugnant, outrageous, sordid, and revolting. Courts have at times failed to describe the specific homosexual events in question because, as one court put it, "the records of the courts [should not] . . . be defiled with the details . . ." or, as another stated, description of such events should not "stain the pages of our reports." (Dressler, 1979a, p. 22)

Despite rampant judicial homophobia and ignorance, some scholars (e.g., Dressler, 1979b; Harbeck, 1992) suggest more promising future prospects for fair and enlightened treatment of gay and lesbian educators in the courts. For example, in a survey of law students' attitudes toward homosexual teachers conducted in the late 1970s, Dressler (1979b) suggested that law students were more tolerant of the rights of gay/lesbian individuals to teach than was the existing judiciary (as manifested in prior court decisions). Dressler found that the majority (particularly women) of a national sample of 528 law students would not fire a homosexual teacher on status alone or for noncriminal sexual acts; however, higher percentages favored firing a teacher for conviction of criminal sexual acts. As with the school administrators in Dressler's 1985 study, results suggest that a substantial factor in respondents' discharge decisions is not homosexual status per se, but the violation of laws that prohibit specific kinds of sexual activity, again pointing to the necessity of eliminating the sodomy laws in protecting the rights of gay teachers. This study suggests more progressive attitudes in the judiciary in the future (particularly as more women enter the field), and despite the conservative Supreme Court appointments of the Reagan/Bush era, there is clear indication of "remarkable advances" (Harbeck, 1992, p. 123) made by lesbian women and gay men in the justice system over the past several decades.

Harbeck (1992) outlined a number of cultural, legal, and educational changes since World War II that have challenged the power of school administrators in hiring/firing decisions regarding gay and lesbian educators: changing sexual mores; decreasing social and legal consensus on definitions of "immoral" conduct; emerging political power of the gay rights movement and increased acceptance of homosexuality; growth in the collective power of teachers' unions and special interest litigation organizations; and increased concern for the procedural rights of criminals and sympathy for people accused of victimless crimes. Such changes have made gay/lesbian teacher litigation a difficult, lengthy, costly process, and one that few school systems willingly undertake (Harbeck, 1992). In fact, Harbeck (1992) asserted that the major obstacle in lesbian/gay teacher litigation at present is the tendency for educators to resign at the first indication of conflict; the broad discretionary powers of employers during hiring make reinstatement (re-hiring) much more legally difficult to accomplish than protecting the position of an employee who has the power of contractual rights, union clout, and a history of professional excellence and community support in her/his favor.

Interestingly, gay and lesbian educators of color may be in the most favorable position in both hiring and firing disputes, because already-existing legal protections accord them greater safety and judicial recourse (Harbeck, 1992). Regardless of the future direction of legal activity relating to gay and lesbian educators, however, there are important educational and professional concerns that are beginning to be asserted and heard; these issues are covered in the following section.

## EDUCATIONAL AND PROFESSIONAL ISSUES

Newton and Risch (1981) outlined four reasons why homosexuality is a legitimate concern of educators: (a) many educators are gay or have homosexual feelings, and must work in an environment that denies and denigrates a fundamental aspect of their being; (b) many students are gay or have same-sex feelings, and providing accurate, fair information to help all students deal with confusion and anxiety about sexuality allows them to self-actualize into healthy adults; (c) homosexuality involves issues of fact and information, and the responsibility of schools is to expose people to the most accurate, timely, complete information available; and (d) fundamental moral issues are involved, and because education is by its nature a moral endeavor, students must be provided with the tools (information, support) to help them decide, clarify, and problem-solve in relation to lifestyle and sexuality. Borrowing from Newton and Risch's

(1981) classification, this section reviews issues of teaching, students, and knowledge within the context of fostering an effective, inclusive educational climate.

## Teaching Issues

In addition to both overt and insidious discrimination, probably the most pernicious problem facing lesbian and gay educators is the fear of disclosure and the perceived need to maintain a dual identity, accompanied by the stress of maintaining a secret and protected private life within a very public profession (Griffin, 1992; Woods & Harbeck, 1992). Fear of job loss, compromised collegial and/or student rapport, and violence or other reprisals forces thousands of gay and lesbian educators to hide and deny their sexual orientation in order to maintain acceptance in a homophobic environment: "Entire lifetimes and careers are conducted through a veil of fear and dishonesty, rendering open communication with peers, colleagues, and families impossible" (Grayson, 1989, p. 137). Homophobia and resultant dual identity problems in educational institutions have been well documented (e.g., Evans & Wall, 1991; Grayson, 1989; Griffin, 1992; Hall, 1989; Newton, 1987; Olson, 1987; Parmeter & Reti, 1988; Woods & Harbeck, 1992), and the individual stories are poignant.

Some describe the pain of being cut off from authentic encounters with students, because of the preoccupation with hiding one's personal life and the habitual silence that keeps one from sharing personal experience:

> . . . one of my most basic premises about education is that a teacher should work to make the learning relevant to a student's life. Yet I have to censor relevant aspects of my own life. . . . What I believe in pedagogically, I am unable to practice. . . . My relationship with students is based on developing mutual trust. . . . However, I don't enter into this relationship based on trust with complete integrity. While I do not consciously lie about my life, my interactions in the classroom do not feel as authentic as I would like them to be. Good teaching involves inspiring kids to ask lots of questions and to explore ideas in depth. However, I often cut discussions short, for fear of revealing my sexuality. . . . I am always occupied with being closeted. . . . I feel detached at school, because internally I am rehearsing what to say in case a student asks an "incriminating" question. (Stein, 1988, pp. 10–11)

Another writes, "My biggest disappointment is the inability to get really close to my students. I am afraid to take individual students—if they're boys—on trips, or to my house, as some colleagues do. I'm afraid to hug them. I feel I'm cheating the kids by not offering a closeness they need and may not get from anyone else. If there were no barriers or fears between us, I could be doing a better job" (Trent, 1978, p. 136). Similar concerns were voiced by a sample of 97 gay/lesbian individuals who were or had been teachers (Olson, 1987), where respondents stated that they were careful of physical contact with students, afraid to approach administrators with student problems for fear of calling attention to their homosexuality, and "angry," "resentful," "sad," and "frustrated" about their constricted contacts with students.

Ironically, as Grayson (1989) points out, many of these teachers are the finest in the educational system, recipients of awards and honors for excellence, and outstanding potential role models for students. Such enforced secrecy deprives students, particularly gay and lesbian students, of positive and healthy role models, reinforces invisibility, and perpetuates stereotypes of gay people as a minority of perverts on the fringes of society. One teacher remarked: "Here I am, a happy, healthy, and competent person, who also happens to be a lesbian, and I cannot present to my students a real example of who lesbians are. Since they don't realize that they know healthy lesbians, because many of us are forced to be closeted, they grow up thinking that they've never known any of us" (Stein, 1988, p. 12).

Another dual-identity issue involves collegial support, including day-to-day exchanges of gossip and information about personal lives, as well as pedagogical advice and support. Gay and lesbian educators often are on the fringes of such exchanges, and many practice deception regarding their personal lives in order to maintain peer relationships. As one individual put it: ". . . social isolation is still the reality at school. The kidding conversations in the teachers' room may not be that interesting—still I'd like to take part. But I can't mention . . . my lover . . . my friends, where I go, what I do. When my personal life comes up, I get flustered and defensive. I feel awkward when I hear teachers or kids laughing about gays, and I'm frustrated by discussions on gay rights because I can't join in" (Trent, 1978). Another teacher remarked: ". . . I know that both my students and I could benefit from my spending more time with other teachers. My teaching experience is limited to my nine-hour-a-day encounters with 12-year-olds. Obviously, the kind of feedback they can give me is different from what a colleague might have to offer. . . . But at my site, I have no real allies" (Stein, 1988). Similar concerns have been echoed in other studies (e.g., Griffin, 1992; Olson, 1987; Woods & Harbeck, 1992), and coping behaviors include complicated identity management strategies (such as "passing" for heterosexual, avoiding peers, and declining to reveal personal information), seeking out other teachers for support, focusing on professional excellence, moving to a different location, resigning from their positions, or disclosing identity.

The social isolation of gay/lesbian educators in their professional settings becomes even more critical when these are the same individuals for whom association with gay peers outside the work environment is risky; cut off from all sources of social support, lesbian and gay educators often are left to wrestle with professional problems and conflicts alone. Interestingly, one-third of the teachers in Olson's (1987) study felt that, despite the risks, more lesbian/gay teachers should disclose identity at work and begin educating their nongay peers, and Sears (1992) found widespread support among prospective teachers and counselors for the necessity of proactive efforts to decrease homophobia in the schools. Although some nongay teachers may harbor negative attitudes (Sears, 1992), and others may hesitate to be supportive in a homophobic climate for fear they themselves will be suspect (Grayson, 1989), studies have generally found self-disclosure to colleagues to be a positive experience (e.g., Griffin, 1992; Olson, 1987). It seems clear that only by breaking their enforced silence will lesbian and gay educators begin to merge their dual identities into honest, congruent (and probably more productive) expressions of personal and professional life; the collective power of gay and lesbian professionals, either in organizations or informal support groups, is crucial in providing the necessary help during this professional "coming out" process.

### Student Issues

Although detailed discussion of homosexual issues related to students is beyond the scope of this chapter, it is worth noting several important educational concerns. Because populations in the nation's classrooms involve gay and nongay students, students struggling with sexual identity, and students who have same-sex feelings, it is imperative to make lesbian/gay experience visible in non-judgmental ways. All students benefit from accurate information about sexuality and diversity in people; however, the needs of the millions of gay and lesbian students currently in elementary, secondary, and higher education are particularly salient because their position as targets of oppression puts them at risk in a number of ways. Sexual minority youth, for example, are at high risk for alcohol and drug use, school problems, family difficulties, sexual abuse, prostitution, sexually transmitted diseases, homelessness, conflict with the law, and antigay violence (Uribe & Harbeck, 1992). In addition, sexual minority youth are five times more likely to attempt suicide than their heterosexual peers, and it is estimated that more than 30% of the more than 5,000 young adult suicides annually are compounded by issues of sexual identity (Uribe & Harbeck, 1992). Moreover, families are unlikely to be supportive; a recent poll indicated that one-third of respondents would try to change a gay child, and other studies have suggested that almost 40% of the violence directed at lesbian/gay teens was inflicted by their families (cf. Fassinger, 1991). Half of 2,000 homeless teens in one urban youth center and one-third of Los Angeles's 25,000 homeless children are homosexual, underscoring the inability of many families to meet the needs of their gay and lesbian children.

Sexual minority youth are also unlikely to fare well in the school systems, where hatred and discrimination are often overt, where their needs are ignored or silenced, and where they are at high risk for dropping out (Sears, 1992); in San Francisco and Los Angeles, for example, where dropout rates exceed 40%, many tens of thousands are sexual minority youth. Grayson (1989) pointed out that discrimination and lack of response to the needs of gay and lesbian students essentially denies their right to a free and safe public education: "Responsible educators . . . can no longer ignore the . . . tortured school yard chants, violence, and humiliation inflicted on students who appear to be 'different' " (p. 132).

Unfortunately, most teachers and guidance counselors are ill-prepared, in both knowledge and attitudes, to deal effectively with gay and lesbian youth. Sears (1992), in an extensive study of 142 guidance counselors and 191 prospective teachers in the South, found that "woefully inadequate knowledge" and pervasive, virulent homophobic attitudes and feelings characterized most of these educators. Almost two-thirds of the counselors (most holding master's degrees with an average of 10 years of experience) and 80% of the prospective teachers (education majors in both beginning and final stages of a teacher preparation program) expressed highly negative attitudes and feelings toward gays/lesbians, with most knowing very little factual information regarding this population; moreover, one-fourth of the prospective teachers acknowledged their inability to treat a homosexual student fairly or discuss homosexuality in class. In this sample, elementary education majors, women, and African-Americans demonstrated the least knowledge and the greatest homophobia, and, as in similar studies, knowledge and prior association with gays was related to less negative attitudes and feelings. Interestingly, when presented with a hypothetical classroom conflict between two students, most of this sample professed a willingness to treat fairly and protect a gay student from harassment, yet most also reported that they would feel uncomfortable if an openly gay teacher worked at their school. This separation of civil rights issues from personal fears and discomfort was documented by Norris (1992) as well, in a study of one liberal college in which high levels of victimization of gays were coupled with positive attitudes overall. The "paradox" (Norris, 1992) of the competing values of equal rights (requiring rational response) and heterosexual orthodoxy (involving strong affective responses) suggests that increased knowledge may result in greater fairness and less overt information in the treatment of sexual minority students by educators, but probably will not produce the commitment to advocacy necessary for effective interventions with these at-risk youth (Sears, 1992).

In higher education as well, gay students are subjected to silencing and discrimination. A 1984 survey at the University of California (UC) at Berkeley indicated that 82% of the gay and lesbian students surveyed had been subjected to perjorative stereotypic comments about gays by instructors, and were more uncomfortable in the classroom than any other minority group. In addition, a 1983 survey of nine UC campuses found that 44% of students refrained from doing research or coursework on homosexual issues for fear of negative reactions, and 14% were actually advised by faculty not to pursue these topics (cited in Hart, 1988). Victimization of gay and lesbian students on college campuses is well documented (see Norris, 1992), as is the pain of isolation and invisibility (see Evans & Wall, 1991).

Professional education and counseling associations have called for school systems and universities to develop support services, to adopt antidiscrimination and antiharassment guidelines, and to take other measures to improve the educational climate for sexual minority students; in addition, the professional literature is beginning to document recommendations regarding the educational needs of these students (e.g., Sears, 1987, 1992; Evans & Wall, 1992). Several very successful special school environments and services for lesbian/gay students, such as New York's Harvey Milk School and Los Angeles's Project 10 (see Uribe & Harbeck, 1992), have been established. Rofes (1990) noted that the needs of sexual minority youth are becoming increasingly difficult to ignore as sexual behavior becomes a more critical concern in the schools and as gay/lesbian students begin to assert their rights. In colleges and universities across the nation, for example, gay students are "waging aggressive civil-rights campaigns," demanding the protection accorded other minority groups (Dodge, 1991); issues include the right to free speech and assembly, funding for lesbian/gay organizations, homosexual couples' access to university housing, inclusionary language in campus nondiscrimination policies, deliberate hiring of openly gay faculty and staff, inclusion of gay content and gay studies in current curricula, and the right to participate openly in college activities such as fraternities, sororities, athletic teams, and student government. One student commented: "I'm heartened to see a lot of people coming out and becoming politically active. It's hard to live with secrecy and shame. We want to live our lives with a modicum of dignity" (Dodge, 1991, p. 32).

Regardless of the sexual orientation of individual students, many educators are beginning to argue that schools must provide a climate that values diversity in *every* form, and where all students can articulate their experience freely in order to achieve their optimal development and growth (Chamberlain, 1985; Grayson, 1989; Hart, 1988; Newton & Risch, 1981; Selverstone, 1991). Some assert (e.g., Chamberlain, 1985) that protecting the legal rights of and providing services to individual lesbian/gay students (and teachers) is critical, but inadequate. Such an approach maintains the focus on homosexuality as an individual problem and fails to address the sources of pervasive homophobia and heterosexism in the schools, thus validating prejudice and discrimination against others and preventing students from "growing into tolerant and compassionate members of a harmonious and pluralistic society" (Grayson, 1989, p. 136). Unfortunately, most educators demonstrate little willingness to become personally involved in transforming the educational environment into one more hospitable to sexual minorities; Sears's (1992) respondents, for example, generally indicated agreement that more educational efforts were needed to increase awareness of homosexual issues, but fewer than one-third indicated any willingness to take direct action (such as attending a professional development workshop). Interestingly, many lesbian and gay teachers believe that their unique contribution to education lies in their sensitivity to differences and their ability to relate to diverse students (Griffin, 1992; Olson, 1987; Woods & Harbeck, 1992), suggesting that effective role models and sources of information for this increasingly important aspect of the educational process already are present in the schools, with experience, perspectives, and knowledge that can deeply enhance efforts to help students achieve "the fullest understanding of what it means to be human" (Newton & Risch, 1981, p. 201).

### Issues of Knowledge: Curriculum and Scholarship

Hart (1988) pointed out that sexuality represents much more than sex, that it is integral to identity, social organization, and culture, and therefore something that clearly belongs within the purview of necessary education. Likewise, homosexuality is not a private act that belongs outside the classroom; it represents a way of living, of creating homes, communities, and culture (Hart, 1988). Comprehensive education thus demands the inclusion of accurate information about homosexuality and the infusion of gay/lesbian perspectives throughout the curriculum (Chamberlain, 1985; Grayson, 1989; Newton & Risch, 1981; Rofes, 1990), allowing students "to develop values based on knowledge rather than prejudice and dogma" (Hart, 1988, p. 31). Attempts at curriculum change will not only need to address issues of homophobia and heterosexism, but also sexism and sex-role stereotyping, because rigid gender roles (which are built directly into the educational system) are enforced through the stigma of homosexuality (Grayson, 1989); when homophobic stereotypes are tied to gender nonconformity, the fear that one might be perceived as lesbian or gay can prevent a young woman from participating in sports or a young man from pursuing the arts, further validating the sex-role status quo and limiting options for all students (Garnets & Kimmel, 1992; Grayson, 1989). Unfortunately, such issues rarely surface in existing curricula, and nowhere is this omission more apparent than in the sex education curriculum.

Although 89% of adults apparently favor sexuality education in the schools (Selverstone, 1991), it has also been noted that sex education is currently under siege as schools have become targets for the New Right and conservatism sweeps the nation (Chamberlain, 1985). Schools are thus put in the difficult position of having a mission that is being directed by fears and myths, and sexuality education is being eliminated from some schools or addressed through human service agency contracts in others (Chamberlain, 1985). Sexuality education has been much criticized for its focus on the mechanics (and dangers) of heterosexual copulation and reproduction (with the goal of reducing teen pregnancy), and for its avoidance of homosexuality, AIDS and safe sex practices, sex roles and sexual scripts, masturbation, abortion ethics, birth control, and other topics concerning sexual and lifestyle choices (Chamberlain, 1985; Sears,

1991). As one scholar observed, the curiosity of young people regarding sexuality is a response to a natural and important developmental need, and students will go on trying to figure out how they feel about sex roles, practices, and preferences regardless of prohibitions (Chamberlain, 1985). Most students do not have access to complete and accurate information about sexuality in general, and particularly about homosexuality; responsible educators must provide this information and help students solve problems, clarify values and attitudes, and make decisions based on facts, as well as full acceptance of selves and others (Selverstone, 1991). Sears (1992) argued that lack of information and support from educators creates a climate of guilt and isolation for students confronting same-sex feelings (which, in adolescence, may be the majority of a school's population), and conveys to all students the legitimacy and desirability of heterosexual standards, thus making educators "silent conspirators in sexual oppression" (p. 74).

Because inadequate and erroneous information regarding homosexuality is pervasive, even among gay people themselves (Fassinger, 1991), curriculum transformation based on accurate facts will be difficult to achieve. Newton and Risch (1981) outlined several content areas with which they believe every educator should be familiar, including origins of homosexual behavior and the issue of "normality" or "naturalness," psychological correlates of homosexual behavior, and the role of gay people in education. This author would add content that includes developmental issues, community and social support, relationships (including families), homophobia and heterosexism, and the unique strengths of gay and lesbian people. Of course, in determining an appropriate knowledge base regarding homosexuality, issues of scholarship and research inevitably arise. Unfortunately, accurate and informed research on homosexuality largely is still in infancy stages, and much of the existing research is based on white male and/or pathological samples, thereby limiting its usefulness (Garnets & Kimmel, 1992).

Two kinds of issues are salient in attempts to increase quality scholarship and research on homosexuality: methodological and political. Methodological issues primarily concern sampling a largely invisible population and therefore obtaining nonrepresentative samples, the difficulty and complexity of assessing sexual orientation, the absence of useful constructs, and the paucity or irrelevance of existing psychometric work (Chung, 1991; Eldridge & Gilbert, 1991). Related methodological problems include the lack of knowledgeable and supportive colleagues who can effectively review one's work, and the poor quality or irrelevance of much of the existing research on which one's work is built (Eldridge & Gilbert, 1991; Garnets & Kimmel, 1992).

More difficult, however, is the political climate surrounding research and scholarship related to sexuality and homosexuality (Eldridge & Gilbert, 1991; Hart, 1988; Newton, 1987; Ruprecht, 1991; Troiden, 1987). A 1983 survey of nine UC campuses (cited in Hart, 1988) revealed that 36% of the faculty for whom gay/lesbian topics would be relevant in their fields refrained from doing research on these topics because they feared negative reactions, and 41% refrained from including such material in their courses. In addition, a survey of 1,000 members of the Society for the Scientific Study of Sex revealed that 32% of its members had experienced discrimination as a result of their occupational focus (Troiden, 1987). Troiden (1987) used stigma theory to describe sex researchers as "marked" and "sexually suspect," and described the personal and professional difficulties a sex specialist encounters. In academic settings, risks are encountered that make one's work suspect or devalued, such as the multidisciplinary nature of the field, the controversial nature of some of the topics, and bias in evaluation of one's work. Troiden also noted that homosexuality as both identity and topic leads to greater levels of stigmatization in an already stigmatized field.

More positively, there are indications that the gay studies discipline is gaining acceptance in many areas of scholarship and teaching, and that newly emerging work has moved from documenting "great homosexuals in history" toward social constructionist work that "charts the proliferation of sexual meanings in a culture" (Heller, 1990, p. A4). Finally, one lesbian academic commented on the voice she has found in scholarship on homosexuality:

> [Academic] homophobia has forced me to define my life by its imperatives. Without it, I would not identify so strongly with other homosexuals. My work might have been on paleolithic arrowheads instead of on people who are marginal and different. Although the kind of writing and teaching I do best—interdisciplinary, controversial—has been scorned by some colleagues, it has gained me the respect of others, and the admiration of students. I have found my intellectual voice in the silence society has tried to impose on me. (Newton, 1987, p. 104)

## SUMMARY AND RECOMMENDATIONS

This chapter has reviewed the issues surrounding gays and lesbians in education. Discrimination, legal action and arguments, and educational and professional concerns were addressed. Following are recommendations for individual, systemic, and societal action that might be taken to improve the experience of lesbian and gay people in education.

### Individual

1. In applying for a position, the lesbian/gay educator should carefully consider the location—size of the community and likely level of visibility, general political climate and attitudes, gay/lesbian school and community resources, and history of administrative action and policies regarding promotion, legal disputes, and treatment of other minorities. Professionals in higher education can explore campus commitment to diversity, and ask questions regarding those

issues in the interview (see Evans & Wall, 1991). Note that legal precedent is clearly punitive regarding misrepresentation on employment applications.

2. In deciding when/whether to come out in the workplace, nongay (as well as other gay and lesbian) allies are important, and a network of support at home or in the community is vital as well. Learning factual information and possessing a knowledge base to counter the stereotypes and myths of others is often helpful, and possible consequences must be considered. Having a solid professional record and wide support among colleagues, students, and parents may offer some protection to lesbian/gay educators who disclose identity. Note that most educators who have come out to colleagues have found it to be a positive experience.

3. Involvement in professional organizations, particularly the gay/lesbian caucuses and task groups of major educational organizations, is critical in building support systems, accessing information, and feeling empowered. Less formal "support" groups (a monthly luncheon with a few other lesbian/gay educators, for example) are also highly recommended as a way to address feelings of isolation and marginality.

4. In the event of litigation, the lesbian/gay educator should remember that the cost of such action for a school system to bear is high, politically and financially. Pressure to resign should be resisted in favor of educating others—colleagues, administrators, boards, and parents and students (if appropriate). Nongay colleagues, union officials, and other professional associates may be particularly useful in resolving such conflicts.

### Systemic

1. Raising the awareness of educational personnel regarding homosexuality *must* be a priority in the schools—through informal discussion, professional workshops, invited speakers, training programs, conferences, task forces, faculty meetings, and the like, with attitude examination (versus merely imparting information) at the root of training and education efforts. Undergraduate and graduate training programs for teachers, school counselors, and student personnel professionals must also include issues related to sexual orientation in their content.

2. The open presence of gay and lesbian professionals (and students) in educational settings must be seen as an equity issue and treated as such. Antidiscrimination clauses should be added to current policies, with concommitant efforts to hire openly gay educators and form gay student organizations. Forging strong alliances with other minority colleagues, and with school administrators and state legislators, is extremely important.

3. Curriculum development regarding homosexuality must begin, providing ready-to-use materials and clear guidelines. The resources and power of professional organizations can be used to assist in everything from materials

development to professional (re)training. Teachers who develop or enhance courses should be amply and publicly rewarded. Note that parents and school boards are likely to be more supportive if they have been involved in the process, and administrative support (funding, special activities, recognition, etc.) is critical. In curriculum transformation, materials on racism and sexism can be very effectively modeled and adapted (see Grayson, 1987; Chamberlain, 1985, for detailed discussion and excellent resources).

4. Counseling and support services must be developed for students struggling with sexual orientation concerns (see Sears, 1987, for suggestions). Libraries should have current literature available and easily accessible. Schools should review current student organizations for exclusionary policies and take appropriate action (see the *Washington Blade,* September 27, 1991, for an account of the San Francisco school board's decision to ban the Boy Scouts of America from school activities due to antigay discrimination).

5. Research on topics related to sexual orientation should be encouraged in academic settings, with administrative support in funding, recognition, and tenure/promotion reviews. Individuals who wish to conduct such research should consider joint projects with nongay or more senior colleagues, who may offer some measure of protection and credibility, as well as mentoring and social support. Note that published guidelines for nonsexist, nonracist, and gay-affirmative research can be consulted for a review of the issues involved in ensuring culturally sensitive studies.

## Societal

1. It is critically important that the sodomy laws be repealed and homosexual acts decriminalized. The fundamental right of privacy to consensual voluntary sexual behavior between adult men or women must be extended to gay/lesbian people (i.e., the *Bowers v. Hardwick* decision must be overturned). Same-gender sexual orientation also must be designated as a "suspect classification" under the law, requiring strict scrutiny in judicial action. States must pass laws prohibiting discrimination based on sexual preference (as of this writing, only five states offer such protection). Antidiscrimination legislation should also be passed at the county and city levels.

2. Law students must be provided with accurate information regarding homosexuality and related case law as part of their training. Textbooks and other materials should be examined for exclusion and bias.

3. Visibility of sexual minority people and issues will continue to be critical to social and educational change. The gay rights movement of the past several decades successfully brought many issues to public attention, but educators alone face the challenge of translating that new consciousness into educational practices and institutions that support the growth of *all* people into fulfilled, productive, compassionate members of the human family.

## REFERENCES

Bersoff, D. N., & Ogden, D. W. (1991). APA Amicus Curiae briefs: Furthering lesbian and gay male civil rights. *American Psychologist, 46,* 950–956.

Bradford, J., & Ryan, C. (1987). *National health care survey: Mental health implications.* Washington, DC: Naitonal Lesbian and Gay Health Foundation.

Chamberlain, P. (1985). Homophobia in schools or what we don't know will hurt us. *Radical Teacher,* April, pp. 3–6.

Chung, Y. B. (1991, August). *Difficulties of research on lesbian and gay issues.* Paper presented at the American Psychological Association Annual Convention, San Francisco, CA.

Dodge, S. (1991, April 3). Vigorous civil-rights drives by homosexual students bring both changes and resentment on campuses. *Chronicle of Higher Education,* A31–32.

Dressler, J. (1979a, January/February). Judicial homophobia: Gay rights biggest roadblock. *Civil Liberties Review,* 19–27.

Dressler, J. (1979b). Study of law student attitudes regarding the rights of gay people to be teachers. *Journal of Homosexuality, 4,* 315-329.

Dressler, J. (1985). Survey of school principals regarding alleged homosexual teachers in the classroom: How likely (really) is discharge? *University of Dayton Law Review, 10,* 599–620.

Eldridge, N. S., & Gilbert, L. A. (1991, August). *Researching same-sex couples: Some problems and solutions.* Paper presented at the American Psychological Association Annual Convention, San Francisco, CA.

Evans, N. J., & Wall, V. A. (Eds.). (1991). *Beyond tolerance: Gays, lesbians, and bisexuals on campus.* Alexandria, VA: American College Personnel Association.

Faderman, L. (1991). *Odd girls and twilight lovers: A history of lesbian life in twentieth century America.* NY: Columbia University Press.

Fassinger, R. E. (1991). The hidden minority: Issues and challenges in working with lesbian women and gay men. *The Counseling Psychologist, 19,* 157–176.

Garnets, L., & Kimmel, D. (1992). Lesbian and gay male dimensions in the psychological study of human diversity. In J. Goodchilds (Ed.), *Psychological perspectives on human diversity in America.* Washington, DC: American Psychological Association.

Grayson, D. A. (1989). Emerging equity issues related to homosexuality in education. *Peabody Journal of Education, 64,* 132–145.

Griffin, P. (1992). From hiding out to coming out: Empowering lesbian and gay educators. In K. Harbeck (Ed.), *Coming out of the classroom closet* (pp. 167–196). Binghampton, NY: Harrington Park Press.

Hall, M. (1989). Private experiences in the public domain: Lesbians in organizations. In J. Hearn, D. L. Sheppard, P. Tancred-Sheriff, & G. Burrell (Eds.), *The sexuality of organization* (pp. 125–138). Newbury Park, CA: Sage.

Harbeck, K. M. (1992). Gay and lesbian educators: Past history/future prospects. In K. M. Harbeck (Ed.), *Coming out of the classroom closet* (pp. 121–140). Binghampton, NY: Harrington Park Press.

Hart, E. L. (1988). Literacy and the lesbian/gay learner. In S. Parmeter & I. Reti

(Eds.), *The lesbian in front of the classroom: Writings by lesbian teachers* (pp. 30–43). Santa Cruz, CA: Herbooks.

Harvard Law Review. (1990). *Sexual orientation and the law,* 74–93.

Heller, S. (1990, October 24). Gay- and lesbian-studies movement gains acceptance in many areas of scholarship and teaching. *Chronicle of Higher Education,* A4.

Levine, M. P. (1979). Employment discrimination against gay men. *International Review of Modern Sociology, 9,* 151–163.

Levine, M. P., & Leonard, R. (1984). Discrimination against lesbians in the work force. *Signs, 9,* 700–710.

Newton, E. (1987, March 11). Academe's homophobia: It damages careers and ruins lives. *Chronicle of Higher Education,* 104.

Newton, D. E., & Risch, S. J. (1981, February). Homosexuality and education: A review of the issue. *High School Journal,* 191–202.

Norris, W. P. (1992). Liberal attitudes and homophobic acts: The paradoxes of homosexual experience in a liberal institution. In K. M. Harbeck (Ed.), *Coming out of the classroom closet* (pp. 81–120). Binghampton, NY: Harrington Park Press.

Olson, M. R. (1987). A study of gay and lesbian teachers. *Journal of Homosexuality, 13,* 73–81.

Parmeter, S.-H., & Reti, I. (Eds.). (1988). *The lesbian in front of the classroom: Writings by lesbian teachers.* Santa Cruz, CA: Herbooks.

Rofes, E. (1990, November). Opening up the classroom closet. *The Education Digest,* 16–19.

Rubinstein, R. A., & Fry, P. B. (1981). *Of a homosexual teacher: Beneath the mainstream of constitutional equalities.* Frederick, MD: University Publications of America.

Ruprecht, L. J. (1991, August). *Politics and policy in researching lesbian- and gay-related topics.* Paper presented at the American Psychological Association Annual Convention, San Francisco, CA.

Schneider, B. E. (1987). Coming out at work: Bridging the private/public gap. *Work and Occupations, 13,* 463–487.

Schneider-Vogel, M. (1986). Gay teachers in the classroom: A continuing Constitutional debate. *Journal of Law and Education, 15,* 285–318.

Sears, J. (1987). Peering into the well of loneliness: The responsibility of educators to gay and lesbian youth. In A. Molnar (Ed.), *Social issues and education: Challenge and responsibility* (pp. 79–100). Alexandria, VA: American Association of Counseling and Development.

Sears, J. T. (1991, September). Helping students understand and accept sexual diversity. *Educational Leadership,* 54–56.

Sears, J. T. (1992). Educators, homosexuality, and homosexual students: Are personal feelings related to professional beliefs? In K. M. Harbeck (Ed.), *Coming out of the classroom closet* (pp. 29–79). Binghampton, NY: Harrington Park Press.

Selverstone, R. (1991, September). Sexuality education can strengthen democracy. *Educational Leadership,* 58–60.

Stein, A. (1988). What's a lesbian teacher to do? In S. Parmeter & I. Reti (Eds.), *The lesbian in front of the classroom: Writings by lesbian teachers* (pp. 4–17). Santa Cruz, CA: Herbooks.

Trent, M. (1978, April). On being a gay teacher: My problems—and yours. *Psychology Today,* 136.

Troiden, R. R. (1987). Walking the line: The personal and professional risks of sex education and research. *Teaching Sociology, 15,* 241–249.

Uribe, V., & Harbeck, K. M. (1992). Addressing the needs of lesbian, gay, and bisexual youth: The origins of Project 10 and school-based intervention. In K. M. Harbeck (Ed.), *Coming out of the classroom closet* (pp. 9–28). Binghampton, NY: Harrington Park Press.

*Washington Blade.* (1991, September 27). *S.F. school board bans Boy Scouts, 22*(39), Washington, DC.

Woods, S. E., & Harbeck, K. M. (1992). Living in two worlds: The identity management strategies used by lesbian physical educators. In K. M. Harbeck (Ed.), *Coming out of the classroom closet* (pp. 141–166). Binghampton, NY: Harrington Park Press.

Chapter 8

# Homosexual Relationships in a Unique Setting: The Male Prison

**Gary Thomas Long**

Late one fall afternoon I was touring a medium security prison in the southern Piedmont district of North Carolina. I was part of a team of potential "expert witnesses" observing the conditions at the prison on behalf of the plaintiffs in a federal law suit against the state of North Carolina. There were prisonologists, safety engineers, lawyers, and a psychologist (me) on the tour, which was being conducted by the prison administrators. The first residential area we saw consisted of two dormitory rooms, which housed over sixty men each. The beds were triple-bunked and the bunks lined each of the three walls that were solid rather than bars. In addition to the beds around the walls there was a double row of triple bunks filling most of the center of the room, leaving only a narrow walkway between the center beds and the beds along the wall. As I walked down this corridor between the beds I had to turn my shoulders at an angle to avoid bumping against the bedframes. Over 90% of the inmates were housed in these two rooms, separated by a corridor of walls of bars from which the guards could view only some of the men during their sundown to sunrise lockup.

After walking through these rooms and talking with some of the inmates, we went down the barred corridor and through a steel door into a hallway of 10 or 12 single-occupancy cells. This is where prisoners were housed for disciplinary reasons, or because they were thought to be in some danger from the other prisoners. Several of the cells were empty, but soon we came to a cell occupied by a prisoner who was startlingly different in appearance from the others. This particular inmate, who had been assigned to one of the few single cells for his own protection, had somehow fashioned the pale denim material of the clothing issued to prisoners into a short, tight dress. He had long curving fingernails with a flashy crimson coating. Curly black hair hung in ringlets around his head and his legs were bare and hairless down to the thongs he wore. The guards conducting the tour acted as is he were not unusual. He was in the single cell in what they call "protective custody."

Of course, as a social psychologist, I was reasonably familiar with transvestism, and as a tourist in New Orleans I had observed numerous men who dressed as women for the pursuit of their own sexual gratification, as well as female impersonators who performed for the amusement of others. This instance, here inside the men's prison, seemed intriguingly different. How did this man relate to other prisoners? Why did the usually conservative prison administration tolerate this lifestyle in this setting? Was this the inmate's way of escaping from the threatening environment of the dormitories? Was this man a transvestite before prison? Many transvestites are heterosexual, but in this setting was this possible? In general, how was sexuality expressed in this single-sex world? These were some of the questions that quickly passed through my mind while I was passing through the single-cell area.

My main purpose in visiting the prison was to assess the social and physical population density to determine whether the level of crowding in this environment was likely to be damaging to the inmates; so, although the presence of this transvestite was thought-provoking for several reasons, I did not immediately pursue the questions about sexuality in prison that occurred to me at that time. This pursuit waited until my colleague, the editor of this volume, Louis Diamant, asked if I would write a chapter on homosexuality in prison. Having some experience in writing about homosexuality and some experience researching and writing about some aspects of the prison environment, I agreed. This was my opportunity to apply my experiences to the literature on homosexuality in prison.

In this chapter some of the literature on homosexuality in men's prisons will be described and some general implications of what we know about this topic will be proposed.

In 1990 there were over 688,000 prisoners in state prisons, over 50,000 in federal prisons, and over 405,000 in city and county jails across the country (U.S. Department of Commerce, 1992). About 80% of the state prisoners had had prior sentences. The federal, city, and county prisoners would likely have had prior sentences at a rate near that in the state prisons. The number of people who are exposed to jail and/or prison experiences is tragically large. These places of incarceration are the homes, the job settings, and the places of recreation for more than a million people in the United States. The literature on homosexuality to be discussed here will include studies that are done in prisons as well as in jails with no general distinction between the two.

The effects of the prison and jail experiences are felt not only by those who serve time, but also by those who come in contact with the people who leave incarceration damaged, or dangerous, or both.

On August 30, 1992, CNBC television network interviewed a male rape victim who described his experiences in prison.

On September 2, 1992, WSOC-TV in Charlotte, North Carolina, reported that a man in the local viewing area was raped by another man that day. Further details were lacking. Had this male rapist been in prison? Several of the articles that will be reviewed here indicate that the effects of the homosexual experiences in prison spill out into the society at large.

It should be noted at the outset that the study of homosexual behavior in prison may have at most an indirect relationship to homosexuality outside of prison. The uniqueness of the setting and the differences between the prison population and the general population make generalization from the inside to the outside a risky process. The vast majority of those who engage in homosexual acts in prison may not be homosexuals at all; at least not in the way the term is used for the nonprison population. The writings about homosexuality in prison suggest to me a problem in defining homosexuality. Obviously homosexual acts can be and are performed by those whose sexual preference is heterosexual. In the prison setting there is no opportunity for heterosexual contacts, while homosexual opportunities are plentiful. Further, most homosexuals who are in prison are probably much more similar to prisoners than they are to homosexuals who have never been in a prison population (West, 1967).

The writings about "homosexuality" in prison would perhaps be better described as about "homosexual behavior" in prison. Much less is written about consensual homosexuality in prison than about the sexual victimization of prisoners who happen to be of the same sex as the aggressor. However, the issue of consensual homosexuality in prison is somewhat controversial in itself, as we will see later. The literature covers about 30 years and includes adult male institutions, adult female institutions, and juvenile institutions. This chapter will deal only with adult male institutions.

## SEXUAL BEHAVIOR OF INCARCERATED ADULT MALES

On September 10, 1990, an associated press story appeared in *The Charlotte Observer* headlined "Jail IDs Homosexual Prisoners" ("Jail IDs," 1990). The story describes the policy of a county jail in Fort Worth, Texas. In this jail all prisoners are required to wear colored wristbands: red for felons, blue for misdemeanor offenders, orange for those awaiting transfer to a federal prison, yellow for those with medical problems, and gray for gay prisoners.

As prisoners enter the jail they are asked whether they are homosexual. If they say they are, protective custody is offered because (the jail officials say) homosexuals are likely to be abused by other inmates. If they choose, those who say they are homosexual are housed in isolated groups, although they are mixed with the other prisoners during meals and exercise periods.

Jail administrators argue that the policy is for the benefit of the prisoners. It may be, but of course the administrators are primarily interested in keeping order and it is a common attitude among those who run corrections facilities that homosexuals cause trouble. Gay activists are challenging the jail's policy on the grounds that the wristbands cause more abuse than would occur without them.

This situation illustrates a dilemma for both the homosexual and for the prison administration. What conditions of incarceration are best for the individual and for the institution? For over 35 years the literature on homosexuality in prison has wrestled with this problem. It is interesting to look at how the changes in attitude toward homosexuality in the society as a whole are reflected in the writings about homosexuality in prison over these 35 years. I will try to illustrate these changes as well as the nature of male homosexuality in prisons over the last third of a century by describing some of these writings in chronological order beginning with 1955. The earlier writings on the subject, such as *Sex in Prison* (1930) and *Prison Days and Nights* (1933), are frequently quoted in the writings of the 1950s, and the thinking seems to be mostly unchanged over this period.

A series of papers on sex in prison was published as a symposium in *Corrective Psychiatry and Journal of Social Therapy* in 1955. The papers dealt with: "social pressures toward deviation"; prison pornography; and, in a separate paper, sex literature; masturbation; and homosexuality in general; as well as homosexuality in prison. Homosexuals and homosexual behavior are described in pejorative terms that reflect the attitude of the times.

Herbert Bloch, in his discussion of social pressures toward sexual deviation, proposes that the men in prison can be divided into three groups that will differ with respect to their sexual behavior in the prison. The largest group is called "a predominantly normal" group. Bloch believes that long sentences and the loss of positive relationships outside the prison may cause these men to engage in homosexual acts, but that most of them will not. The second group is called "a quasi-abnormal group." This group is said to constitute about 37% of the population and consists of those who under the proper aggravating and provocative circumstances may be unable to resist "abnormal," homosexual behavior. The third group is said to be quite small and consists of the "frankly abnormal" or homosexual population. They will, of course, seek the opportunity for homosexual relationships.

William Haines, in his paper "Homosexuality," says that homosexuality will occur whenever groups of the same sex are confined together and have no opportunity for "natural" sexual expression (Haines, 1955). He notes that in the distant past homosexuality has been accepted by other cultures. He says that in ancient Rome and Greece, intercourse between two persons of the same sex was almost as common as normal intercourse, but today (1955) it is not condoned morally or legally. He divides the inmate homosexual population into three groups: (1) The frank homosexual; (2) The feeble-minded, mentally ill, or insane; and (3) The occasional or situational.

Frank homosexuals are described as having obvious feminine mannerisms, speech, and clothing. These are not a behavior problem but they are to be "segregated, guarded and sometimes protected." He includes in this group another type of person who does not necessarily have these feminine characteristics. The "prison wolf" is a crafty, sly, and dangerous homosexual who dominates or owns a punk. These are likely long-term prisoners who are so jealous of their punks that they will commit murder "not infrequently."

The second group is described as the "frank psychotic or feeble-minded," some active, aggressive, and dangerous and some passive and preyed upon.

The third group is called the "latent, situational, or occasional homosexual" who under the deprivation and stress of confinement, or the threats of others will vent his sexual tensions through homosexual acts. This may be followed by emotional disturbance.

Haines concludes that the only way to control homosexuality in prison is to have a well-trained staff that is aware of the situation and will not tolerate or condone any semblance of this form of behavior.

Donald Webster Cory (1955) in "Homosexuality in Prison," the last paper in the symposium, offers views that seem unusually tolerant given the attitudes of the other writers in the 1950s. He recognizes the difficulty in devising a rational policy for handling homosexuality in prison because doing so would require reconciling our culture's hostility toward homosexuality and the assumption that men in prison must have no sex life whatsoever. For purposes of analysis he divides the men in prison into four groups of unknown size and discusses the implications of confinement for each.

**1** Exclusive heterosexuals who do not yield to the pressures of confinement by engaging in homosexual acts.

**2** Exclusive or almost exclusive homosexuals before prison.

**3** Those who had no homosexual experiences before prison, but who begin to have such contacts in prison.

**4** Those who are primarily oriented toward the opposite sex, but have had some occasional sexual contacts with same-sexed partners before incarceration.

Cory is most concerned about the long-term effects of homosexual behavior on those who had no such experiences before prison. He notes that homosexuality is thriving in prisons and that authorities do little to prevent it. He says even if we accept the assumption that homosexuality is neither good nor bad, neither moral nor immoral, that the ex-prisoner who has acquired homosexuality as a result of his prison experience will have greater difficulty readapting to the outside world because of the added social, psychological, and legal difficulties he will encounter as a result of this new lifestyle. He does not accept the argument that these people were "latent homosexuals" in the first place or they would not have changed. He feels that sexual development is dynamic rather than static and that a lengthy period of sexual contact with one sexual outlet while all others are blocked will lead to a psychological adjustment that involves the available outlet becoming more desirable through familiarity, while the original outlet becomes less needed because of the substitution. In other words he feels homosexuality as a sexual preference can be acquired as a result of this prison experience and will increase the difficulties of adjustment for the prisoner after release. The personal experiences reported by Donald Tucker, which will be described later in this chapter, will illustrate what is suggested here by Cory.

Cory makes four recommendations for a policy toward homosexuality in prison.

**1** Prison officials should arrange for conjugal visits or home visits by trustworthy prisoners.
**2** So long as homosexual activities in prison are voluntary they should not be punished.
**3** Prison officials should not exhibit a derogatory attitude toward homosexuals.
**4** Prison officials should do everything possible to protect prisoners from coercive homosexuality.

Cory's recommendations have only rarely been adopted even in the 1990s. They are unusually progressive for the time he made them. Most of the earlier writers seem to view homosexuality as a sickness that should be prevented or isolated from "normal" people. Their writings are somewhat theoretical and distant from the behavior itself. They develop categories largely based on conjecture. The writings of the 1960s will show a greater tendency to describe the homosexual behavior in prisons in vivid terms, often relying upon first-person accounts of prisoners and ex-prisoners.

## WRITINGS ON HOMOSEXUALITY IN MEN'S PRISONS IN THE 1960s

In 1960, Arthur V. Huffman, the supervising sociologist of the Illinois Department of Public Safety, published "Sex Deviation in a Prison Community" in the *Journal of Social Therapy.* He states his awareness that prison authorities probably know less about sexual behavior in prison than they do about any other aspect of prison behavior. Inmates do not trust the authorities and fear the reprisals of other inmates so they will rarely report what goes on. When inmates do give accounts of sexual experiences, their veracity cannot be counted on. Administrators of prisons may not want the extent of the problem in their own institutions to be known as it would not reflect well on them. Each of these circumstances makes getting accurate information about the matter difficult.

One indication that there is a wide range of sexual activity taking place in prison is the existence of a highly developed vocabulary for the various types of homosexual acts and relationships. Huffman lists the following terms as part of the vernacular of Stateville-Joliet prisons: punk, brat, queer, handshakes, leggins or slick leggins, jocker, wolf, gunsel, head-hunter, cannibal, kid-fruit, stud, and sissy. Punks and brats may be any age and take the passive role in sodomy. Handshakes refers to mutual masturbation, while leggins consist of one man inserting his penis between the legs of another, usually face-to-face and horizontal. Jockers and wolves are the active partners in sodomy. When a jock or wolf is teamed with a particular punk or brat he is a gunsel. Headhunters and cannibals are fellators. A kid-fruit is an older inmate who fellates a younger one. Stud and sissy are expressions used by blacks to refer to white jockers and brats, respectively. If an inmate is "geared," or "wired-up," he is available for a homosexual relationship.

Huffman interviewed a long-term inmate for information about the sexual scene in the Illinois prisons. The inmate tells the story of a hypothetical inmate to illustrate one of the typical sexual scenarios, the seduction of the virgin. This is one of several scenarios that will be described in this chapter. These are the accounts of inmates who may or may not have been involved in the scenes they describe. We cannot know whether these experiences are typical, or how accurate the accounts are. It does seem useful to know what inmates tell us about sexuality in prison, however, because it is the best source of information available.

A new inmate, Sam, arrives with 25 other "fish." He is assigned to B cellblock in a two-man cell with a total stranger. Sam is an ordinary fellow in every respect. He is not "feminine" looking, he is not unusually "handsome," nor is he unusually small or weak. He is, however, younger than most inmates (21 years old). Sam has little in common with his cellmate and is depressed and lonely. He is from a small town that sends few men to this institution so it is unlikely he will find a "homeboy" with whom he might socialize.

Bud is a prison-wise jocker who is the commissary runner for B block. Bud is between romances. His previous brat has been paroled, so he surreptitiously cases the new fish for a replacement. He decides to explore the possibilities of turning Sam into a punk, beginning the process in a very subtle manner. He wants to find out how much resistance to expect so he becomes superficially acquainted with Sam, walks to the yard with him as an oldtimer showing the newcomer around. Bud makes sure that while in the yard he introduces Sam to several "married couples" of jockers and punks. In most cases the newcomer will be curious about the nature of these relationships, having never encountered such before. Bud casually explains that this is the way in prison, stressing the normality and acceptability of these relationships in the prison setting.

These first few weeks in prison are very difficult for Sam. His loneliness and depression leave him highly vulnerable to the supportive attentions paid him by Bud. Bud makes himself available to Sam at every opportunity, all the while "educating" Sam about the homosexual scene in prison. Bud becomes Sam's constant companion, doing him favors like supplying him with erotic literature. Finally, after a courtship of several weeks, the stage of "laying on of hands" begins. This takes the form of horseplay, backrubs, and wrestling. Bud is waiting for some sign of an erotic response to the touching. When this happens Bud moves as quickly as possible to consummate the sexual relationship. He may get Sam transferred to his cell or maneuver him into a private place where sodomy is possible. In this scenario, if Sam resists vigorously, the seduction ends. As a matter of pride, no jocker would seduce a brat after being say, punched in the nose. This would result in ridicule from the other jockers, characterized by snide remarks suggesting that they were "flipflopping" (interchanging roles in the sex act). This is not acceptable among jockers. They want to be the "man of the house." Seducing a punk who is "manly" enough to offer physical resistance suggests that the marriage is not between a clearly dominating jock and a submissive punk. According to the inmate giving this account, these values are important to the jockers and punks and they are critical of relationships that deviate from this norm.

This seduction pattern is said to very rarely fail. Further, these marriages usually last for extended periods. It appears that the single consummation is sufficient for the punk to define himself as a punk and to remain a punk as long as he is in prison, even if he breaks up with the original seducer.

The inmates do not believe that either the jockers or the punks were homosexuals on the outside. Inmates who enter the prison as known homosexuals are avoided by those in this scene. Known homosexuals are said to be "too hot" and association with them would indicate that the jocker is homosexual. Prisoners on the whole denigrate frank homosexuals. The jockers seem to totally deny that they are homosexual themselves even though in prison they are "married" to another man.

It should be reiterated that this is the scene described by one inmate in Illinois who was in prison through the 1950s even though his account was published in 1960. Some of the other case studies will support parts of what this inmate said and contradict other parts. This nonviolent style is clearly not the only way a punk is made, as we shall see in the following accounts.

In 1968 a Philadelphia County judge was told by an attorney that his male client had been gang-raped while being transported in a sheriff's van. A few weeks later the same judge was told that a slender 21-year-old man who was sent to Philadelphia detention center for pre-sentence evaluation had been sexually assaulted within minutes of his arrival. The judge, Alexander F. Barbieri, appointed the Chief Assistant District Attorney of Philadelphia, Alan J. Davis, to investigate these allegations. The results of the three-month investigation, which studied the period from June 1966 to July 31, 1968, were shocking (Davis, 1968). About 60,000 inmates passed through the Philadelphia prison system during that period, of these 3,304 were interviewed, in addition to 361 custodial employees. There was a serious attempt to determine the truthfulness of the accounts of both the inmates and the employees. When an interview yielded critical information the respondent was asked to take a polygraph test. If they refused or failed the test their accounts were disregarded. During the two-year period that was studied there were reports of 62 assaults in the institutional records. Interviews of a sample of about 5% of the inmates who had passed through the institution during that period found 94 additional verifiable assaults that were not in the records. Extrapolation from this sample indicates that nearly 2,000 assaults probably occurred during those two years. This is almost three every day. The authors of this study excluded any accounts of consensual homosexuality from their count. They were only interested in coercive homosexuality, although they commented on the difficulty in determining what is purely voluntary in the prison setting. The atmosphere of fear created by the frequent sexual assaults could make many inmates give in to sexual overtures to avoid becoming one of the assault victims.

The account of a 19-year-old named Charles is typical of the incidents. Charles said that he was in his cell about 9:30 one Tuesday morning in June. He was cleaning up when a tall, heavy-set man came in and asked for a mirror that Charles's cell partner had said he could borrow. The stranger remarked that he had heard something about Charles engaging in homosexual acts, and Charles immediately denied it. The stranger threatened to hurt him if he wouldn't have sex and Charles hit him with his fist in the face. Three other men came into the cell and they all punched Charles until he fell down and then they kicked him in the ribs. They tore his pants off and each one in turn sodomized him while the others held him down.

Victims like Charles usually do not report what happened to them for several reasons. The guards sometimes discourage such reports because the guards will look bad as a result of them. Inmates don't trust the guards to protect them from retaliation. Victims don't want others to know what was done to them. Of the 2,000 estimated assaults in the Philadelphia system 96 were reported to prison authorities, only 64 were mentioned in prison records, 40 resulted in internal discipline against the aggressor, and 26 were reported to the police for prosecution.

The aggressor who attacked Charles was described by him as tall and heavy-set. There are on the average physical differences between the aggressors and the victims identified in the Philadelphia study. Aggressors are older, taller, heavier, and convicted of more serious crimes than their victims. Victims averaged less than 21 years old, while aggressors were just under 24. Both these ages are several years below the prison average of 28.8 years. The height advantage of the aggressor is less than an inch (5′8.25″ vs. 5′9″), but the weight difference is over 15 pounds (141 vs. 157).

Eighty percent of the inmates at the time of this study were black; and 85% of the sexual aggressors were black. However, even though only 20% of the inmates were white, whites made up 71% of the victims. There were no white aggressor/black victim incidents.

These violent incidents are obviously in stark contrast to the story of the careful seduction of the virgin in the Illinois prison. These are acts of domination and humiliation. They are often expressions of anger reflecting social conflicts that were brought from the outside, such as racial conflict. The differences between these rapes and the seduction described earlier illustrate only some of the range and variety of the sexual behavior behind prison walls. We will see further variations in the later writings.

Also in 1968, a paper was published in *Federal Probation* by two senior research sociologists at the Institute for Sex Research at Indiana University, John H. Gagnon and William Simon, Ph.D. Their paper was titled "The Social Meaning of Prison Homosexuality." These authors estimate the frequency of homosexuality in the male prison population to be between 30–45%, which they feel is quite low. It is interesting to me that many other authors on the subject agree with Gagnon and Simon on the percentage of occurrences, yet the others interpret the percentages to indicate that homosexuality is "rampant" in men's prisons. Obviously, they have different standards for the expected level of homosexuality in prison. People who work in the corrections field as administrators or researchers probably compare the 30–45% figure to an expectation of near zero, so they feel that homosexuality in prison occurs at a high rate. Gagnon and Simon are sex researchers and their stated comparison level is the frequency of sex outside of prison. They say that sex is much less frequent inside prison than it was for these same people when they were outside so their frequency in prison is low by comparison. They feel that the desire for sex is stifled in prison by the anxiety, the lack of appropriate stimuli and opportunity for sex, the absence of females and other sexual cues, and a general limited ability to generate complex fantasies. They feel these situational characteristics explain the low incidence of sexual behavior in prison and that the homosexual behavior that does occur is not motivated by sexual needs. They propose two motivations that are the force directing and energizing the inmate's homosexual behavior, the need for meaningful relationships, and a man's need to have his masculinity validated.

The former motivation is the force behind the nonviolent relationships that are the prison parody of the heterosexual relationships on the outside. The jocker and punk "marriages" are characterized by intimacy and affection, and also have clearly distinguished masculine and feminine roles. The jocker here can satisfy both the intimacy needs and some of the need for masculinity as well. The punk is able to achieve intimacy and protection, but must relinquish any masculinity needs he may have. Homosexual assaults with their domination and physical abuse associated with an aggressive masculinity are motivated by the latter of the motivations alone.

These authors feel that the only solution to the problems caused by homosexuality in prison is to allow the inmates periodic home visits that will allow them to retain intimate contacts with those outside and to allow them to feel more control over their lives to help maintain their feeling of masculinity. Both these steps are probably impractical for the majority of inmates. Home visits should only be granted to those who are safe and trustworthy. These people should not be in prison. Allowing control over their lives is not impossible, but is a practical problem for prison administrators. What control can they be given?

## MALE PRISON SCIENCE IN THE 1970s

Essays by prison researchers and first-person accounts of inmates continue to appear in the literature, but the frequency of more structured studies increased in the 1970s. An example was published in April 1971 in *The American Journal of Orthopsychiatry.* Loren H. Roth, a physician on the staff of the Federal Penitentiary in Lewisburg, Pennsylvania, authored an article titled "Territoriality and Homosexuality in a Male Prison Population."

Roth made a map of the Federal Penitentiary at Lewisburg, which indicated the housing location of all individuals known by the administration to engage in homosexual acts. Because the housing locations were largely the result of inmate requests, Roth was interested in how aggressive inmate "rapists" and passive homosexuals distributed themselves among the dormitories and the single-cell blocks. Out of the 1,220 men in the institution, 107 were known by the administration to engage in homosexual behaviors. Of the 107 known to engage in homosexual behaviors, 14 were known to forcibly rape other inmates. It is interesting to me that the administration apparently made no effort to control the housing locations even of those known to be the rapists of other prisoners. It is also of interest to note that the administration records show only 9% of the inmates to be involved in homosexuality, when most other studies indicate that a 30–40% rate is more typical. These matters were not, however, the subject of Roth's study. He was interested in detecting patterns of territoriality in the inmates, particularly in the aggressive rapists.

Roth found what he described as a parallel of animal territoriality in the spacing of the inmates. With only one exception, each rapist had his own territory in a cell block. There were always three or four of the nonaggressive homosexuals in his territory, but no other aggressive homosexual. This arrangement was said to serve the same function as animal territoriality in aggressive species, to reduce conflict and increase the survival of the species. This reduction of conflict served a function for the administration as well as for the homosexuals. It reduced violence in the prison.

A 1974 publication in *Prison Behavior* (Akers, Hayner, & Gruninger, 1974) is another example of the scientific approach to studying homosexuality in prison. The authors are comparing two theoretical models of the inmate system for explaining homosexual and drug behavior in prison. They compare a "functional" explanation of prison behavior to an "importation" model. The functional model would explain homosexual behavior in prison as an adaptation to the prison environment. The importation model sees the nature of homosexuality in prison as primarily derived from the roles and values the inmates bring with them from the outside. Of course, these two models are not mutually exclusive, and homosexuality likely results from both kinds of influences in prison. However, the results of their rather extensive study covering seven prisons are interpreted by them to indicate that the type of prison environment the inmate inhabits has a greater influence on the frequency of inmate homosexual behavior than do the social characteristics the inmates bring with them from the outside. They base this conclusion on the finding that about three times as many inmates in more repressive prison environments (compared to more "open" ones) report knowing of six or more inmates who have engaged in homosexual acts in the past year. Even though there is concern that the reports of the inmates may not provide an accurate rate of homosexual behavior, these data do suggest that much of the homosexuality in prison is caused by the prison situation rather than by any individual predisposition of the prisoner. It is of course possible, even likely, that the situational influence of the prison environment interacts with the characteristics of the individual to produce homosexual behavior in those who had never or rarely experienced it before.

Several studies indicate that many men have their first significant homosexual experiences in prison. What are the long-term effects of these experiences? Dr. Edward Sagarin, past president of the American Society of Criminology, published a systematic attempt to answer this question in 1976 (Sagarin, 1976). Dr. Sagarin was interested in whether those who frequently engaged in homosexual behavior in prison continued to do so once they were outside. In spite of his efforts he was able to find only nine released inmates who would participate in his research. Five of these ex-inmates were voluntary participants who were the aggressors or "inserters." The remaining four were involuntary recruits known as "jailhouse turnouts" or JTOs. JTOs come into prison with a self-image of themselves as heterosexuals. They are raped or seduced into the role of passive sexual partner or "insertee." Once this happens they are identified in the institution as boy-girls, punks, fairies, homosexuals. The aggressors, as long as they were inserters, maintained or even increased their manly image in the prison society. A composite of their stories after prison indicates some major differences between the effects of the experiences on the members of these two groups.

The five aggressors were tall, muscular, and tough-looking. They admitted to their homosexual experiences in prison, but were adamant in the insistence that they were always the inserters. They denied any positive feelings for their sexual partners and referred to them in the most negative of terms. Even though their descriptions of some of their sexual encounters included physical threats made to force compliance, they insisted they never forced themselves on a "kid." Their story is that the "kid" is always a queer who doesn't know it yet himself. The aggressors expect initial resistance, but after "they are broken in, they're dying for it." When asked whether they have had any homosexual experiences after release from prison they are astonished at the question. "Why would I want a fairy, when I can get a broad?" is the reply. Sagarin's interviews with some of the post-prison female sex partners of these aggressors indicated there was violence and brutality in their sexuality. This was not considered to be very unusual because it is not infrequent in the social class to which they belong.

The involuntary recruits have a dramatically different story. Their accounts of their introduction to homosexuality in prison are like the horror stories that appear elsewhere in this chapter. They report being either physically raped or so completely terrified by physical threats that they were unable to resist. They recalled the pain, humiliation, and disgust they felt in their first sexual encounters and afterward. They recall the shame of being identified as punks. They report this shame and disgust in reflection, even though each one had chosen to continue exclusive homosexuality after prison. They recalled with disgust and humiliation their homosexual roles in prison, yet they were continuing in voluntary homosexuality outside of the prison. It should be noted that no JTOs were found who had returned to heterosexual behavior after prison, but this may be because these people are extremely reluctant to discuss the homosexuality they experienced in prison.

Although we must be concerned about the representativeness of the sample in Sagarin's study, taken as nine case histories the results are provocative. Because some of these accounts are corroborated by several of the other accounts presented previously, and some to be presented later, the proposition that the prison experience can cause previously heterosexual men to become homosexual even after prison has considerable support.

In January 1977, Leo Carroll published a 15-month study of a maximum security prison that housed an average of 200 men daily (Carroll, 1977). Although he states that consensual homosexual activity is more frequent than coercive relationships, his focus was on sexual assault. His informants indicated that there were 40 or more assaults per year. The large majority of these assaults were perpetrated by black inmates on whites (75%), even though only 22% of the inmates in this prison were black and 78% were white. Assaults on black prisoners were unheard of. The prisoners reported that this was typical for other prisons as well as this one. The effect of the sexual assault is, as in the other accounts, a lasting one. After the assault the victim is considered to have been "turned" and usually then becomes a "JTO," continuing in the passive role in homosexual activities.

The most common assault style in ECI, where Carroll's study took place, was a combination "hard and soft sell." In this approach, prospective victims are taunted by being called names like "girls," "bitches," and "whores." They are threatened with sexual assault. This allows the aggressors to ascertain whether the potential victim has any allies who will come to his aid. If other white prisoners come to the victim's aid, the process ends. If no one comes to the defense of the victim, the process continues. The next step is maneuvering the victim into a position of trust and dependency on a black inmate. Once this relationship is established, the taunting ceases. This gives the victim a feeling of security for which he is indebted to his black protector. The protector, called the "ripper" in this prison, eventually maneuvers the victim into a place where he is raped by the ripper and perhaps a few of his associates. After this, the victim is told he will be killed if he reports the rape, or if he asks for protective custody. The ripper promises that he (and perhaps a few others) will be the only ones who the punk will have to service. Gradually the ripper introduces the punk to more sex acts and to more participants until he is generally available to the entire prison population.

Carroll interprets the predominant black on white pattern of these assaults as an expression of racial hostility in response to white domination in the outside world. Blacks are a small minority in this prison (22%) and their domination of whites could be discouraged by the white majority if they wanted to do this. The early stage of the "hard and soft sell" is taunting to determine whether the victim has any support from other white prisoners. If he does, he does not become a victim. The whites who become victims are those with no friends. Some of these are kids who some of the white prisoners will eventually use as punks. One interviewee indicated that he would have his eye on a kid and just wait till the blacks worked him over, then take him under his wing. After what the kid had been through he was a willing punk to his new protector. So these black assaults may be serving some function for the white population. In addition, it is possible that there are general differences in the races' attitudes toward homosexuality; and, therefore, a difference in the likelihood of "turning" in prison. The data do not provide a test of this proposition. It is mentioned only as a possibility.

In 1977, Edwin Johnson's account of his observations during his incarceration in San Quentin was published (Johnson, 1977). Johnson served three years in the California prison before he was cleared of the charge that sent him there.

His story is unlike other first-person accounts in that he does not report his own victimization, nor his own aggression. His report is that of an observer of the homosexual scene in two prisons in which he was housed. Johnson proposes that homosexuals are necessary in the prison society. They take the place of women filling the roles of "wife" and "mother." He says that in the abnormal inmate culture homosexuals are normal. He believes that the prison world is a more comfortable place for homosexuals than the world outside of prison. They get the best jobs in prisons and are more secure and more valued than on the outside.

Among the types of homosexual relationships he saw, was the "class" courtship. This begins with a date between an inmate and a known homosexual. (Here, too, the one playing the "male" role in the relationship is not viewed as homosexual.) The inmate will bring a gift of candy or a favor as an introductory present. The courtship proceeds much as the outside relationships of men and women, ideally progressing to the point of marriage. Marriage certificates as well as ceremonies including the friends of both parties were part of the ritual. A honeymoon, followed by setting up a home cell, would lead to the prison equivalent of marital life. Cells were often decorated by the "wives" with rugs, curtains, paintings, and colored lights. The "wife" kept house and the "man" provided the security and extra material goods needed.

The violent encounters of the type described earlier were also observed by Johnson, in addition to homosexual prostitution. Johnson concludes that homosexual behavior is learned behavior, and that homosexuality is essential to the functioning of a male prison. A further conclusion is that the homosexual's role in prison is more complete and more valued by others than it is outside the walls.

This article, like some of the others, is based on one man's observations. Caution is required in generalizing from his experiences to other places and times. However, by taking his observations as one piece of information and comparing his impressions to those of others, we can add to the picture of the homosexual scene in prison.

The nature of the 1980s writings on male homosexuality in prison is exemplified by Anthony Scacco, Jr.'s book entitled *Male Rape* (Scacco, 1982). He edits 26 chapters, about 15 of which deal with adult-male-prison experiences. Several of his chapters are reprints of the writings mentioned earlier, such as the study of the Philadelphia prison system in the 1950s. There are additional instances of the first-person accounts of men who were raped and then adopted homosexuality as a lifestyle, not only during their incarceration, but after release.

The most recent new trend in the area is that of prison officials being held legally liable for the rapes of inmates held in their custody. This is likely to change the permissive attitude toward violent homosexuality that was said to prevail.

## OVERVIEW

The literature on homosexuality in male prisons over the last 35 years indicates that there are several types of homosexual relationships that are common. The variety of relationships is likely a reflection of a range of needs in the male prisoner that require satisfaction.

The need for validating and expressing the prisoner's own view of masculinity (Wright, 1991) is evidenced in aggressive and dominating homosexual relationships, such as the sexual assaults (Long & Sultan, 1987). Many of the sexual assaults can be expressions of racial hostility, frequently including a desire by black inmates for revenge against whites.

The more tender "marriages" in the prison setting appear to be expressions of a need for intimacy and closeness with another person.

There also appear to be homosexual relationships that are largely motivated by a need for sex. The existence of homosexual prostitutes indicates this. The man who was a homosexual before entering prison is, of course, motivated by a desire for sex, as well as security.

Another general implication from the literature is that heterosexuals can, as a result of being "turned" in prison, adopt the sexual preference of homosexuality both while they are incarcerated and after they are released. This is in conflict with those who insist that homosexuals are born and not made. It appears that at least some are likely to be made, but this does not preclude the possibility that others are born.

## REFERENCES

Akers, R. L., Hayner, N. S., & Gruniger, W. (1974). Homosexual and drug behavior in prison: A test of the functional and importational models of the inmate system. *Social Problems, 21,* 411–422.

Bloch, H. A., Smith, C. E., Zuckerman, S. B., Haines, W. H., Cory, D. W., & Ellis, A. (1955). Sex in prison: A Symposium. *Corrective Psychiatry and Journal of Social Therapy, 1,* 112–144.

Carroll, Leo. (1977). Humanitarian reform and biracial assault in a maximum security prison. *Urban Life, 5,* 417–437.

Cory, Donald W. (1955). Homosexuality in prison. *Corrective Psychiatry and Journal of Social Therapy, 1,* 137–140.

Davis, Alan J. (1968). Sexual assaults in the Philadelphia prison system and sheriff's vans. *Transaction, 6,* 8–16.

Gagnon, J. H., & Simon, W. (1968). The social meaning of prison homosexuality. *Federal Probation, 32,* 23–29.

Haines, William H. (1955). Homosexuality. *Corrective Psychiatry and Journal of Social Therapy, 1,* 132–136.

Huffman, Arthur V. (1960). Sex deviation in a prison community. *Journal of Social Therapy, 6,* 170–181.

Jail IDs homosexual prisoners. (1990, September 10). *The Charlotte Observer,* 2A.

Johnson, E. (1977). The homosexual in prison. In R. Leger & J. Stratton (Eds.), *The sociology of corrections: A book of readings* (pp. 254–255). New York: John Wiley.

Long, G. T., & Sultan, F. E. (1987). Contributions from social psychology. In L. Diamant (Ed.), *Male and female homosexuality* (pp. 230–231). New York: Hemisphere Publishing.

Roth, L. H. (1971). Territoriality and homosexuality in a male prison population. *American Journal of Orthopsychiatry, 41*, 510–513.

Sagarin, E. (1976). Prison homosexuality and its effect on post-prison sexual behavior. *Psychiatry, 39*, 245–257.

Scacco, A. M. Jr. (Ed.). (1982). *Male rape.* New York: AMS Press.

U.S. Department of Commerce. (1992). *Statistical abstracts of the United States 1992.* Washington, DC: Bureau of the Census.

West, D. J. (1967). *Homosexuality.* Chicago: Aldine.

Wright, K. N. (1991). The violent and victimized in the male prison. *Journal of Offender Rehabilitation, 16,* 1–25.

Chapter 9

# The Homosexual Athlete

**Robert L. Barret**

Like gay fathers (Barret & Robinson, 1990), the idea of a homosexual athlete clashes with the stereotype of gay men and lesbians. The notion of a gay man as a physically strong and gifted athlete who can be nonsexual while having physical contact with heterosexual men is a challenge for many people. Our nation's discomfort with homosexuality in general does not leave room for the kind of idolization and positive image that accompanies successful athletes. On the other hand, for a lesbian to enter the world of sports does not seem quite so revolutionary and, in fact, many women athletes are able to become successful in spite of their lifestyle. Tennis stars like Billie Jean King and Martina Navratolova seem to be able to maintain a following in spite of the often negative publicity that accompanies their openness. Like other public figures, most gay professional athletes keep their gay lives carefully hidden out of a fear that coming out will destroy their ability to maintain their careers.

The world of sports, just like American society as a whole, suffers from a strong homophobic bias that refuses to acknowledge homosexuality as an alternative lifestyle. While movement away from such negative stereotyping can be seen in a few places, the predominant attitude toward homosexuality continues to be stuck between viewing gay men and lesbians as either sick or sinful. This uneasiness with public acknowledgment of homosexuality as an acceptable expression of self also reflects our culture's discomfort with discussions of human sexuality in general.

This homophobic attitude can be seen in the National Olympics Committee's (NOC) successful suit to stop gay men and lesbians from using the term "Gay Olympics" for their national games. The courts upheld the NOC's ownership of the word "olympics" when used to describe athletic competitions. The NOC has not challenged the use of the term "Special Olympics" by groups supporting athletic events for mentally handicapped individuals. In the gay community, such discrimination is a source of further alienation, especially because the term "Gay Olympics" more clearly defines who is competing than the term "Special Olympics." Nevertheless, the competition does continue as the "Gay Games," held in different locations around the world every four years.

The reality of discrimination reminds athletes that coming out can seriously detract from their career hopes. Finding professional athletes who are comfortable talking about their gayness and the experiences they encountered in the sports world is difficult. Dave Pallona (1991), an umpire in baseball's National League, has written a book detailing his career as a gay man involved in professional sports. In his book, he points out that many baseball players are, in fact, gay. Dave Kopay, whose book, *The David Kopay Story* (1977), chronicles his years as a professional football player in the National Football League, is another professional who tells his story of coming out as a gay man shortly after he quit playing. His athletic career as a running back for the San Francisco Forty-Niners, the Detroit Lions, the Washington Redskins, the New Orleans Saints, and the Green Bay Packers ended as a result of injuries. In the years since his retirement in 1976, Kopay has settled in Los Angeles where he runs a successful flooring store called Linoleum City. He continues to speak to civic groups on gay issues and to lend his support to other gay athletes.

In order to tell the story of homosexuality in the world of sports, Kopay gave the following interview for this book chapter.

*RB:* Begin by telling me a little bit about your background, just in terms of sports, how you came to professional sports.

*Kopay:* I grew too fast. My bones really didn't support my weight correctly and my knees hurt a lot. It was very painful for me to do sports, but I absolutely loved sports in school and continued to do them even though I had this incredible pain. I was a fairly decent student, won a scholarship to a Catholic all boys high school. I had a number of college scholarship offers and really didn't have the confidence to think I could play at the major level so I chose a small Catholic school in the Midwest, Marquette University. They turned around and canceled football at the end of my first semester and said they would continue my scholarship or I could transfer out and not lose my eligibility, and that's what I chose to do. My brother, Tony was going to the University of Washington. He was a junior college player at the same time I was a senior in high school. Tony was going to the Rose Bowl and I saw all those players and looked at those guys and said, "Hell, I could be as good as any of those guys, so let me go to the University of Washington." That's where I decided to go.

*RB:* While you were not thinking you had the skill to play professionally, there still was a thought somewhere in your mind that maybe you could?

*Kopay:* No, not even remotely in my mind. I didn't think I could play professional football until my senior year in college, and even then everybody said they questioned my ability in terms of raw talent and speed. They didn't question the intensity it takes. You have to be a little, you know, at the extreme end of the scale to have the intensity to make it in professional football, and I was really intensified. I played at the University of Washington and had a very up and down career in football, started as a sophomore, didn't letter as a junior, and captained the team as a senior when we went to the Rose Bowl. I missed out being drafted and made it as a professional athlete as a free agent.

*RB:* How about your awareness of your sexual orientation in college? Did that influence your decision?

*Kopay:* Well, it was . . . I was definitely attracted to men, and I was, you know, having most sex with women. I had an ongoing relationship with a fraternity brother that was only consummated under a drunken haze. We never talked about it. It was just something we did. I didn't really label it. I guess I mean that I thought I couldn't be queer, you know, that word just totally freaked me out, a word that I can cherish now. But I knew I was different, and then again, I looked around and thought, "Well, maybe I'm not so different." I saw other major athletes who had those close, close friendships at the fraternity house, and I was thinking, "Well, maybe they're doing the same thing with their buddies and still making love to women and dating women and doing the whole fraternity bit." He was a very competitive athlete in basketball. We used to have some knock-down, drag-out one-on-one basketball games, and they always resulted in going to a bar, drinking beer, and then going home and holding each other. It was a safe passion that involved touching and hugging.

*RB:* So, being gay did not seem to be an issue that would interfere with your ability to participate in sports?

*Kopay:* No, it didn't. All along the way you're competing and socializing and other people are drawn to you. You find out whether you can mix publicly and be accepted. Now, I was accepted by graduate people from my fraternity house. But, I wasn't holding hands with some guy.

*RB:* So, you decided to try professional football?

*Kopay:* Well, I didn't go to Wall Street. All of a sudden it was like instant gratification. Imagine what it feels like to run out onto a football field with 60,000 people going nuts, 100,000 people at the Rose Bowl. It was an incredible, incredible rush and a high. But, the odds on making it as a free agent were very high, but once I got asked to come in as a free agent and I went to training camp, I never even doubted that I would make it. I was relaxed about my sexuality and was still dating women and certainly didn't see myself as gay.

*RB:* What was it like being a free agent?

*Kopay:* What you respect in the other players is their ability to perform out on the football field, whether they shy away from physical encounters. You learn to respect players that are tough. I came in weighing 225 pounds and being able to squat 800 pounds. I had an intense tunnel vision as to what I wanted to do, and I hustled all the time. I had all of these aggressive masculine qualities that people don't usually associate with a gay man. I think true masculinity is homosexuality. I was like unofficial captain of special teams before they had captains of special teams, and I think I was in a special sense liked and loved by my teammates. I worked hard in sports and had a lot to overcome all along the way. But, I made the team and went on to play on several NFL teams over the ten years of my career.

*RB:* When did you begin to come out?

*Kopay:* I didn't come out until like, really until I went back to Detroit, that was my fourth or fifth year in professional football, and I was coming out to myself all along. Of course, the real bomb came in 1976 when I went public in the *Washington Star.* Along the way several of the players suspected that I might be gay, and there were comments made from time to time, but usually I didn't respond.

*RB:* Were they suspicious because you were not having a lot of sex with women?

*Kopay:* Right, and bragging about it.

*RB:* What led them to suspect?

*Kopay:* Well, locker room talk is a lot about sex. I was in good shape and a pretty good looking guy and women were always throwing themselves at me, but I wasn't interested. Several of them noticed that and would comment from time to time. No one who was my friend ever challenged me about it. One time while I was in my last year with Green Bay, there was an all-pro player who was kind of hinting about me being queer, and I said to him, "Listen, you got some questions, why don't you ask them?" Well, he didn't do that. He would say things like, "Do you ever get laid? Why do you stick to yourself so much?" I've always been pretty much of a loner but was more to myself in football because I had to keep my private life safe. When I got to Detroit I tore up my knee and couldn't play and got real depressed. People on the team were definitely suspicious, but some others were real supportive, at least in terms of being friendly to me. There was a faction of guys, kind of like picking on me. "How come Kopay doesn't go out drinking and raising hell with all of us and hang out with the broads the rest of us are hanging out with?" That's kind of what it was, and Alex Karras and Bill Munson backed me up. I think Karras knew what was going on with me before I did. People in Detroit definitely were suspicious.

*RB:* But it was in Washington with the Redskins where it finally came out publicly? It seems like you had almost decided that you would complete your coming out there.

*Kopay:* Well, you know probably in a way too the fact that Lombardi was there, you know, here's the toughest coach in football wanting me to come play for him. It gave me a real sense in a way, "Damn it, I'm OK." After this really struggling year in Detroit where I was injured and really freaked out by my first experience in a gay bar and began to think that I must be gay, I found myself in a very cosmopolitan city. It's funny, like when people say how come you didn't know you were gay? It's like when I was twelve years old, I knew and I didn't know. So, here I was with Lombardi and knowing that I could play for him, and here was a fellow teammate, Jerry Smith, who later died of AIDS, who was also not going out with women. I was, like, following him around like a little puppy dog. Here was this single guy who was not constantly talking about the broads and who had a lot more sensitivity than I had seen in other people, and he was hinting around about what was going on. There was another player too. I ended up being a roommate with a guy who was handsome and a real ladies' man. This guy was such a ladies' man, it was amazing, yet he was never put off by the fact that I wasn't trying to get laid all the time and I felt comfortable with him. It's funny, looking back, why I really didn't let him more into my life.

*RB:* So you began to come out?

*Kopay:* I had my first real encounter with seeking somebody out for sex.

*RB:* But you didn't tell anyone?

*Kopay:* I started admitting what was happening to some of the players. One of the players that I admitted to later told me of his own bisexuality that's never been fulfilled. I didn't know at that time and he was very supportive to Jerry and me, and the most respected member of the team. I think there was lots of support. Looking back, I think what was really bugging me was my religious background, in terms of my guilt about being queer, you know?

*RB:* You did a lot with Jerry Smith? Did you talk openly with him?

*Kopay:* Not at first, but eventually, yes. Jerry couldn't make a big deal of it himself at first. He was a really very, very closeted gay. My first real love experience was supposedly with Jerry, but it wasn't that at all. It was just really a sexual thing for Jerry, and he couldn't deal with the responsibility of someone who's coming out, I mean, it's a real gentle, fragile time. He had much more experience than I. For many years, he was flying off to different cities on the weekends.

*RB:* So, due to injuries, your football career was winding down and you didn't have a career?

*Kopay:* Now it's over, now no career. I felt that in interviewing for coaching jobs that it was useless because they're gonna find out. But I never really applied anywhere. I kept getting more and more frustrated because I knew what the answer was going to be. I ended up going to Idaho and working there for a while and trying a thing with National Football League properties and selling beer, but I finally decided that I would set things straight knowing I didn't have a chance. I decided to come out in the *Washington Star*.

*RB:* Once you went public, how did the sports people react?

*Kopay:* I was distant from them at the time because I was no longer on the team. I was not going to team meetings, and I did not see them. But, all this commotion was going on and I ran into people. I think some of the players respected my courage, but I also knew that I could forget about ever getting a coaching job. I had decided that I had to be me and that meant expressing myself and being honest. I was just tired of being deceitful and all that crap. A lot of the players had led double lives, using drugs and running around with women. When the opportunity arose with the *Washington Star,* I felt, "Here's something I can at least do," but I didn't tell anyone in advance that I was going to do it. I knew they would make a fuss, but I didn't expect so much commotion. Still, I never wished that I could take it back because I was just wanting to be me. I was wanting to be able to express myself, wanting to just be able to be honest. I just got tired of being deceitful and all that crap. "Give me some room to breathe," you know? I knew that they'd make a fuss, but I didn't know, I had no idea that it was going to be that kind of fuss. I didn't know which way I was going.

*RB:* So you became a public figure?

*Kopay:* I was on TV and the David Susskind Show. Everybody said the media would tear me apart. Here's this big studio in New York with no audience. Looking back at the tape of the show, I can't believe how totally peaceful I felt at the time. Coming out made me realize that I had power. I mean that sounds sort of corny. But I was also embarrassed about having so much attention paid to me. It was a real rush, but I was really nervous. I think I came across really well. I was worried about my folks and my friends. But, on the whole, things have turned out OK.

*RB:* What about people in sports? How did they react? You had done somethings that at one level demonstrated a lot of courage.

*Kopay:* Well, some of the players let me know they were supportive. Yet, they also knew that, you know, I could forget about ever having a coaching job. "You've had it. No way. Zero." And that proved right after I did my book, and I did try to seek out a couple of positions. I just didn't get any offers.

*RB:* Is that the business side of sports?

*Kopay:* There's the business side of sports that can't seem to tolerate gay people. It's the stereotype that people hold in their minds that keeps them from meeting the real gay man and realizing he is just like everybody else. So, in the locker room and in the board room, wherever, there's this notion, "Oh, we can't have them in here cause that's bad for our image, bad for morale, or something." There's this myth that the gay person on the team wants to have sex with all his teammates. Coaches keep their distance from the players and really don't want to get to know them as persons. And the owners never come around.

*RB:* The business side of sports sounds pretty rough.

*Kopay:* It is a real cold business. I mean, no matter how good a player I was, if I missed a week's practice, I would never have made the team. Some people were out to get me after I came out, but most just kept quiet. I chose the people I wanted to be around because I was upset and depressed some of the time.

*RB:* Some people attacked you?

*Kopay:* Some of it was hard to take because some of those who attacked me were the same ones who would have sex with a man on the quiet. The NFL has acted like I just don't exist. When I was working on the book we went to Seattle and I went back to the locker room to face my former teammates. It was my most fearful experience. But, there wasn't one teammate from my past when I was at the University of Washington that was like, they were a little standoffish, but there wasn't one guy who, like came up and attacked me, and I found that interesting because, you know, the public can be brutal. The *Star* was attacked incredibly after they ran the series, and they had more negative mail than anything they had ever done. My mail was one or two letters that were negative and hundreds that were positive.

*RB:* It sounds like you managed all of this real well.

*Kopay:* I chose who I wanted to be around carefully. I have a good friend from my past who really helped me a lot. She really didn't want to hear all of the stuff I talked with her about, but she really saved my life. I was so depressed, I thought maybe I would just dive into the river. I really felt like I was under a dark cloud at that time. Eventually I sought help to deal with the depression.

*RB:* It was hard to take all the criticism?

*Kopay:* You know, it wasn't hard to take that. I knew other players who used to brag about having sex with men. I knew I wasn't the only one, and I felt good that at least I was telling the truth.

*RB:* But the NFL treated you badly?

*Kopay:* It was like I had an infectious disease. I was trying to get a settlement on my contract, and there were strikes going on. I went to the Players Association trying to get some help in getting the money that was owed to me. It was like I was really a nonentity almost. In fact, I got a chance to go in front of a board and there were a few of the NFL owners on it. They couldn't understand that I was a positive reflection of their business. I tried to tell them why there is a need for a change of laws to protect the rights of gay men in the workplace and so on. I wanted to give them something like practical training in dealing with gay men. I said, "I am not a threat to you people at all. Here you turn around and give jobs to ex-addicts but you don't want me." They just kind of didn't say anything. They didn't support me in the grievance either. They said they would get back to me.

*RB:* You did get a pension from them?

*Kopay:* Yes, eventually. I really felt totally put off and I felt hostility toward me from the owners. I backed away from all my former football friends. I didn't want to cause them any problems. After a few years I finally began to miss them and decided to call my friend, Howard Mudd. He asked me to come over to the hotel and visit him. We chatted about old times and what was going on with me. Last year I was going to see him again, and I got on the elevator, and one of the players looked at me and recognized me and said, "I read your book. I thought it was pretty good." Another player or two got on and there was polite chit-chat. When we got to the lobby it was time for the team to have dessert and a little get together for the evening. I met the head coach, and he asked how I was. A number of the coaches who had attacked me when I first came out came over and asked me to join the team for dessert. Many of them wound up coming over to the table to say hello. Howard asked me back later and one of the coaches invited me to join the team for dinner. I thought to myself, "Thank God, there's at least one coach in the National Football League that is not afraid of me."

*RB:* Why do you think this is happening?

*Kopay:* Well, I think it was this guy who just happens to be a very bright, secure man who can see that Howard respects me. This coach respects his friend. I think he knows who I am. There were a couple of players at that meal who came over and visited a little bit and kind of kidded Howard about our friendship. Howard turned around and kidded them about their special friendship. So, it was like no big deal, because Howard is the kind of person that makes it no big deal and also has the credibility behind him to make it no big deal.

*RB:* Do you hear from other players who are gay?

*Kopay:* No, I haven't heard from any of the pro ball players. On occasion I've had some people in my past tell me about their sexual experiences and I've had letters from some college players.

*RB:* Have you had any contact with athletes in other sports who want to come out?

*Kopay:* No. Most of them know that they would not get the $250,000 beer commercials if they came out.

*RB:* But, Jerry Smith seemed to retain professional respect even after he died of AIDS.

*Kopay:* He had a low profile, but people also liked his total casualness. He was a California sun boy, the kind of beach boy people dream about. He was so loose with himself that some of the other players got jealous. He was tolerated because he was great.

*RB:* What is your career today?

*Kopay:* I sell floor covering, carpet, linoleum to the stars. Linoleum City is a store that's been there for almost 45 years, near the center of Hollywood, a good store. We're the largest stocking dealer of floor covering this side of the Mississippi. We sell most of your sitcoms and TV shows, tour specials, and so on.

*RB:* Your being gay is not an issue with your customers?

*Kopay:* It's not an issue at all. In fact, it's probably helped because on occasion when they really need a price, they'll ask me because they respect some of things I've done for our "community." My visibility has really helped this business out.

*RB:* Do you continue to speak as a gay activist?

*Kopay:* Yeah, I speak around the country, Florida, Virginia, Washington, and frequently in California. I just do whatever I can do to help out.

*RB:* Are you ever asked to speak to high school students?

*Kopay:* Not high school students. I've spoken to a lot of different church groups, parent groups, that kind of thing. It seems like it's real important for things to change, and I hope I can do something to make life easier for other gay men and lesbians. My visibility really changes people's attitudes. All of a sudden they think this guy is no more crazy than we are. I can see their attitudes change.

*RB:* As you look at your life as a single gay man, what is it you would hope that the public at large would understand about being gay?

*Kopay:* Well, I don't think it's any different. I think all of us are out to achieve some peace and happiness and it comes around in lots of different ways, but we're not so different. I think the whole AIDS thing has created a space where we are seen as exotic, erotic beings. I don't think we're all so different. Everybody's out to try to achieve some peace and happiness and it comes around it lots of different ways, but we're not so different, that's it.

The literature on professional gay athletes is limited to Kopay's book and other first-person accounts. It is clear that public homosexuality and professional sports do not seem compatible. Even a superstar like Magic Johnson, who played basketball for the Los Angeles Lakers, was emphatic that his HIV disease did not result from homosexual behavior. Rather than deflect questions about his sexuality as unimportant, he chose to repeatedly deny any homosexual experience. The fact that these statements offended many in the gay community who work toward creating an attitude that HIV disease is a potential threat to all persons was largely unnoticed in the popular press. Johnson's need to state that he had had no homosexual encounters reflects the anxiety that the sports world has about gay men as athletes.

Professional sports is big business. Coaches and owners are aware that their players' image can mean financial windfalls to the industry as a whole.

The homophobic attitude that Dave Kopay encountered as he came out is representative of the prevailing attitude throughout the country. While many people in powerful places may have friends who are openly gay, they rarely come to the defense of gay rights issues or see the need to make public statements that reflect a more accepting attitude toward homosexuality. The public is not likely to begin to embrace homosexuality as an alternate lifestyle until more respected and visible men and women come out and challenge the negative stereotype that is so pervasive.

## REFERENCES

Barret, R., & Robinson, B. (1990). *Gay fathers.* Boston: Lexington Books.
Kopay, D., & Young, P. (1977). *The David Kopay story.* New York: Anchor House.
Pallona, D. (1991). *Behind the mask.* New York: Viking Penguin.

Part Four

# AIDS in the Workplace

Chapter 10

# Risk Perception and HIV Legal Issues in the Workplace

**Nancy L. Roth**
**Judith Carman**

In a recent United States 5th Circuit appeal (*Leckelt v. Hospital District No. 1,* 1990), the court upheld a hospital's decision to fire a licensed practical nurse (LPN) who refused to disclose the results of his HIV antibody test. The hospital had requested that the nurse be tested because it was known that his roommate (with whom he had a homosexual relationship) had AIDS and had been treated at the hospital. The LPN was informed that he could not return to work until he

The first author, now an Assistant Professor of Communication at Rutgers University, gratefully acknowledges the support of the National Centre for HIV Social Research, University of New South Wales, Sydney, Australia where she was a visiting Research Fellow when she participated in the design of the protocol used to collect data reported in this chapter. Other members of the team participating in this data collection project include: the second author, now at the Department of Clinical Biochemistry, Royal Prince Alfred Hospital, Missenden Rd., Camperdown, NSW Australia; Michael Ross, Associate Director, National Centre in HIV Social Research, University of New South Wales; Lesley Painter, Area HIV/AIDS Coordinator, Central Sydney Area Health Service; and Trish MacLeod, Health Promotion, Central Sydney Area Health Service. Many thanks to Title IIB Fellow Hester Stephenson for assistance with background research and to Michael Ross and Peter Sandman who commented on earlier drafts of this chapter.

submitted HIV test results, that if the results were positive he would be placed on leave with pay, and that if he refused to submit the results he would be fired.

At approximately the same time, a registered nurse (RN) suffered a needle stick while attending to the LPN's roommate, an AIDS patient at the hospital. She was asked to take an HIV test, but was not placed on leave pending the results of her test. The hospital claimed that the LPN posed a greater risk to patients than the RN because he was a hepatitis B carrier, had had a case of syphilis in the previous six months, and was undergoing treatment for a cyst under his arm. Although none of these conditions is particularly related to HIV, the court agreed that the LPN could not be considered to be "asymptomatic" and found that the hospital was justified in requesting the LPN to take leave until his test results were available. They also ignored evidence that it may be easier to transmit HIV during seroconversion than at any other time. Therefore, the RN may, in fact, have posed a greater risk to her patients than the LPN.

In making this judgment, the court contradicted an earlier Supreme Court case, *School Board of Nassau County v. Arline,* which established a precedent of measuring the "significant risk" of transmitting a contagious disease using the American Medical Association's (AMA) standards (Barnes et al., 1990). AMA standards suggest that the "Public health department must make findings of fact, based on reasonable medical judgments about mode of transmission, the duration of the risk, probability that the infection will be transmitted, and the seriousness of harm" (Gostin, 1991, p. 665). In part, the court's decision to uphold the LPN's firing rested

> on the appellate court's conviction that if he were HIV-infected, he would present a "significant risk" to patients under the Arline standard. In applying that standard, the court incorrectly ignored the interrelationship of the four factors in the "significant risk" calculus . . . failing to view the four factors as equal parts of an overall risk equation. Instead, the court concentrated only on the severity of a transmission and found that regardless of the "extremely low" probability of transmission to patients . . . [the LPN] presented a "significant risk" because HIV transmission would be "fatal." (Barnes et al., 1990, p. 318)

In this chapter, we explore some factors that may influence perception of risk by the courts, by employers, and by receivers of services. We suggest that such factors may influence perceptions of risk probability and risk severity differently as exemplified by the outcome of *Leckelt v. Hospital District No. 1.* We review traditional, psychological, and cultural conceptions of risk. We then focus specifically on perceptions of risk in the workplace, particularly in health care settings surrounding HIV/AIDS. We present preliminary results of a study of perceptions of HIV transmission in health care settings by hospital workers in Sydney, Australia, which raise additional questions about how risk is perceived.

## CONCEPTIONS OF RISK

Traditionally, risk was conceptualized as the product of the probability of an event occurring and the magnitude of its result if it did occur. Risk was seen as a neutral accounting of the probability of gains and losses, particularly in gambling contexts. However, in recent times, the concept of risk is most often associated with negative outcomes and has come to mean "bad risks" (Douglas, 1990, pp. 2–3).

In the past 20 years, cognitive psychologists Daniel Kahneman and Amos Tversky conducted a series of studies on how people make judgments under conditions of uncertainty (many of which are reprinted in Kahneman, Slovic, & Tversky, 1982). Their work was built on Paul Meehl's comparison of clinical and statistical prediction, Ward Edwards's study of subjective probability in the Bayesian paradigm, and Herbert Simon and Jerome Bruner's investigations of heuristics and strategies of reasoning. The cleverly designed experimental laboratory studies of Kahneman and Tversky investigate the influence of one variable at a time (for example: availability, representativeness, and overconfidence) on the judgments people make in simulated circumstances of uncertainty.

Building on the work of Kahneman and Tversky, Paul Slovic, Baruch Fischoff, and Sara Lichtenstein study the psychological factors that influence people to perceive events or situations as risky (e.g., Slovic, Fischoff, & Lichtenstein, 1982; Fischoff, Slovic, Lichtenstein, Read, & Combs, 1978). They suggest that people perceive a risk as "likely or frequent if instances of it are easy to imagine or recall" and that people are quite confident in their perceptions of risk even when they are quite different from "accepted" estimates of risk (1982, pp. 465, 472). Weinstein and his colleagues (Weinstein, 1987; Weinstein, Klotz, & Sandman, 1988) find that individuals have unreasonably optimistic perceptions of personal risks if they have been exposed to the risk in the past and have not been affected, if the event is perceived as infrequent, or if they have not experienced exposure to the risk. Starr and his colleagues (Starr, 1969, 1972; Starr, Rudman, & Whipple, 1976) suggest that individuals are more likely to accept personal risks that are voluntary, that provide more benefits to offset potential costs, and that have negative effects that affect few people.

While psychologists stress the individual factors that influence perceptions of risk, Mary Douglas and Aaron Wildavsky (Douglas, 1985, 1990; Douglas & Wildavsky, 1982; Wildavsky & Drake, 1990) suggest that perception of risk is influenced by societal or cultural rather than individual factors. Douglas (1990) argues that modern Western culture values the individual over the community, thus influencing the perception of risk. Events or situations that threaten individual goals are seen as risky while those that encroach on community attainment are disregarded. Wildavsky and Drake (1990) find that political ideology is of primary importance in determining which situations or events are considered risky. Douglas and Wildavsky (1985, p. 7) argue that community consensus can "relate some natural dangers to moral defects."

In research conducted both by those concerned with individual influences on perceptions of risk and those concerned with societal or cultural influences, scholars have viewed risk as a singular variable, and have asked respondents to rate their perception of "risk" without distinguishing between perceptions of the probability of the event occurring and the magnitude of the event should it occur. Indeed, Fischoff, Slovic, Lichtenstein, Reed, and Combs (1978) found that the nine characteristics hypothesized by various authors to influence judgments of perceived and acceptable risk were highly correlated and could be reduced to two dimensions: (1) high and low technology (with high being characterized by new, involuntary, and poorly known activities); and (2) certainty of death. These dimensions bear interesting resemblance to the traditional view of risk as influenced by probability and magnitude, with death being the ultimate in magnitude. Yet few scholars have assessed to what extent perceptions of "risk" are based on perceptions of probability, perceptions of magnitude, or some combination of the two.

## PERCEPTIONS OF RISK IN WORKPLACES

Most work on risk perception employs experimental techniques in laboratory conditions. There has been little published research on risk perception among people who work in jobs that pose specific risks about their perceptions of the risks they encounter in their daily tasks. One exception to this dearth of literature is the work of Sjoberg and Drottz-Sjoberg (1991). In their recent study of risk perception among nuclear power plant employees, they find that more employees define risk as "mainly a question of how probable an event is" than define it as "mainly a question of how large the consequences of the event are likely to be" (p. 612). Yet, those employees who consider magnitude of the outcome as important see their jobs as riskier overall than those who consider probability as important (Sjoberg & Drottz-Sjoberg, 1991). They also find that those employees who have the least knowledge about nuclear radiation perceive their job risks as being higher, and that employees "accurately" rate the risks associated with their jobs, but overestimate the risks associated with other risk situations or events including disease, accidents, and natural disasters, thus suggesting that some "risk denial" is at work (Sjoberg & Drottz-Sjoberg, 1989).

Sjoberg and Drottz-Sjoberg's (1991) study makes several important contributions. Their finding that employees vary on the extent to which they evaluate risk based on perceptions of probability and magnitude suggests that future studies should account for such differences. Their finding that psychological factors have little influence on risk perception suggests that other factors, including social and cultural factors, should be considered in future studies. And their finding that level of knowledge is inversely related to perception of risk suggests that future work should further test the relationship between employee risk perception and knowledge.

### Perceived Risk of HIV/AIDS in the Workplace

There have been few studies published to date that explore perceptions of HIV transmission risks in the workplace. Much of the literature on HIV in the workplace is directed toward human relations practitioners and managers and provides guidance concerning HIV and legal issues in the workplace (Gostin, 1990; Kirby, 1989; Neave, 1988; Parmet, 1989; Perkins, 1988; Thomas, 1989; Waters, 1990), HIV/AIDS policy and education programs (Backer, 1988; Bauman & Aberth, 1986; Cacioppe, 1988; Ryan, 1986), studies of seroprevalence among members of the United States' armed forces (Cowan et al., 1991), and studies of knowledge of HIV transmission routes, attitudes about HIV/AIDS, and working with HIV positive coworkers (Barr, Waring, & Warshaw, 1992; Sheehan, Lennon, & McDevitt, 1989).

Of these, only the studies of knowledge and attitudes begin to address the issue of perceived risk of HIV transmission in the workplace. Barr, Waring, and Warshaw (1992) find that high scores on HIV/AIDS knowledge scales are often associated with "negative" attitudes. One-third of their corporate and public service employee questionnaire respondents believe that their workplace should not hire people who are HIV positive and one-quarter would be afraid of getting HIV from people at work even though they are aware that their "risk" of being infected in the workplace is low. Respondents question the accuracy of pubic information about HIV, fear that scientists will make future discoveries that reverse current knowledge, distrust scientific authority, and worry that messages about negligible risks are merely attempts to calm employee fears. Sheehan, Lennon, and McDevitt's (1989) laboratory study of college students' reactions to working with coworkers who are HIV positive in hypothetical situations finds that respondents are less willing to interact with HIV positive coworkers than with coworkers who have other illnesses perceived as "controllable," such as lung cancer and hepatitis. Regression analysis suggests that these findings are in part due to respondents' empathy, attitudes toward homosexuals, and attitudes and knowledge about HIV.

This research suggests that knowledge and attitudes about HIV are often widely divergent. Although workers "know" that the risk of HIV transmission in their workplaces is negligible, they still would prefer that their workplaces not hire HIV positive workers and prefer not to interact with such coworkers. This research makes preliminary identification of some of the factors that might influence perception of HIV-related risk. Further work is required to determine whether such factors influence perceptions of increased probability or increased magnitude of risk.

### Perceived Risk of HIV in Health Care Settings

Concern about the risk of HIV transmission in health care settings began long before the first known case of transmission from a dentist in Florida to one of his patients was reported in the summer of 1990 (Centers for Disease Control, 1990). Medical clients, their health care providers, and nonmedical staff have expressed concern about HIV transmission, and the Centers for Disease Control has issued four sets of guidelines concerning prevention of such transmission (Centers for Disease Control, 1982, 1983, 1987, 1991; Gerbert, Maguire, & Sumser, 1991; Gerbert, Maguire, Hulley, & Coates, 1989; Gostin, 1990a, 1990b; Landesman, 1991; Worksafe Australia, 1990). Debate about the risks of transmission from HIV positive health care workers to their clients also received much media attention (e.g., Kantrowitz et al., 1991).

Estimates of the probability that an HIV positive health care worker will transmit the virus to a client are very low—they range from 1 in 40,000 to 1 in 400,000 (Armstrong, Miner, & Wolfe, 1987; Klein et al., 1988; Mishu, Schaffner, Horan, Wood, Hutcheson, & McNabb, 1990). Yet, 18% of a stratified sample of 2,000 United States' adults reported that they believe that transmission of the virus is "very likely" if they are operated on by a surgeon who is HIV positive, 8% believe transmission is "very likely" just being treated in a dental office, and 3% believe that transmission is "very likely" if they live near a home or hospital for HIV/AIDS patients (Gerbert, Maguire, & Sumser, 1991, p. 325). Even the 12% of respondents who believe that it is definitely not possible for physicians to transmit the virus to patients believe that HIV-positive physicians should not be allowed to work. "The public's desire to avoid people with HIV disease seems much stronger than their perception of risk of transmission would 'rationally' predict" (Gerbert et al., 1989, p. 1971).

Health care workers are not immune to concerns about HIV transmission risks at work. At a 1989 symposium on the medical and legal ramifications of HIV transmission to hospital employees at San Francisco General Hospital, employees expressed concerns about transmission from needle stick injuries and about policies that place more importance on protecting the confidentiality of clients than on making known each client's HIV status so that hospital workers will know when precautions are necessary (Sowa, 1989). The most likely route of transmission is from accidental punctures from needles on syringes that have been used on HIV positive patients. The estimated probability of transmission if a needle stick occurs is 0.4% or about 1 in 200 (Gerberding et al., 1989).

A number of studies have reported on the HIV/AIDS knowledge, attitudes, and behaviors of physicians, nurses, and other hospital employees (Henry, Campbell, & Willenbring, 1990; Hunter & Ross, 1991; Kerr & Horrocks, 1990; Gallop, Lancee, Taerk, Coates, Fanning, & Keatings, 1991; Storosum et al., 1990). Few studies have addressed perceptions of risk of HIV transmission. Bliwise, Grade, Irish, and Ficarrotto (1991) find a high correlation between perceived personal risk and negative attitudes toward patients with HIV/AIDS. They also find that while some negative attitudes may be attributed to homophobia and the social stigma associated with groups at high risk for AIDS, others may be based more on fear of contagion and anxiety about death. Working with the heuristics of risk assessment suggested by Kahaneman, Slovic, and Tversky (1982) and Heath, Acklin, and Wiley (1991), study the impact of availability and simulation on physicians' perceptions of the risk of HIV transmission from clients. Ability to imagine oneself being exposed to HIV on the job related significantly to perceived risk. None of these studies explored the impact of the various factors that may influence perceptions of risk on perceptions of probability and magnitude separately.

## A STUDY OF THE INFLUENCE OF HIV/AIDS KNOWLEDGE, FEARS, DISCOMFORT, COMPLIANCE WITH INFECTION CONTROL PROCEDURES, AND DEMOGRAPHICS ON HOSPITAL WORKERS' PERCEPTIONS OF HIV TRANSMISSION RISK FROM CLIENTS

The *Leckelt v. Hospital District No. 1* decision that began this chapter raises questions concerning the factors that influence perceptions of the probability of HIV transmission from provider to client occurring in medical settings and those that influence perceptions of the magnitude of HIV transmission, should it occur.

In this chapter we report the preliminary results of an investigation of medical facility personnel (both health care professionals and other, nonmedical staff). We investigated their perceptions of risk of HIV transmission from patients. The study examines the influence of a number of variables (knowledge, discomfort, fear, compliance with infection control procedures, and a number of demographic variables) on perceptions of the probability of becoming infected with HIV on the job and on perceptions of the seriousness of becoming infected with HIV.

### Sample

The data for this study are a subset of data collected from 1,056 employees of health care units in Sydney, Australia in 1992. The units include acute and subacute care, general medical, psychiatric, hospice, and home-based services. The 1,056 responses comprise a 75% response rate to a questionnaire that was sent to every fifth name on the organizations' payrolls, with oversampling of smaller units. The subsample reported in this study is the first 400 responses received. Of that group, 168 or 42% of respondents reported working with needles and syringes or other "sharps" on the job and fall into such occupational categories as physicians, clinical nurses, laboratory workers, sterile supply, and cleaners. (Fifty-two percent of the entire sample of 1,056 reported working with sharps, so the smaller sample is similar, but not identical to the full sample.)

## Method

Respondents were asked to complete an anonymous paper and pencil questionnaire that was mailed to them at their place of work and that they were asked to mail back. The questionnaire contained seven scales that assessed the amount and type of HIV/AIDS education received; means of infection control enforcement; organizational culture; HIV/AIDS attitudes, fears, and risk perceptions; HIV/AIDS-related discomfort; and level of HIV/AIDS knowledge and use of infection control procedures. The last four scales are included in the analysis for this chapter.

All scales were composed of Likert type questions with five possible responses scored 1 to 5 with 1 representing the low response (e.g., strongly disagree) and 5 representing the high response (e.g., strongly agree). Attitudes and fears were measured using a 28-item scale for which factor analysis revealed 5 factors with eigenvalues greater than or equal to 1 ($p < .05$): (1) moral attitudes (e.g., HIV/AIDS is God's punishment for immoral acts.); (2) uncertainty (e.g., Even if I follow infection control procedures, I might catch AIDS from a patient with HIV/AIDS.); (3) rejection attitude toward HIV-infected patients (e.g., I would prefer it if patients with HIV/AIDS were sent to another hospital.); (4) infection control (e.g., I believe most people here follow infection control procedures carefully.); and (5) secondary stigma (e.g., If I got HIV/AIDS, I would lose my job.). Discomfort was assessed on a 21-item scale that measured 3 factors: (1) secondary stigmatization (e.g., If I talk to or touch a homosexual or bisexual person, people will think I am homosexual or bisexual.); (2) fear of AIDS (e.g., If I got (or had) HIV/AIDS, I would be concerned about dying.); and (3) primary stigmatization (e.g., If I talked to or touched a person with HIV/AIDS, I would be concerned about getting HIV/AIDS.). Knowledge was measured on a 16-item scale that addressed modes of transmission and health care related items including use of disinfectants to kill the virus and necessity of obtaining client consent before testing for HIV antibodies. Use of infection control procedures was explored using a three-item scale that asked if sharps were carried properly and disposed of safely and if they were recapped by hand (a) if the worker knew the client had HIV/AIDS and (b) if the worker did not know the client's HIV/AIDS status. All scales were scaled by reversing the questions that were scored in the opposite direction and simply summing the results.

### Results and Discussion

We performed 2 stepwise regression analyses. The first used perceived probability of transmission as the dependent variable. The second used perceived magnitude as the dependent variable. In both cases, independent variables were entered into the equation so that those with the highest correlation with the dependent variable were entered first.

None of the independent variables entered the first equation ($p < .05$). However, of the demographic variables entered to control for demographic differences, practicing a religion entered the equation ($p < .05$) and accounted for 6.8% of the variance. In the second equation, only knowledge entered into the equation ($p < .05$). Age and gender also entered into the equation with young men with high HIV/AIDS knowledge assessing the impact of contracting HIV/AIDS most highly.

## DISCUSSION

Our preliminary findings suggest that discomfort, attitudes, fears, and use of infection control procedures have a negligible effect on both perception of probability of transmission and on perception of magnitude of impact of being HIV positive. Yet, although 73% of respondents report that they have little or no risk of getting HIV/AIDS at work and only 10% believe that they have a high or very high chance of getting HIV from work, 56% believe that even if they follow infection control procedures, they might get HIV/AIDS. This finding is quite different from the results Sjoberg and Drottz-Sjoberg (1991) discovered among nuclear plant workers. Their work suggests that perception of risk is mostly influenced by perception of probability that the risky event or situation will occur. Our results suggest that our respondents perceive that the probability of transmission is relatively low, yet their overall risk is fairly high.

Our findings concerning the influence of education on perceptions of magnitude met our expectations. We hypothesized that higher education would be associated with higher perceptions of magnitude. This hypothesis is opposite the findings of Sjoberg and Drottz-Sjoberg because we anticipated that unlike nuclear energy, where education emphasizes the treatments available for radiation exposure, education about HIV/AIDS emphasizes prevention activities because there is no known cure and because, although current treatments allow people to live with the virus for 10 or more years, the syndrome is still generally considered to be fatal. This would suggest that the effects of education on perceptions of magnitude will vary, depending on the type of risk being studied.

Our findings concerning attitudes and fears about HIV/AIDS were consistent with the literature. Thirty-five percent of our respondents would not be willing to eat in a restaurant where they know the chef has HIV, 17% would not want to send their children to school with a child who has HIV, and 58% do not believe that scientists know all there is to know about how HIV is transmitted. Such results suggest that while discomfort, fears, and attitudes may not influence perception of the probability of the risky event occurring or of the magnitude of the risk, they might influence an overall perception of "risk." Perhaps there are other factors than probability and magnitude that affect perception of "risk." Sandman and his associates (Sandman, 1987; Sandman & Miller, 1991) suggest that risk can be seen as being a function of what he calls "hazard"—defined as the product of probability and magnitude (the traditional definition of risk) and "outrage"—defined as the extent to which the activity or situation is: voluntary, natural, familiar, memorable, dreaded, potentially catastrophic, knowable, controllable, fair, moral, handled by people who are trustworthy, or handled by people who are responsive to concerns expressed.

This formulation would explain our results by suggesting that the factors we tested do not have a significant impact on respondents' perceptions of hazard, but that such factors might have an impact on respondents' level of outrage, as evidenced by responses to some attitude questions: Twenty-one percent of the sample agree that HIV positive people should be quarantined; 25% believe that people who get HIV through medical means deserve better care than those who get it through sex or drugs; 58% do not believe that scientists know all there is to know about how HIV is transmitted; and 6% believe that HIV is God's punishment for immoral behavior. Desire for quarantine might be seen as an operationalization of "dread," differentiating among those infected based on mode of transmission might be viewed as an operationalization of unfamiliarity, concern that scientists have not identified all transmission routes might be seen as an operationalization of unknowability, and viewing HIV/AIDS as evidence of God's wrath might be seen as an operationalization of moral outrage. As Sandman's model has not yet been thoroughly tested empirically, future research concerning perceptions of HIV/AIDS transmission risks should consider formal operationalization and testing of this model. Those concerned with developing educational programs concerning HIV/AIDS in the workplace might also benefit from application of this model, which suggests that rather than highlighting the low probabilities of HIV transmission in the workplace, which are well known by workers, education programs might focus on discussion of the sources of employee "outrage."

An alternative explanation for our results is offered by Sitkin and Pablo (1992). They describe a model that suggests that in organizations, individuals' risk perception is influenced by: (1) such individual characteristics as their own propensity to take risks and the extent to which they have encountered similar issues in the past; (2) such organizational characteristics as homogeneity within the top management team and the extent to which organizational rewards are based on the process used versus the outcome achieved; (3) such issue characteristics as the extent to which the issue is positively framed; and (4) such cultural factors as the way in which organizational leaders perceive the risks and the types of risk values encountered in the organization (Sitkin & Pablo, 1992). This model's accounting of organizational factors in risk perception provides important insights. Future research into perceptions of HIV transmission risks in health care organizations should include measures of organizational culture and the influence of management, coworkers, unions, and other groups on perception of risk.

## CONCLUSIONS

Our work suggests that although the legal standards applied to cases of HIV/AIDS in the workplace often appear to be clear cut and straightforward, perceptions of "risk" may influence how the legal standards are interpreted and can thus have a potentially devastating effect on employees who are or are perceived to be HIV positive. Our work suggests that the ways in which risk is perceived may indeed influence not only legal issues associated with HIV, but also more legalistic (Sitkin & Bies, forthcoming) issues concerning how HIV is treated in the workplace. Indeed, research on legalization in the workplace suggests that legal forms and procedures are often repeated at the organizational level, sometimes with the effect of escalating the problem rather than resolving it (Sitkin & Bies, forthcoming; Sitkin & Roth, forthcoming). In addition, organizational factors such as culture and management influence must be taken into account when studying perceptions of HIV/AIDS risks in the workplace.

The analysis presented in this chapter suggests that although factors that influence perceptions of "risk" do not appear to influence perceptions of probability or perceptions of magnitude directly, they appear to influence some component of the perception of "risk"—perhaps the component that Sandman and his associates label "outrage." In the example with which we began this chapter, the court upheld the nurse's firing because it perceived that the fact that HIV/AIDS is seen as a fatal illness (magnitude) outweighed consideration of the other factors that were established by precedent to be considered to be part of a risk analysis. Our work suggests that neither the courts nor individual employers are immune to the influence of "outrage" when applying established standards.

## REFERENCES

Armstrong, F. P., Miner, J. C., & Wolfe, W. H. (1987). Investigations of a health care worker with symptomatic human immunodeficiency virus infection: An epidemiologic approach. *Military Medicine, 152*, 414–418.

Backer, T. E. (1988). Managing AIDS at work: Psychology's role. *American Psychologist, 43*(11), 983–987.

Barnes, M., Rango, N. A., Burke, G. R., & Chiarello, L. (1990). The HIV-infected health care professional: Employment policies and public health. *Law, Medicine & Health Care,* 18, 311–330.

Barr, J. K., Waring, J. M., & Warshaw, L. J. (1992). Knowledge and attitudes about AIDS among corporate and public service employees. *American Journal of Public Health, 82*(2), 225–228.

Bauman, L. J., & Aberth, J. (1986). Health educators in the workplace: Helping companies respond to the AIDS crisis. *Health Education Quarterly, 13*(4), 395–406.

Bliwise, N. G., Grade, M., Irish, T. M., & Ficarrotto, T. J. (1991). Measuring medical and nursing students' attitudes toward AIDS. *Health Psychology, 10*(4), 289–295.

Cacioppe, R. (1988). AIDS in the workplace: A frightening disease poses delicate questions for employers. *Human Resources Management Australia, 26*(3), 52–67.

Centers for Disease Control. (1982). Acquired immune deficiency syndrome (AIDS): Precautions for clinical and laboratory staffs. *Morbidity and Morality Weekly Report (MMWR), 31*(43), 577–579.

Centers for Disease Control. (1983). Acquired immunodeficiency syndrome (AIDS): Precautions for health-care workers and allied professionals. *MMWR, 32*(34), 450–451.

Centers for Disease Control. (1987). Recommendations for prevention of HIV transmission in health-care settings. *MMWR, 36*(2-S), 3–17S.

Centers for Disease control (1990). Possible transmission of human immunodeficiency virus during an invasive dental procedure. *MMWR, 39,* 21–27.

Centers for Disease Control. (1991). Recommendations for preventing transmission of human immunodeficiency virus and hepatitis B virus to patients during exposure-prone invasive procedures. *MMWR, 40*(RR-8), 1-9.

Cowan, D. N., Brundage, J. F., Pomerantz, R. S., Miller, R. N., & Burke, D. S. (1991). HIV infection among members of the U.S. army reserve components with medical and health occupations. *Journal of the American Medical Association, 265*(21), 2826–2830.

Douglas, M. (1985). *Risk acceptability according to the social sciences.* New York: Russell Sage Foundation.

Douglas, M. (1990). Risk as a forensic resource. *Daedalus, 119*(4), 1–16.

Douglas, M., & Wildavsky, A. (1982). *Risk and culture: An essay on the selection of technical and environmental dangers.* Berkeley: University of California Press.

Fischhoff, B., Slovic, P., Lichtenstein, S., Read, S., & Combs, B. (1978). How safe is safe enough? A psychometric study of attitudes towards technological risks and benefits. *Policy Sciences, 9,* 127–152.

Gallop, R. M., Lancee, W. J., Taerk, G., Coates, R. A., Fanning, M., & Keatings, M. (1991). The knowledge, attitudes and concerns of hospital staff about AIDS. *Canadian Journal of Public Health, 82,* 409–412.

Gerberding, J. L., Bryant-Leblanc, C. E., Nelson, K., Moss, A. R., Osmond, D., Chambers, H. F., Carlson, J. R., Drew, W. L., Levy, A., & Sande, M. A. (1987). Risk of transmitting the human immunodeficiency virus, hepatitis B virus, and cytomegalovirus to health/care workers exposed to patients with AIDS and AIDS-related conditions. *Journal of Infectious Diseases, 156,* 1–8.

Gerbert, B., Maguire, B. T., Hulley, S. B., & Coates, T. J. (1989). Physicians and acquired immunodeficiency syndrome: What patients think about human immunodeficiency virus in medical practice. *Journal of the American Medical Association, 262*(14), 1969–1972.

Gerbert, B., Maguire, B. T., & Sumser, J. (1991). Public perception of risk of AIDS in health care settings. *AIDS Education and Prevention, 3*(4), 322–327.

Gostin, L. (1990). The HIV-infected health care professional: Public policy, discrimination, and patient safety. *Law, Medicine & Health Care, 18*(4), 303–310.

Gostin, L. (1990). The AIDS litigation project: A national review of court and human rights commission decisions, part II: Discrimination. *Journal of the American Medical Association, 263*(15), 2086–2093.

Gostin, L. (1991). The HIV-infected health care professional: Public policy, discrimination, and patient safety. *Archives of Internal Medicine, 151*, 663–665.

Heath, L., Acklin, M., & Wiley, K. (1991). Cognitive heuristics and AIDS risk assessment among physicians. *Journal of Applied Social Psychology, 21*(22).

Henry, K., Campbell, S., & Willenbring, K. (1990). A cross-sectional analysis of variables impacting on AIDS-related knowledge, attitudes, and behaviors among employees of a Minnesota teaching hospital. *AIDS Education and Prevention, 2*(1), 36–47.

Hunter, C. E., & Ross, M. W. (1991). Determinants of health care workers' attitudes toward people with AIDS. *Journal of Applied Social Psychology, 21*(11), 947–956.

Kahneman, D., Slovic, P., & Tversky, A. (Eds.). (1982). *Judgment under uncertainty: Heuristics and biases.* Cambridge: Cambridge University Press.

Kantrowitz, B., Springen, K., McCormick, J., Hager, M., Denworth, L., Bingham, C., & Foote, D. (1991). Doctors and AIDS. *Newsweek, 118*(1), 48–57.

Kerr, C. I., & Horrocks, M. J. (1990). Knowledge, values, attitudes and behavioral intent of Nova Scotia nurses toward AIDS and patients with AIDS. *Canadian Journal of Pubic Health, 81*, 125–128.

Kirby, M. (1989). AIDS and law. *Daedalus, 118*(3), 101–121.

Klein, J., Phelan, K., Freeman, K., Schable, C., Friedland, G. H., Trieger, N., & Steigbigel, N. H. (1988). Low occupational risk of human immunodeficiency virus infection among dental professionals. *New England Journal of Medicine, 318*, 86–90.

Landesman, S. H. (1991). The HIV-positive health professional: Policy options for individuals, institutions and states. *Archives of Internal Medicine, 151*, 655–657.

Leckelt v. Board of Commissioners of Hospital District No. 1, 714 F.Supp. 1377 (E.D.La. 1989) aff'd 909 F.2d 820 (5th Cir. 1990).

Mishu, B., Schaffner, W., Horan, J. M., Wood, L. H., Hutcheson, R. H., & McNabb, P. C. (1990). A surgeon with AIDS: Lack of evidence of transmission to patients. *Journal of the American Medical Association, 264*, 467–470.

Neave, M. (1988). Anti-discrimination laws and insurance: The problem of AIDS. *Insurance Law Journal, 1*, 10–29.

Parmet, W. E. (1989). Legal rights and communicable disease: AIDS, the police power and individual liberty. *Journal of Health Politics, Policy and Law, 14*(4), 741–771.

Perkins, N. (1988). Prohibiting the use of the human immunodeficiency virus antibody test by employers and insurers. *Harvard Journal of Legislation, 25*, 275–315.

Ryan, C. (1986). AIDS in the workplace: How to reach out to those among us. *Public Welfare, 44*(3), 29–33.

Sandman, P. M. (1987). Risk communication: Facing public outrage. *EPA Journal*, 21–22.

Sandman, P. M., & Miller, P. (1991). *Outrage and technical detail: The impact of agency behavior on community risk perception.* Division of Science and Research, New Jersey Department of Environmental Protection, Trenton, New Jersey.

*School Board v Arline,* 480 U.S. 273 (1987).

Sheehan, E. P., Lennon, R., & McDevitt, T. (1989). Reactions to AIDS and other illnesses: Reported interactions in the workplace. *The Journal of Psychology, 123*(6), 525–536.

Sitkin, S. B., & Pablo, A. L. (1992). Reconceptualizing the determinants of risk behavior. *Academy of Management Review, 17*(1), 9–38.

Sitkin, S. B., & Bies, R. J. (in press). The legalistic organization: Definitions, dimensions, and dilemmas. *Organization Science.*

Sitkin, S. B., & Roth, N. L. (in press). Explaining the limited effectiveness of legalistic "remedies" for trust/distrust. *Organization Science.*

Sjoberg, L., & Drottz-Sjoberg, B.-M. (1991). Knowledge and risk perception among nuclear power plant employees. *Risk Analysis, 11*(4), 607–618.

Slovic, P., Fischhoff, B., & Lichtenstein, S. (1982). Facts versus fears: Understanding perceived risk. In D. Kahneman, P. Slovic, & A. Tversky (Eds.), *Judgment under uncertainty: Heuristics and biases* (pp. 463–489). Cambridge: Cambridge University Press.

Sowa, P. E. (1989). Medical and legal ramifications of HIV transmission to hospital employees: Questions and answers. *American Journal of Hospital Pharmacy, 46,* S16–18.

Starr, C. (1969). Social benefit versus technological risk: What is our society willing to pay for safety? *Science, 165,* 1232–1238.

Starr, C. (1972). Benefit-cost studies in sociotechnical systems. In Committee on Public Engineering Policy, *Perspective on Benefit-Risk Decision Making.* Washington, DC: National Academy of Engineering.

Starr, C., Rudman, R., & Whipple, C. (1976). Philosophical basis for risk analysis. *Annual Review of Energy, 1,* 629–662.

Storosum, J. G., Sno, H. N., Schalken, F. A., Krol, L. J., Swinkels, J. A., Najuijs, M., Jeijer, E. P., & Danner, S. A. (1991). Attitudes of health-care workers toward AIDS at three Dutch hospitals. *AIDS, 5,* 55–60.

Thomas, D. K. (1989). The legal status of AIDS in the workplace. *Medical Anthropology, 10,* 193–201.

Waters, P. (1990). The coverage of AIDS-related discrimination under handicap discrimination laws: The U.S. and Australia compared. *Sydney Law Review, 12,* 377–419.

Weinstein, N. D. (1987). Unrealistic optimism about susceptibility to health problems: Conclusions from a community-wide sample. *Journal of Behavioral Medicine, 10*(5), 481–500.

Weinstein, N. D., Klotz, M. L., & Sandman, P. M. (1988). Optimistic biases in public perceptions of the risk from radon. *American Journal of Public Health, 78*(7), 796–800.

Wildavsky, A., & Dake, K. (1990). Theories of risk perception: Who fears what and why? *Daedalus, 119*(4), 41–59.

Worksafe Australia (1990). HIV/AIDS and the workplace: Information for health workers and others at risk. (cat. no. 90 07196). Canberra, Commonwealth of Australia: National Occupational Health and Safety Commission.

Chapter 11

# Human Resources: Policies and Practices

**Sue Margaret Norton**
**Kim Buch**

Acquired Immune Deficiency Syndrome (AIDS) first came to the attention of the American public in the early 1980s. In several separate instances, mostly in the Los Angeles and New York City areas, young homosexual men required treatment for unusual types of cancer and/or pneumonia generally seen only in a small percentage of elderly men. Eventually, medical experts determined that the complex of such otherwise unusual illnesses was indicative of a weakened or deficient immune system, which caused the young victims to fall prey to a variety of otherwise unusual diseases. The term AIDS was eventually coined to refer to this disease complex, and, in short order, became part of common language.

The two basic stages of AIDS are now well known. The first stage is characterized solely by a positive test for the human immunodeficiency virus (HIV) in an otherwise healthy person. An HIV-positive person may eventually develop a variety of different (often serious) diseases, and can transmit the virus to others even before any such diseases develop, but is otherwise in good physical health. The second stage is thought to comprise two different forms of the disease: AIDS-Related Complex (ARC), which is characterized by decreased vitality and increased vulnerability to illness; and full-blown AIDS, which is characterized by progressively deteriorating health, weakness, emaciation, and eventually (in fact, thus far inevitably) death due to a secondary, opportunistic infection such as pneumocystis carinii (a rare type of pneumonia) or Kaposi's sarcoma (a rare type of cancer). Although life expectancy varies tremendously (some AIDS patients die within months of the first symptoms, while others are still living as long as 10 years after their first symptoms appear), current prevailing medical opinion is that the disease is invariably fatal, as there is not yet any cure available. While AIDS (or, more precisely, the AIDS-causing HIV) is technically communicable, transmission of the virus has been found to occur only through direct blood-to-blood or semen-to-blood contact.

From the handful of cases first reported, the frequency of AIDS has increased dramatically. By the end of this year (1991), the Surgeon General's office estimates that there will be more than 270,000 cases reported in this country, and more than 179,000 people will have died. The Centers for Disease Control (CDC) estimates that the number of reported cases will have increased to approximately 480,000 by the end of 1993. As frightening as these numbers are, they may severely underestimate the real scope of the AIDS problem: The number of people who are HIV positive may be as high as 1.5 million. The CDC estimates that as many as 50% of these people will progress to full-blown AIDS and die within seven years. Another 25% is expected to develop ARC, and an increasing number of medical experts predict (cf. Zilg, 1989) that virtually 100% of ARC patients will develop AIDS within 12 years of their first ARC symptoms.

The magnitude and effects of the AIDS epidemic may be especially significant for employers. Because approximately 90% of those with AIDS are people between 25 and 49 years old, AIDS-related problems will extract a high price from the most vital segment of the workforce. Although the total costs are difficult to estimate, some sources say that AIDS and related problems may cost employers $56 billion (in turnover, reduced productivity, etc.) by the end of 1991 (cf. Zilg, 1989).

A major complication for employers who must deal with AIDS involves the stereotypes and myths about the nature of the syndrome. Among the many AIDS-related myths that exist, several may be especially significant in the workplace.

A popular myth holds that AIDS is solely a "gay" concern. Gay men are, statistically, the largest risk group. It is estimated (cf., Zilg, 1989) that approximately 70% of AIDS victims in this country are either homosexual or bisexual males. However, the virus is being reported with increasing frequency among intravenous drug users, hemophiliacs, and even heterosexuals without specific identified risks.

The workplace problems associated with the misconception of AIDS as a purely "gay" disease may be twofold. First, the gay male employee may be unfairly victimized (i.e., ostracized by other employees or even denied employment opportunities) if organizations or other employees assume (usually incorrectly) that he is a carrier of the AIDS-causing HIV merely because of his sexual orientation. Sexual preference in and of itself is not, however, actionable under such federal laws as Title VII of the 1964 Civil Rights Act; thus the gay male who is the victim of unfair employment discrimination because of his sexual orientation may feel (sometimes correctly) that he has no legal recourse.

Second, many employees may prefer (often unrealistically) to avoid dealing with AIDS if they consider it purely a "gay" problem. Some may assume that it has no relevance to them, that there is no possible way they could ever get the virus. Others may fear that any show of interest on their part will be construed as evidence of a nontraditional sexual preference, when, in fact, information about the nature of the disease may be relevant to anyone, regardless of sexual orientation (cf. Kronenberger, 1991).

The pervasiveness of an antigay bias in the context of the AIDS epidemic was empirically demonstrated by St. Lawrence, Husfeldt, Kelly, Hood, and Smith (1990). Three hundred undergraduate students were asked about their attitudes toward different fictionalized characters described in short vignettes. These characters differed only on their specific illnesses (AIDS versus leukemia) and their sexual orientation (gay versus heterosexual). Homosexual patients were considered more responsible for, and more deserving of, their illnesses, more deserving of employment loss, and less deserving of sympathy and even medical care. While the authors note that previous research has demonstrated that gay people in general are socially stigmatized, there also appears to be little public sympathy for AIDS patients. In particular, the authors hypothesize that the gay male with AIDS, more so than individuals in the other vignettes, was thought to be responsible for (and hence deserving of) his disease. In other words, a gay male AIDS victim may be seen as someone who has brought his health crisis on himself, and does not deserve any sympathy or support. Such strong antigay sentiment, taken with the general hysteria that has surrounded AIDS, could have significant implications for all gay males in the workplace, regardless of their physical health.

Another myth is that AIDS is easy to catch. As noted above, AIDS is, technically, communicable. In reality, however, the AIDS-causing virus simply is not transmitted by the kind of casual, nonsexual contact that generally occurs between employees in the workplace. There is no evidence whatsoever that the virus is transmitted by touching people who are HIV-positive or from dishes, utensils, drinking fountains, or telephones. Uninformed or fearful employees may refuse to work with an HIV-positive person, fearing, incorrectly, that they themselves will become victims of AIDS merely by proximity. Misinformation about the nature of contagion may also translate into efforts to screen applicants for the presence of the HIV virus (i.e., attempts to screen applicants who are openly homosexual). It could also possibly result in overt discrimination against gay males, if it is assumed that all have and will easily transmit the virus.

People with AIDS do not belong in the workplace is another misconception. In actuality, a job may provide an important source of stability for a person who is coping with AIDS. In fact, some experts (i.e., Ritter, 1989) argue that work may be palliative and help to maintain/improve not only attitude but also life expectancy. Patterson (1989) notes that work is physically and mentally therapeutic for AIDS patients. For many, work may be the only outlet for social interaction.

The question of whether people who are HIV-positive belong in the workplace may also turn on legality. In addition to humanitarian concerns, an employer may, depending on applicable laws, be legally obligated to accommodate an HIV-positive person as long as that person is able to work. Also, employers may be legally required to be flexible about accommodating employees whose health is suffering due to opportunistic illnesses (just as they may be required to accommodate employees with a variety of other sorts of temporary or permanent health problems). The issue of whether people with AIDS "belong" in the workplace may thus be a moot point. Not only do they belong; the workplace may also be legally obligated to accommodate them.

Given the potentially overwhelming burden of AIDS and its implications for employers, it is essential that employers consider development of formal AIDS policies. Former Surgeon General C. Everett Koop recommended in 1987 that some sort of AIDS policy exist in the workplace *before* the first AIDS case forces the issue. By establishing an AIDS policy a priori, the number of complaints and workplace disruptions related to AIDS will obviously be reduced.

The number of employers who have actually developed policies on AIDS is difficult to estimate. According to Patterson (1989), many employers seem to take an "it can't happen here" attitude, and are thus not motivated to develop viable corporate policies. Jones and Johnson (1989) report the same philosophy, as they note that many organizations may prefer to operate under the illogical (but human) assumption that only *other* organizations will have to face the AIDS crisis. Further, they note, some organizations may feel that any formal policy on AIDS will detract from a company's image (i.e., imply that the company has a serious AIDS problem).

Given such attitudes, many companies initially chose to ignore the AIDS problem, at least in terms of policy development. Koch (1990) cites a study reporting that only 4–10% of U.S. businesses have a written policy for employees who test HIV-positive. Another recent survey, however, reported by Ross and Middlebrook (1990), indicated that 58% of companies polled had some kind of AIDS policy. Obviously, increasingly more employers are exploring ways to deal with a variety of AIDS-related issues, including the development of viable corporate policies on AIDS to ensure that all employees are treated legally and ethically, the most effective approaches to educating employees about the nature of the disease, and the options available to provide support and accommodation for both the HIV-positive employee and his or her coworkers.

Interestingly, the necessity for corporate AIDS-related policies is increasing as life expectancy for AIDS victims improves. Temple (1990) points out that in 1982, less than 30% of those diagnosed with AIDS lived longer than 18 months. Unfortunately, this meant that many AIDS victims who were denied job opportunities never had the chance to take action, and corporate policies on AIDS may have been considered unnecessary. Many organizations may have assumed, somewhat coldbloodedly, that AIDS victims would die so quickly that policies on AIDS would be unimportant. As expected survival time has increased, however, the need for viable corporate policies has also increased. AIDS victims are surviving long enough that their demands for fair treatment in the workplace need to be addressed formally.

## LEGAL STATUS OF AIDS

To fully understand the importance of corporate AIDS-related policies, a brief review of the current legal status of AIDS is necessary. According to DiLauro (1989), AIDS victims themselves, HIV-positive individuals, and those in high-risk groups (most significantly, gay men) have been denied employment or even discharged because of the fear that they would spread the disease to others. The legality or illegality of such actions was unclear until 1987. In that year, the first significant case addressing the problem of a contagious disease in the workplace reached the U.S. Supreme Court. While the case itself (*Arline vs. School Board of Nassau County, Florida*) did not specifically address AIDS, the Supreme Court did conclude that a different contagious disease (tuberculosis) is a protected handicap under the terms of Section 504 of the 1973 Vocational Rehabilitation Act (which applies to all private employers who receive financial assistance from the federal government and requires such employers to make reasonable accommodation for people with protected handicaps). The plaintiff in the case, schoolteacher Gene Arline, had to be hospitalized three times for tuberculosis relapses, after having shown no symptoms of the disease for some 20 years. The school board insisted that he resign from his job, citing a fear of contagion as their reason. In a footnote, the court agreed that when a major life activity is impaired by a disease, even a contagious disease, the person in question is to be considered handicapped. Specifically, the court noted that

> few aspects of a handicap give rise to the same level of public fear and misapprehension as contagiousness . . . the fact that some persons who have a contagious disease may pose a serious health threat to others under certain circumstances does not justify excluding from the coverage of the Act all persons with actual or perceived contagious diseases. (p. 94)

Note that while the court did not specifically mention either AIDS or its precursor (being HIV-positive), the implication of the above quote is that *both* conditions are to be considered a handicap, and thus protected by the Rehabilitation Act. AIDS, of course, is an "actual" contagious disease, and testing HIV-positive could reasonably be assumed to constitute a perceived contagious disease.

The Rehabilitation Act obviously covers only a subset of all employers. Individuals with AIDS are also protected in the employment area by a number of other federal statutes and agencies such as the Employee Retirement Income Security Act of 1974 (ERISA), the Comprehensive Omnibus Budget Reconciliation Amendment of 1986 (COBRA), and the Occupational Safety and Health Act of 1974 (OSHA). ERISA prohibits an employer from discharging an employee with AIDS in order to deny him or her entitled pension or retirement benefits. COBRA makes an employee with AIDS eligible for continuation of medical benefits for up to 18 months after termination. Because medical evidence overwhelmingly indicates that AIDS is not transmitted by casual contact and does not present a risk in the workplace, the employment of a person with AIDS does *not* violate OSHA standards for a safe workplace. Further, as long as an employer educates employees about AIDS, an employee's refusal to work with an AIDS-infected coworker is not protected by OSHA. In other words, an employee who refuses to work with an HIV-positive coworker (or with one who has full-blown AIDS) may actually be fired, provided that the organization has an AIDS education program that clarifies the nature of the disease and its transmission. While Title VII of the 1964 Civil Rights Act says nothing specific about any kinds of physical disabilities or problems, the fact that the HIV affects disproportionately more minorities means that organizations must be wary of the possibility of disparate impact (which may occur when a facially neutral employment policy adversely affects disproportionately more members of a protected class) when evaluating the employment status of individuals who are HIV-positive (or who have ARC or AIDS). Finally, in terms of federal legislation, the Americans with Disabilities Act (ADA), which took effect in July 1992 for all organizations with 25 or more employees, requires covered employers to employ people with disabilities who can perform the work required with reasonable accommodation. In July 1993, the ADA will be extended to cover all organizations with 15 or more employees. Obviously, AIDS education in the workplace is not only desirable, but essential, for legal reasons.

State laws regarding the status of AIDS (and the status of homosexuals in general) in the workplace vary widely. Currently, only two states (Massachusetts and Wisconsin) and the District of Columbia specifically prohibit employment discrimination on the basis of sexual orientation. However, 24 states (as well as the District of Columbia) have included HIV-positive, ARC, and AIDS within the definition of handicap or disability in their state human rights, civil rights, handicapped rights, or fair employment legislation. One state, Kentucky, has specifically ruled that AIDS is *not* a protected handicap. In addition, 14 states have enacted laws concerning HIV testing and confidentiality. Typically, such laws prohibit employers from testing present or potential employees for the presence of HIV. They also prohibit employers from firing individuals who are HIV-positive or those who are afflicted with ARC or AIDS. Typically, an employee may be dismissed only if he or she poses an unreasonable risk to the health and safety of coworkers or to the pubic, and if no reasonable accommodation is possible.

## POLICY DEVELOPMENT

Many employers develop AIDS policies reactively—in other words, because they are forced to deal with the problem. This may be especially pertinent depending on where a company is located. Although AIDS has been reported in every state, the preponderance of cases (approximately 50% of the national total) are in either New York or California. New York City, in fact, had reported 13,874 cases by the end of 1990, making it the metropolitan area hardest hit by the disease thus far. Such statistics have meant that many employers are forced to deal with the AIDS problem before they have developed clear policies for doing so, and any policy development is post hoc, or done out of dire necessity. For example, the vice president for Employee Relations at Bank of America in San Francisco explained (Koch, 1990) that the company was forced to deal with the problem after an employee who had been temporarily incapacitated with an AIDS-related illness wanted to return to work. Two pregnant coworkers complained; one eventually threatened an action under OSHA. Despite the fact that medical experts consulted by the bank determined that there was no danger to the coworkers, the two women chose to resign. At that point, the bank decided that some kind of formal corporate policy on AIDS was necessary and formed a task force to develop such a policy.

A similar situation occurred at Morgan Guaranty Trust in New York City (Koch, 1990). Several employees, after reading somewhat sensationalized descriptions of AIDS, demanded that a gay coworker be either reassigned or fired. The problem was not the coworker's sexual preference in and of itself; rather, the employees were operating under the doubly mistaken assumption that all gay men have HIV and can therefore transmit the disease via casual work interaction. This scenario was repeated at Levi Strauss, where a manager contacted the Employee Assistance Program (EAP) office, concerned that all gay people carried the disease.

According to Wagel (1988), organizations that recognize the AIDS issue as pertinent (either with foresight or out of necessity) to them typically take one of two different approaches to developing a corporate AIDS policy. Many simply subsume AIDS and related problems under existing policies that deal with life-threatening illnesses. This approach has the advantage of efficiency: It is simply assuming that AIDS can be approached like any other life-threatening illness, such as cancer or heart disease, and that policies for dealing with those types of illnesses will be adequate for dealing with AIDS. A second possible advantage of such an approach may be the removal of the stigma of AIDS are merely a "gay" disease. It may instead by portrayed as a serious disease that can affect anyone, much like cancer or heart disease.

Other organizations take an alternative approach to policy development, which is to recognize AIDS as a disorder with unique characteristics and formulate policies that address these characteristics. This type of approach may also have some merit, as AIDS is, in some significant ways, much different than cancer or heart disease. Commonly cited differences, as noted above, include the inevitable (thus far) fatality of the disease, the perception (not entirely correct) that it is mostly a "gay" disease, and the fact that it is communicable, if only via exchange of bodily fluids. Obviously, perceptions about AIDS make it different from cancer or heart disease, and many experts argue (cf. Culpan, 1990) that approaching it as "just another potentially fatal disease" is a gross oversimplification. This line of reasoning may have some merit: heart disease is typically perceived as an illness that can afflict anyone, regardless of such factors as sexual orientation or drug use, and heart disease is not assumed to be communicable. Indeed, it would be highly unusual for an employee to insist that a coworker with heart problems be reassigned or fired; heart disease is usually regarded as a universal problem that might afflict anyone and does not cast aspersions on the victim's moral integrity. [This is not meant to imply that gays are morally reprehensible. Many people, however, unfortunately see homosexuality as an expression of perversity rather than as one expression of the possible diversity among human beings. This was obvious in the St. Lawrence et al. (1990) research described above, where gay males with AIDS were blamed for their disease.]

Multiple benefits of an AIDS-specific policy have been cited (cf. Chapman, 1986; Koch, 1990). Significant benefits may include the maintenance of high worker productivity (from both the AIDS patient and the other employees, all of whom can recognize the organization's support for AIDS issues), the management of health care costs (which may be especially high with AIDS, even more so than with other serious diseases), and the development of a responsible, sympathetic public image (as the public recognizes the organization's commitment to dealing with AIDS in a responsible manner).

A possible drawback to specific policies, however, is that they may contribute to the stigmatization of AIDS as purely a "gay" disease. The Catch-22 is that an AIDS-specific policy does recognize the uniqueness of AIDS, but by doing so, places it in a category by itself. This, as noted above, may have negative implications not only for all gay men, but for others who will continue to believe that the disease is irrelevant to them.

Regardless of which approach an organization takes, several components consistently appear in corporate AIDS policies. A major focus of any AIDS-related policy is education. By its nature (it is a communicable disease that is thus far invariably fatal), AIDS has, as noted above, created a great deal of fear and panic. An effective education program may provide several important benefits for an organization. First, it may allay fears and misconceptions about the nature of the syndrome. If employees are provided with credible medical information about transmission and treatment, they are less likely to be overwhelmed by fear. Second, education may benefit employers who are obligated to comply with the Vocational Rehabilitation Act and with OSHA requirements concerning education of employees. If an organization has an AIDS education program in place, employers cannot file safety complaints with OSHA alleging that AIDS is a danger to them. Third, education could help decrease costs associated with turnover. In a 1988 poll reported by Nowlin and Stockham, 66% of 2,000 workers surveyed indicated that they were concerned about using the same bathroom facilities as an AIDS victim. Forty percent were concerned about eating in the same cafeteria, and 37% were concerned about sharing equipment or tools. Obviously, decreasing or eliminating groundless fears might help reduce (or eliminate) possible workplace conflict and turnover associated with unreasonable fears. An essential tool for combating panic is information. The approach to education will, of course, vary according to the organization's structure, philosophy, size, and resources, but should definitely be a key part of any AIDS-related corporate policy.

A second important focus of an AIDS policy involves feasible accommodations for victims. Work itself may contribute positively to the victim's physical and emotional stability; however, depending on the health status of the victim, some flexibility in work assignments or schedules may be necessary. Ideally, all employees should be aware of their rights in this context, as legally, employers are required to accommodate HIV-positive employees and ill employees (those with ARC or AIDS) as they would any other employees with disabilities, provided that there is no risk of contagion. In addition, willingness to accommodate an employee whose health is suffering can have a positive impact on productivity and morale for all employees.

A third important component of AIDS policies often addresses the long-term consequences of dealing with victims. Although the primary concern is obviously for the physical and emotional health of the HIV-positive employee (and, of course, the employee with ARC or AIDS), employers also need to recognize the fears and concerns of other employees. Some employees may simply be fearful of catching the virus; others may need emotional support as they try to accept and deal with the fact that a valued coworker is seriously (or fatally) ill. Cochran and Mays (1990) use the term "worried well" to refer to individuals who are not themselves HIV-positive, but are concerned about their risk of being infected. Extrapolating from what is known about the reaction of gay men to possible infection with AIDS, the worried well may experience acute or chronic anxiety with panic attacks, agitated depression, and hypochondriacal reactions that may actually mimic AIDS symptoms.

## POLICY CONTENT

One example of the first approach (handling AIDS as simply one type of life-threatening illness) is used at Bank of America. In 1988, the bank modified its written policy on life-threatening illnesses to include AIDS. The written guidelines emphasize that any employee with a life-threatening medical problem (included but not limited to cancer, heart disease, and AIDS) may continue to work as long as acceptable performance standards are met and as long as the employee's condition does not present a health or safety threat. Resources available through the bank's Personnel Relations Department include information and education on a variety of life-threatening illnesses (including AIDS), referral to support services, and benefit consultation for employees who may need help in managing health insurance, disability leave, etc.

Because Bank of America is a large, decentralized organization, it does not have centralized health facilities at which to aim its AIDS education programs. Instead, it provides information about many different health matters through various means, such as videotapes and a monthly newsletter to all employees. The bank's goal is to provide at least some basic AIDS information to every employee at least once a year. In addition, the bank makes information about health matters (including AIDS) available on request (with full confidentiality maintained). Finally, the bank makes an effort to evaluate and assist (through its corporate Employee Assistance Program) those who may be working with an HIV-positive coworker.

A similar policy exists at the San Francisco-based Levi Strauss. In 1982, a group of concerned employees approached Strauss's CEO to discuss the logistics of distributing AIDS information in the company's atrium plaza. These employees wanted to share the information with other potentially interested employees but were concerned that others would interpret their efforts as evidence that they were infected. The CEO and other management representatives decided to join the information campaign, reasoning that information coming from upper management would be perceived as official concern on the part of the company, rather than as evidence of disease. In 1983, the company, faced with increasing concern from employees about the nature of the disease and confusion about the company's "official" policy, developed a "no-policy" policy, treating AIDS like any other life-threatening medical condition. Ongoing education programs reinforce the company's official philosophy: AIDS can kill, but all employees suffering from potentially life-threatening illnesses are entitled to work as long as they are able. Initially, the company brought in local experts from the San Francisco AIDS Foundation to talk with fearful managers.

The company then launched a general education campaign, first for managers and then for other employees. Eventually, the company hosted a conference on AIDS in the workplace for other Bay-area companies. According to company officials, this no-policy approach (in other words, no separate policy statement for AIDS) works because the ongoing education programs reinforce the company's position on AIDS and, while recognizing the urgency of the AIDS problem, handle it like any other serious medical problems, rather than treating it as a "gay" disease.

Other organizations, as noted above, prefer to approach AIDS as a unique condition deserving of its own specific policy. The Digital Equipment Corporation (DEC) has been something of a leader in the development of a formal AIDS policy. In 1987, DEC developed one of the first AIDS program offices in the country. The policy at DEC is to treat AIDS specifically, rather than subsuming it under the company's existing policy on life-threatening illnesses. Managers and personnel staff participate in four- to eight-hour training/education sessions that cover basic AIDS information and debunk common AIDS myths. Once they have been thoroughly educated about the disease, they can act as important sources of information for their own subordinates.

The University of California (UC) system issued an AIDS-specific policy in October 1985. While acknowledging that UC personnel policies are adequate for dealing with most ill and/or disabled employees, the policy states that the AIDS/ARC epidemic compels the university to decrease anxiety about the public health aspects of the disease, as well as to be sensitive to AIDS/ARC employee-victims and their coworkers. Implicit in their policy statement is the philosophy that AIDS is not just another potentially fatal disease—that it has unique characteristics (in both medical and social terms) and should be recognized accordingly.

One of the most intensive education efforts is reflected in the policy at Modine Manufacturing in Racine, Wisconsin. Initially, the company took a fairly traditional approach to AIDS education. A series of informational seminars on AIDS was offered (much like seminars on other health-related topics), and employees could attend at their discretion. Eventually, it became apparent that this approach was ineffective for several reasons. Many employees simply skipped sessions; thus only a small number of employees were reached. Of those who did attend, many either did not take the information seriously ("let's go to the queer show" was a remark overheard by the then-personnel director) or felt stigmatized for their interest. Consequently, attendance at AIDS seminars is now mandatory. In fact, according to Modine's former personnel director, if employees choose to skip a seminar, "they might as well just turn in their keys and employee ID card." While such insistence on attendance may seem harsh, Modine's approach seems to be more effective than voluntary seminars. Employees may be understandably reluctant to attend a voluntary information session if they fear that coworkers will interpret their interest as evidence of either infection or nontraditional sexual preference. Obviously, without sufficient motivation, even the best-intentioned education efforts will be ineffective.

Education is obviously not the only necessary element in an AIDS program. Support for employees is also extremely important, and is reflected in the approach taken by Pacific Gas & Electric (PG & E). PG & E's AIDS-specific policy asserts that employees with AIDS do not present a health risk to other employees under normal working conditions. Such employees are to be evaluated solely according to their ability to work and are entitled to coverage under PG & E's benefit policies. Employee Assistance Program (EAP) counselors may provide more comprehensive educational efforts for employees who ask for (confidential) help and/or information.

At PG & E, a confidential employee hotline was set up in 1984 by a group of volunteers from the company's human resources department. The volunteers felt that employees might be hesitant to ask important questions about AIDS if they were concerned about confidentiality. Volunteers from the human resources department (who receive in-depth training about the nature of AIDS) take turns staffing the hotline and returning messages left on the hotline's answering machine.

Accommodation available for unwell employees is also an integral part of many AIDS policies. As HIV-positive employees begin to suffer from various kinds of opportunistic infections, they may be unable to meet the normal demands of the workplace. At Syntex (USA), Inc., in Palo Alto, California, accommodation may include part-time work, flexible hours, a restructured work load, or work done at home. In the case of one employee, for example, the company installed a computer modem in the employee's home so he could work from there while recovering from an episodic illness that had hospitalized him for several weeks. A messenger dropped off and picked up work assignments and the employee remained almost as productive as he had been in the office. The benefits of such accommodation may be multiple: There may be little, if any, interruption in productivity, the ill employee is able to maintain the security of a job, and the image of the company as a concerned employer is enhanced.

An especially unique approach to accommodating AIDS is demonstrated by Multitasking Systems (MTS) in New York City, an office services firm that hires only people with AIDS and HIV infections. MTS specializes in performing such services as word processing, data entry, list management, bulk mailings, and photocopying. MTS has been in existence in various stages since 1987, although it officially opened its doors for the first time in February 1988. Money for start-up costs (approximately $250,000) was solicited from individuals and foundations; several corporations also provided grants. Ritter (1989) describes the company as filling a special void for AIDS patients. For any AIDS patient, the amount of time that must be spent on visits to doctors and on hospital stays makes it difficult to hold a conventional full-time job. At MTS, schedules are flexible, even with new hires. If a newly hired employee is too sick to work, the company will make an effort to hold the job for up to 60 days. All full-time workers receive major medical health insurance, a major source of concern for many AIDS patients.

MTS places a higher priority on employing people with full-blown AIDS than those who test HIV-positive. The company does not discriminate in favor of people with full-blown AIDS. However, HIV-positive people are more likely to be able to meet the demands of the conventional workplace and are thus not as desperate for jobs. Those with full-blown AIDS, on the other hand, may find the conventional workweek impossible to handle and thus have few options in the workplace.

In addition to their unique approach to staffing, MTS emphasizes a specific approach to training. New employees are trained in all of the company's functions, so filling in for an absent coworker (a frequent necessity, given the nature of the employee population) is no problem. Ritter reports that client companies have given MTS "rave reviews," and many continue to do business with the company not only because of the social value of MTS' mission but because of the high quality of service provided.

A third significant aspect of AIDS-related policies may involve emotional support for coworkers. Joseph (1991) notes that an AIDS death can be as devastating for "office survivors" as it is for family members (just as death from any other cause may be). In fact, a person with AIDS may share his or her diagnosis with the "work family" before telling the "real" family. As a consequence, some organizations are now hiring psychologists and/or professional grievance counselors to help employees deal with their feelings of grief and loss. While employers obviously cannot prevent the deaths from AIDS, they can help surviving employees cope with the loss of a valued coworker.

Another trend in the area of emotional support concerns the issue of bereavement leave for domestic partners. Many companies have traditionally allowed employees paid leave to attend the funerals of spouses and immediate family members. Kronenberger (1991), however, notes that often such policies are not helpful for unmarried domestic partners (of gay or straight employees). Given the impact of AIDS, however, organizations will, ideally, recognize the significance of such leave to apply to any domestic partners who may need bereavement leave. (A related issue concerns family leave. In several states, state law requires that covered employers allow employees to take time off to care for seriously ill family members.)

## CONCLUSION

AIDS has had, and will continue to have, a significant impact on employees and organizations. Although it is still considered, to some extent, a gay issue (it has had and will continue to have a significant impact on the gay community), it affects many other people as well. It is more than a gay man's health issue; it is a social and legal issue as well.

Obviously, given the range of organizations and policies discussed above, it is impractical to suggest that any one AIDS policy will work in all organizations. Every organization must be cognizant of its own philosophy and resources, as well as the legal climate (which obviously differs from state to state) in which it exists. But while there is no single best policy for all organizations, some type of AIDS policy is essential.

A number of experts provide specific kinds of checklists that may be of value to organizations struggling with the development of an AIDS policy. Culpan (1990), for example, mentions the following guidelines. Because of the multidimensional nature of the AIDS problem—on medical, managerial, and legal levels—approaching the problem must also be multidimensional. The specific guidelines he suggests include:

> Take measures to support the affected employee. This may include assistance with benefits (i.e., sharing portions of medical expenses not covered by insurance), provision of time off for treatment, counseling, and work accommodations that allow the employee to work as long as possible.
>
> Avoid discrimination. Adherence to laws, at federal, state, and local levels, is essential. It is therefore essential that policy formulation is done in the context of the relevant legal climate.
>
> Launch education programs. Workplace-based education programs can significantly increase employee awareness of the disease and its possible ramifications. Education should, ideally, include information about prevention, as well as information to reduce groundless fears of contagion.
>
> Learn from others. Organizations should make an effort to learn from the successful experiences of other companies, including Bank of America and Levi Strauss.

Patterson (1989) suggests the following elements as essential issues to consider in detail when developing an AIDS policy:

- company policy and philosophy statement
- education
- hiring and continuation of employment
- benefits and insurance
- medical confidentiality
- employee assistance programs
- outside support

Obviously, all of these elements may be of concern to individual employees as well as to entire organizations, and detailed attention to each is warranted. Each organization may have its own unique approach as far as addressing a particular element, but careful planning can help ensure that the needs of everyone—again, both individuals and the organization as a whole—are met.

Corporate policy obviously is a critical factor in dealing with the AIDS crisis in any meaningful way, as corporations have been, and will continue to be, hard hit by the AIDS crisis. Clear, consistent policy development and implementation may have a positive impact not only on productivity and morale, but may also contribute to the recognition that AIDS can be approached constructively and supportively. While the lack of a corporate policy does not preclude dealing with an AIDS-related crisis in a healthy, humanitarian way, rational, unemotional policy development may help ensure that all employees are treated fairly and ethically. Regardless of whether an organization develops a policy reactively (i.e., because they are forced to deal with an AIDS-related problem) or proactively (i.e., in anticipation of possible AIDS-related concerns), a clear policy statement obviously helps guarantee that all employees will be treated fairly, legally, and ethically.

## REFERENCES

*Airline v. Nassau County, Florida.* (1987). U.S. 43 FEP 81.

Chapman, F. S. (1986, September 15). AIDS & business: Problems of costs and compassion. *Fortune, 110*(6), 122–127.

Cochran, S. D., & Mays, V. M. (1989). Women and AIDS-related concerns. *American Psychologist, 44*(3), 529–535.

Culpan, R. (1990, July–September). Guidelines for developing an AIDS policy. *Business, 40*(3), 55–58.

DiLauro, T. J. (1989, Spring). Understanding AIDS in the workplace: Education, legislation and selected arbitrations. *NRECA Management Quarterly, 30*(1), 16–29.

Jones, W. J., & Johnson, J. A. (1989). AIDS in the workplace: Legal and policy considerations for personnel managers. *Review of Public Personnel Administration, 9*(3), 3–14.

Joseph, N. (1991, January 7). Harder days at the office. *Newsweek, 116*(1), 61.

Koch, J. J. (1990, April). Wells Fargo's and IBM's HIV policies help protect employees' rights. *Personnel Journal, 69*(4), 40–48.

Kronenberger, G. K. (1991, June). Out of the closet. *Personnel Journal, 70*(6), 40–44.

McDonald, M. (1990, July). How to deal with AIDS in the workplace. *Business & Health, 8*(7), 13–22.

Nowlin, W. A., & Stockham, E. B. (1988, May–June). The employment policy implications of AIDS. *IM, 30*(3), 24–28.

Patterson, B. (1989, January/February). Managing with AIDS in the workplace. *Management World, 18*(1), 44–47.

Ritter, A. (1989, November). AIDS and the medicinal power of work. *Personnel, 66*(11), 36–39.

Ross, J. K., & Middlebrook, B. J. (1990, Winter). AIDS policy in the workplace: Will you be ready? SAM *Advanced Management Journal, 55*(1), 37–41.

St. Lawrence, J. S., Husfeldt, B. A., Kelly, J. A., Hood, H. V., & Smith, S. (1990).

The stigma of AIDS: Fear of disease and prejudice toward gay men. *Journal of Homosexuality, 19*(3), 85–101.

Temple, T. E. (1990, October). Employers prepare: Hope for AIDS victims means conflict in your workplace. *Labor Law Journal, 41*(10), 694–699.

Wagel, W. H. (1988). AIDS: Setting policy, educating employees at Bank of America. *Personnel, 65*(8), 4–8.

Zilg, R. J. (1989, Winter). AIDS: Implications for employee benefit plans and personnel policies. *Employment Relations Today, 16*(4), 285–293.

Chapter 12

# Mental Health Issues and the Worker with AIDS: The Impact of Work on Psychological Functioning in Men with HIV Disease

**Michael W. Ross**

From an economic point of view, much of the projected cost of HIV disease to the community is associated with the loss of young, productive men. However, further anecdotal clinical evidence suggests that continuing employment also has a significant impact on the quality of life and the clinical progress of an individual with AIDS or AIDS-related complex (ARC) (Rosevelt, 1987). There have been no investigations of the effect of continuing at work on individuals with HIV disease on either their quality of life, the clinical course of the disease, or the interactions of those two variables with the initial disease severity, which may make it difficult to continue work.

Employment is a source of self-esteem, provides a secure reality base, and is one of the most important predictors of positive mental health. Deprivation of work is a source of grief (Vaillant & Vaillant, 1981). Numerous studies on the effect of unemployment confirm that mental health in the employed is high, while that in the unemployed and part-time employed is significantly lower

My thanks go to James Skelton and Emma Wallhead for their invaluable contribution to the conduct and typing of the interviews for the pilot study and Nancy Roth for her help with discussions and study design.

(Furnham, 1983; Warr & Jackson, 1985). Vaillant and Vaillant provide evidence from their 33-year longitudinal study that unemployment is a cause, not effect, of a decrease in mental health. Warr and Jackson found that unemployment has a major impact on mental health in the first three months of unemployment, and mental health improves when the individual regains work. Warr and Jackson also noted that a high commitment to employment leads to a greater decrement in mental health, and, of significance for the situation with HIV disease, the more chronic health impairment initially, the greater the subsequent decline in psychological health. Feather and Davenport (1981) and Feather and O'Brien (1986) also reported that the importance of employment to an individual was related to mental health, and Krupinski (1984) found that the type of work (dependent or independent) has no effect on psychological well-being, but that the nonfulfillment of desires concerning work is a critical variable for mental health.

These data are of greater significance for homosexual men with HIV disease for two reasons. First, because there will usually be a chronic health impairment; and second, because the great majority of homosexual men are not married or rearing children, and usually place more importance on their work as a source of identification and reflection of their competence and social utility (Ross, 1988). AIDS and ARC lend themselves to investigation of the effects of employment on mental health and disease because there is considerable variability in the degree of severity of illness across categories, ranging from incapacitating to minimal effects on work performance. Severity of disease can thus be partialled out or used as a further independent variable. In turn, this allows the effects of disclosure (of disease or of homosexual orientation) on mental health to be investigated.

Only one study has investigated the impact of work-related life events in homosexual men. Ross (1990) found significant correlations between life events related to work and anxiety and insomnia, social dysfunction, and depression as well as global mental health. The correlations for finances (clearly associated with work) were even higher. Correlations were substantially higher than correlations for supposedly nonhomosexual samples and confirm both that employment is more significant for homosexual men in terms of mental health, and that it has a major impact on their mental health. Ross also found that disclosure of homosexual orientation was significantly associated with somatic symptoms and anxiety. For a presumed heterosexual sample, Layton (1986) has also noted that anhedonia and social dysfunction resulted from unemployment, and Donovan, Oddy, Pardoe, and Ades (1986) confirmed that economic change in its own right will increase stressful life events and precipitate behavioral problems.

Apart from anecdotal comments, little is known about the effects of cessation of work on homosexual men with HIV disease. Bauman and Aberth (1986) have reported that employers often dismiss people with HIV disease from work "for the good of the workers' health" or because of concerns about "the safety of others.'' They observed that terminations of employment resulted in some strong negative reactions to the loss of an important source of self-esteem and personal gratification. Rosevelt (1987) notes that of her sample of gay men with AIDS or ARC, 35% were the victims of work discrimination and of these, 64% were unemployed. Rosevelt also found that social supports were associated with a greater ability to cope with HIV disease and longer survival. Of particular importance, 47% of her sample reported that work associates were their most significant supports after friends or lovers. In her sample, half the people with AIDS and 70% of those with ARC were employed; significantly, 74% of those listing work associates as a major source of support were employed. The gay men rated work associates as providing a significantly higher percentage of functional support than her normative (heterosexual male) sample. These data suggest that ability to cope with HIV disease and survival time may be associated with employment status.

These studies on homosexual and apparently nonhomosexual samples lead to the suggestion that the impact of work status (being employed full- or part-time, or unemployed) on both mental health and reported quality of life, and on course of illness, may be significant. No published studies investigate these questions (nor am I aware of unpublished ones).

The impact of the work situation on mental health and particularly the bereavement process has been described by Sowell, Bramlett, Gueldner, Gritzmacher, and Martin (1991) in a phenomenologic study of eight bereaved gay men in the United States. They noted that through fear of a lack of understanding, if not reprisal, some of their respondents were reluctant to disclose their loss to people at work. Concern was also expressed at the possibility of social sanctions from work colleagues if the relationship with a homosexual partner who had died of AIDS was discovered. As a consequence, workplace support was not available. Sowell et al. (1991) note that the survivor (who may often be HIV seropositive himself) may not be prepared to risk the disenfranchisement and sanctions involved in revealing a homosexual relationship and also possible HIV infection. This study suggests that while the sanctions anticipated may be related as much to the respondent's homosexual orientation as to possible HIV infection (the two are frequently co-categorized in public perception), there is not only the foregoing of a significant source of support, but the added complication of the pressure and stresses involved in actively *suppressing* the nature of the relationship. Where a bereavement is involved, the need to also suppress mood and to present a normal facade will undoubtedly also involve significant stress: in such a situation, work may be a significant contributor to poor mental health. Further, Ross (1978, 1985) has found that *anticipated* negative societal reaction to homosexuality is in itself a concomitant of poorer mental health than *actual* negative societal reaction, suggesting that those who anticipate a negative reaction in the workplace may be at double risk of psychological dysfunction. This raises a further question: to what extent are homosexual men with

HIV disease likely to be further discriminated against? There are two studies that bear on this issue. Sheehan, Lennon, and McDevitt (1990) surveyed more than 300 students at a university in the United States, where each was given a scenario relating to interaction in an open-plan workplace in which people interact frequently and collaborate on team projects. There were six endings to the scenario: a colleague had either AIDS (acquired homosexually, or through a blood transfusion), cancer (lung cancer acquired from heavy smoking, or pancreatic cancer), or hepatitis (acquired either through injecting drug use, or through a blood transfusion). In all cases the colleague was male. Data indicated that the pattern of coworkers' interactions with the ill colleague differed by type of illness, but not by the individual's perceived control over acquiring the illness. Interactions with, and appraisal of future job performance of, coworkers with AIDS would be significantly more negative than would their interactions with hepatitis patients, which were in turn likely to be more negative than interactions with cancer patients. However, most respondents indicated that they would help ill colleagues with their work regardless of whether they were perceived to have control over acquiring their illness or not.

Similar findings were reported by Hunter and Ross (1991), who used a similar set of scenarios with health workers. In this study, the illness (HIV or hepatitis B infection) was attributed to sexual contact, intravenous drug use, or blood transfusion. The patient was identified as being either homosexual or heterosexual within each diagnostic category and for each source of infection. Results indicated that regardless of disease, patients infected through intravenous drug use or sexual contact were seen as more responsible for their condition, and those HIV (but not hepatitis B) patients infected by sex or intravenous drug use were seen as having less moral integrity than those infected by transfusion. Source of infection similarly resulted in a lower desire for close social interaction with intravenous drug users compared with those infected via transfusion or sexually. Of particular importance, however, is the fact that sexual orientation was not a significant variable in predicting social distance or blame.

Taking these two studies together, it appears that perceived control over infection is one of the important predictors of interaction and social distance, rather than sexual orientation as such. Thus, while workers with HIV disease, and those who are perceived to have acquired a disease through their own actions, are more likely to be stigmatized, whether they are homosexual or heterosexual appears to be unimportant. The bad news is that people are likely to be stigmatized for perceived control over acquiring HIV (or similar conditions): the good news is that it doesn't seem to matter if they are heterosexual or homosexual. And even where there is a degree of stigmatization, the data from the study of Sheehan et al. (1990) suggest that coworkers are still likely to help regardless of the illness or the person's role in acquiring it.

Such psychological studies, however, do not counter the evidence that discrimination in the workplace does occur. In a comparison of AIDS-related discrimination in the United States and Australia, Waters (1990) notes that people with HIV disease may suffer the added burden of ostracism and prejudice of a fearful and misinformed public. He notes that it is possible to hold a condition to be a handicap solely on the basis of the prejudicial reactions of others to that condition: this would include the psychological component of response to HIV. While U.S. courts have generally held that it would be invalid to allow the prejudices and preferences of customers to determine whether discrimination was valid, there are examples where if the employment of particular persons in the workplace may cause undesirable tension, it may be justified. Thus, while discrimination against homosexual persons may be invalid under the laws of several Australian states, in the United States it may be valid in some circumstances. While the law is uncertain, it does take account of the discrimination that may arise from a status (such as homosexuality) as well as from a condition (such as HIV infection). From a psychological point of view, this is a recognition both that discrimination based on sexual orientation may occur, and that it may have wide-reaching consequences for interaction and tension in the workplace. Given that discrimination based on HIV infection (and further, degree of disease progression) may also occur, and that co-categorization of HIV infection and homosexuality may occur because of the two issues being closely related in the view of much of the general public, the psychological consequences of HIV infection and homosexual orientation in the workplace are likely to be major (and legal protection, depending on the jurisdiction, doubtful).

Backer (1988) has suggested that the role of mental health professionals in managing HIV/AIDS at work may be important in reducing the stress of both the person with HIV/AIDS and of coworkers. In particular, he identifies the problems of the person with HIV/AIDS at work as including the complications of preexisting psychopathology, substance abuse as self-medication for anxiety, AIDS dementia complex, anxiety management, and relationship difficulties related to the medical status. Importantly, Backer also identifies the fact that coworkers need psychological services as well, for example how to work alongside a person with HIV/AIDS, and how to deal with the grief related to the death of a coworker with AIDS. Further, advice to management about the difficulties likely to arise in work teams where there are people with HIV disease is also important.

However, these factors are among the most prominent. It is interesting to document the actual experiences of people with HIV disease to identify what are for them the most psychologically stressful issues related to the workplace. In a pilot study designed to identify the issues associated with mental health, HIV disease, and the workplace, we interviewed 16 people who were working and had HIV disease, using a semi-structured interview schedule, and utilizing the narrative method to identify core categories of workplace response that was associated with stress. A number of core categories were identified and examples from interview transcripts are provided here.

*Using information in workplace battles.* The issue of using the information about a person's HIV status as a weapon in preexisting conflicts was mentioned several times.

> . . . he used that information for his own purposes against me [small laugh] . . . you know, against me. How can I describe it? He made me sort of feel that, under the circumstances, he had me over a barrel, whereas, before, I had him over a barrel.

*Change in attitude of coworkers and management.* One stressful area in the workplace that was reported by several respondents was a radical change in attitude of coworkers and management once it was known that the individual was HIV seropositive. Major alterations in friendships and work relationships developed, which were often unexpected.

> And there were a lot of things that happened, from that, from the point of disclosure. Our relationship altered one hundred and eighty degrees. Um . . . he treated me very shabbily, you know, from then on.

*Inaccurate empathy.* Even when the individual's HIV status was accepted, it was sometimes found that there was not a great degree of empathy with the person's state.

> I came back to work and I burst into tears and I said "Oh, God! my—you know—my doctor thought that I may have had PCP [Pneumocystis carinii pneumonia] and that was just such a shock." And one of the other members of the staff turned around and I would have thought would have known better, turned around and said "Oh, you'd feel a lot worse than that, Robin." And I said, "How on earth do you know how I feel?"

*People with HIV disease seen as being demanding.* One respondent indicated that he felt that there was a sense that when issues relating to HIV status or special needs were raised, it was felt by management that HIV disease was being used as an excuse to get special concessions or be difficult.

> I felt that sometimes it was looked upon us—looked at—we were looked upon as . . . being troublesome. Perhaps just, you know, being, yeah, being troublesome and aggressive. . . .

*Discrimination as co-categorized person.* In several cases, respondents felt discriminated against because of the co-categorization of HIV and homosexuality, because revealing their HIV status had also involved revealing that the source of infection was homosexual activity.

> Well, neither case is discrimination because I'm HIV positive. I think it's discrimination because I'm gay. In one job I had a head of a department who tried very hard not to be homophobic but was. . . .
>
> There were seven people on the committee, and you had to get a positive vote from five of them to be recommended and only three of them were for me. I was told after that two of the others on the committee would not have voted for me under any circumstances because they didn't approve of my lifestyle.

*Anticipated discrimination and insensitivity.* In a number of cases, respondents expressed concern about the possibility of discrimination, particularly because of earlier antihomosexual or anti-AIDS comments, which led them to expect discrimination if their HIV status were revealed. Specifically, antigay and anti-AIDS jokes were found distressing.

> 'Cause they actually joke about me being gay and being HIV positive or having AIDS. So that type of humor, to me, isn't, you know . . . they don't need to know . . . they'll look at it as a negative thing, you know, so . . . I am also looking for another job. I want to remove myself from the catering industry . . . to remove all the stress or the majority of the stress from my life. So I am in the process of looking for a more appropriate job.
>
> (*Interviewer: But the people who make the jokes are making them not knowing you're HIV positive?*)
>
> Well, yes. . . . They don't make it to me, they make it to someone else and then the other person tells me, but they don't make it directly to me.

*Lack of appreciation of situation.* At a lower level of stress, lack of knowledge and education about homosexuality and HIV infection was also found to be disturbing, although manageable.

> It's a negative sort of attitude. But on the other hand, sort of, they know they've got to accept me because I am who I am and what I do is what I do. So they have accepted that in a way, but they are still a little bit uneducated . . . not . . . I wouldn't say prejudiced, but just very uneducated about the whole thing.

*Denial.* More subtle, but also a source of concern, was an insinuated but nevertheless felt level of denial of the problem, which made it difficult or impossible for the individuals to discuss their condition.

> I've worked with the similar group of people for some years now . . . about . . . seven years . . . and they're fairly conservative. It's largely . . . it's male dominated . . . mainly white Anglo-Saxon . . . but there is at another level it is, you know, that . . . there is that sense that people find it . . . difficult. There's never been a thing there. It's been . . . that's good, that part of it. I mean, I think, actually, from that point of view, it's pretty good, for the most part, it's never discussed.
>
> (*Interviewer: But you don't feel that you've been stigmatized?*)

Well it's interesting. I'm just thinking, um [long pause] mmmn, yeah. I mean, it might be there but it's in a subtle sort of way.

*Need to hide illness.* For those respondents who had not revealed their HIV disease at work, the stress of managing to hide their illness was major, particularly the need to juggle medical appointments so as not to arouse suspicion at work.

(*Interviewer: At work, for example, no one knows your true medical status?*)

No.

(*Interviewer: And this was your choice, obviously, not to reveal your illness to anybody?*)

Mmmn [long pause]

(*Interviwer: OK: no one's found out. They know you go off to the hospital. They know you're going to the doctor. What do they think happens to you when you're not there?*)

I, um, try to organize my appointments so that it's not noticeable, um . . . I . . . for instance, this afternoon, um . . . my appointment was at five ten. I left work just after four. I have flextime so, that appointment could be fitted in, um . . . you know, my . . . I see [doctor] at eight o'clock in the morning, or quarter to eight and, you know, I'm out of there by quarter past and on my way to Parramatta [laugh].

*Need to pretend.* Similarly, the need to think up excuses for illness to maintain the pretense was seen as being awkward.

There have been periods where my asthma was so bad that I had really quite a lot, I was really quite debilitated and I had quite . . . I, you know . . . my . . . it was quite sustained that I was having tests, but it wasn't clear it was asthma and I had quite a bit of time off and . . . and so, it . . . what I've had to do is substitute, at times.

*Difficulty of fitting in treatment.* Logistically, even when the respondent was known to have HIV disease, there were major problems associated with trying to organize medical treatments without excessive disruption of the workplace routine and the work day.

It's just been a hassle, trying to sort it out.

(*Interviewer: On the other hand, when you get back from holidays, if you do retire, you won't . . .*)

It won't be a problem, yes. But it has been . . . a . . . it's been, I mean, you . . . it's eighteen treatments and you . . . well, you . . . you imagine trying to find eighteen half-days leave!

From a positive perspective, there was also evidence that workplace response and changes in work practice actually enhanced the individual's psychological functioning. Several individuals responded to questions about workplace response to their HIV disease by indicating that they felt supported by their coworkers and management.

*Positive changes in work life.* On the other hand, a number of positive aspects of being HIV seropositive were also mentioned, particularly self-induced changes in work or work habits.

> So that I slowed down a bit and didn't take so much on . . . and . . . you know, actually spent a bit of time doing things that I . . . want to do, rather than should do. I'm enjoying the job more than I have in quite a while, which is fine.

*Favorable experiences in workplace.* The majority of experiences reported had favorable aspects: some if not all coworkers being more supportive than the respondent had anticipated, and attempts by coworkers and management to make the work situation more comfortable.

> I actually was a bit concerned, at one stage, that people were only nice to me because I was positive [laugh] [cough]. Um . . . but, um . . . I now don't think that's the case.
>
> So, I think . . . while I can talk about positive examples, the negative are harder to come by. By and large, they don't impinge themselves on . . . so much, on my awareness.

These illustrations from the pilot interviews indicate that there are a number of both positive and negative aspects of workplace conditions that are likely to have an effect on the worker's psychological functioning. Generally, these can be summarized as relating to exacerbation of previous workplace issues, discrimination, subtle discomfort, and the stresses of the need to hide one's condition because of anticipated discrimination. Discrimination primarily because of a co-categorized status (such as homosexuality) may also be a secondary effect of being identified as having HIV disease.

Bauman and Aberth (1986) note that there is a need to work, and that work is an important source of self-esteem and personal gratification. People with HIV disease need to feel that they remain valued and accepted members of their workplace community. This encapsulates the importance of work in the psychological functioning of the individual as has been demonstrated generally in terms of the effect of unemployment, and specifically here with regard to HIV disease. We have identified both from the literature and from a series of pilot interviews some of the issues that arise with regard to psychological functioning and how response to HIV disease in the workplace may impact on the individual. The issue of co-categorization illustrates how, for the homosexual person, there may be stresses associated either with a homosexual orientation of HIV disease that will magnify the psychological impact. The homosexual with HIV disease in the workplace is in a particularly sensitive and important confluence of areas that may result in major psychological trauma, and it is critical that this be recognized in HIV-associated logistical, educational, and psychological workplace interventions.

## REFERENCES


Backer, T. E. (1988). Managing AIDS at work: Psychology's role. *American Psychologist, 43,* 983–987.

Bauman, L. J., & Aberth, J. (1986). Health educators in the workplace: Helping companies respond to the AIDS crisis. *Health Education Quarterly, 13,* 395–406.

Donovan, A., Oddy, M., Pardoe, R., & Ades, A. (1986). Employment status and psychological well-being: A longitudinal study of 16-year-old school leavers. *Journal of Child Psychology and Psychiatry, 27,* 65–76.

Feather, N. T., & Davenport, P. R. (1981). Unemployment and depressive affect: A motivational and attributional analysis. *Journal of Personality and Social Psychology, 41,* 422–436.

Feather, N. T., & O'Brien, G. E. (1986). A longitudinal analysis of the effects of different patterns of employment and unemployment on school-leavers. *British Journal of Psychology, 77,* 459–479.

Furnham, A. (1983). Mental health and employment status: A preliminary study. *British Journal of Guidance and Counselling, 11,* 197–201.

Hunter, C. E., & Ross, M. W. (1991). Determinants of health-care workers' attitudes toward people with AIDS. *Journal of Applied Social Psychology, 21,* 947–956.

Krupinski, J. (1984). Psychological disturbances and work fulfillment. *Australian and New Zealand Journal of Sociology, 20,* 56–65.

Layton, C. (1986). Employment, unemployment, and response to the General Health Questionnaire. *Psychological Reports, 58,* 807–810.

Rosevelt, J. (1987). Support for workers with AIDS. *American Association of Occupational Health Nurses Journal, 9,* 397–402.

Ross, M. W. (1978). The relationship of perceived societal hostility, conformity and psychological adjustment in homosexual males. *Journal of Homosexuality, 4,* 157–168.

Ross, M. W. (1985). Actual and anticipated societal reaction to homosexuality and adjustment in two societies. *Journal of Sex Research, 21,* 40–55.

Ross, M. W. (Ed.). (1988). *Psychopathology and psychotherapy in homosexuality.* New York: Haworth Press.

Ross, M. W. (1990). The relationship between life events and mental health in homosexual men. *Journal of Clinical Psychology, 46,* 402–411.

Sheehand, E. P., Lennon, R., & McDevitt, T. (1990). Reactions to AIDS and other illnesses: Reported interactions in the workplace. *Journal of Psychology, 123,* 525–536.

Sowell, R. L., Bramlett, M. H., Gueldner, S. H., Gritzmacher, D., & Martin, G. (1991). The lived experience of survival and bereavement following the death of a lover from AIDS. *Image: Journal of Nursing Scholarship, 23,* 89–94.

Vaillant, G. E., & Vaillant, C. O. (1981). Natural history of male psychological health, X: Work as a predictor of positive mental health. *American Journal of Psychiatry, 138,* 1433–1440.

Warr, P., & Jackson, P. (1985). Factors influencing the psychological impact of prolonged unemployment and of re-employment. *Psychological Medicine, 15,* 795–807.

Waters, P. (1990). The coverage of AIDS-related discrimination under handicap discrimination laws: The U.S. and Australia compared. *Sydney Law Review, 12,* 377–419.

Part Five

# The Individual and the Organization: Social-Psychological Issues in the Workplace

Chapter 13

# Special Problems of Older Gay Employees

**Jo Ann Lee**

The title of this chapter should *not* be interpreted to mean that older homosexuals have inherent psychological problems. Instead, the problems discussed here refer to problems that this segment of the American population often endures because of the conditions imposed on them by society. Older homosexual employees as a group can be said to be in a "double whammy" category, because they are the target of two common types of discrimination: age discrimination and sexual orientation discrimination. The problems they may experience are not unique to them and may be experienced by younger homosexual employees or by older heterosexual employees. However, the intensity of the problems may be greater and the strategies for coping with the problems may be different for persons who are both older and homosexual.

I was unable to find any research conducted specifically on this topic. However, my interviews with older gays and reports by other researchers (Friend, 1990; Kelly, 1977) indicate that the plight of older homosexual employees may warrant further study and closer examination. This chapter is an introduction to issues that should be considered in future research. This chapter is based on related research and interviews conducted with gays and the New

York City organization, Seniors Aging in a Gay Environment (SAGE), the oldest and largest organization serving older gays and lesbians.

This chapter focuses on gay men as opposed to gays *and* lesbians. However, points made in this chapter may also apply to lesbians. I begin by discussing the common stereotypes of older workers and older gays. Other chapters in this book have discussed the common stereotypes of homosexuals and they need not be repeated here. Next, I discuss the problems that may confront older gay employees. I end with discussing the ways older gay employees may cope with these problems.

## STEREOTYPES

### Older Workers

Our society continues to be very youth oriented and biased against older people (Barrow, 1989). Negative stereotypes about older persons are often carried to the workplace (Rosen & Jerdee, 1976) and can affect employment decisions about older workers (Lee & Clemons, 1985). Much research has shown that the negative stereotypes are often unwarranted and that older workers often perform as well as or better than their younger counterparts (Doering, Rhodes, & Schuster, 1983; Hale, 1990; Rhodes, 1983; Robinson, 1986).

The definition of older workers varies across applications and studies. The Age Discrimination in Employment Act of 1967, as amended in 1986, defines older workers as those over 40; the Older Americans Act and the Job Training and Partnership Act define older workers as those older than 55 years; researchers have variably used 45 and 50 years as well as 40 and 55 years as benchmarks for defining older workers. Although the exact chronological age used to define older workers varies, the common finding in the studies has been that older workers, compared to younger workers, are seen as being less able to learn new material, more inflexible, and lacking in technological skills (American Association of Retired Persons, n. d.). On the other hand, older workers are usually perceived as having better interpersonal skills, better work habits, and more job knowledge (American Association of Retired Persons, n. d.).

Older workers may not be offered training to improve their skills as a consequence of the negative stereotypes. Without periodic training, their skills may become obsolete and their employment may be terminated. It usually takes them a longer time for reemployment after losing a job, which can then lead to depression.

It is true that some abilities decline with age (Salthouse, 1986), and the age at which a person becomes a less effective worker depends on the specific job. The abilities that are affected the most by age are physical abilities, but most of today's jobs do not require maximum physical ability. Persons between 40 and 70 years are usually very capable of performing well in many jobs in our society, especially because many jobs require those skills that have been found to be strengths of older workers (e.g., interpersonal skills and job knowledge).

### Older Gays

The common stereotype about older gays is that they are lonely, depressed, sexually deprived, and lacking a social support system of family and friends (Kelly, 1977). However, researchers have found that this negative description does not apply to many older gays (Friend, 1990; Kelly, 1977; Moses & Hawkins, 1986). In fact, many older gays have a very strong network of friends and are not alone or lonely (Moses & Hawkins, 1986). Kelly (1977) found that as gay men age, they accumulate more gay friends and associate less with non-gays.

The negative stereotypes may derive from the gay community's focus on youth and physical appearance. With age, most persons, homosexuals and heterosexuals, lose some physical attractiveness.

## PROBLEMS CONFRONTING OLDER GAY EMPLOYEES

### Age Discrimination

As mentioned earlier (p. 218), employers may discriminate against an individual because of age, regardless of sexual orientation. It is speculated that the loss of a job or promotion by a gay may be more traumatic, because of a broader sense of insecurity. One interviewee explained that older gay men feel a general insecurity about their employment, because many feel that the employer could easily dispose of them, without legal repercussions. Any worker, regardless of sexual orientation, will likely suffer some loss of self-confidence when rejected by his employer. However, the older heterosexual may receive some reassurance from friends and family of his continued cognitive abilities and such reassurance may help to console the person. Given the gay community's emphasis on physical appearance, such reassurance may not be forthcoming to the closeted gay man with few heterosexual friends and may mean very little to the gay man. In other words, it is speculated that gay friends will be less likely to provide reassurance about one's job-related cognitive abilities given their focus on physical attributes.

### The Glass Ceiling

Networking and social contacts are often instrumental to a person's climb up the ladder of success in the world of work. This avenue may be blocked or closed to the gay man, because of his reluctance to come out of the closet. Rapport with coworkers and superiors is often built on social commonalities such as sports or vacations. Such rapport often leads to business contacts and access to important information related to the job. Gay men have two alternatives to coming out: create a fictional heterosexual life or abstain from social events with coworkers and superiors.

Creating and maintaining a fictional heterosexual life can be very stressful and can lead to bitterness, according to one interviewee. However, not attending social events may preclude the development of important business contacts.

The difficulty of socializing with work associates is revealed in the following account. An interviewee, a self-proclaimed gay man, described his conversation with a public official who claimed that sexual orientation did not affect employment decisions in his office. The interviewee asked the official if known gays and lesbians brought their significant others to social events. When the official replied in the negative, the gay man explained that that showed the continued discomfort and fear of discrimination felt by the gays and lesbians.

It appears that self-proclaimed gays and lesbians often find it difficult to build a support network of homosexuals, also, because of the fear of being discovered. An interviewee explained his difficulty in organizing events for gays and lesbians in his place of work, which is supposed to be a relatively liberal and accepting environment. He explained that many gays and lesbians refused to attend the meetings because they did not want to be associated with the group. They feared that their association with other gays and lesbians would reveal their sexual orientation, which would decrease their chances of advancement.

Interviewees explained to me that it is more difficult for older gays to come out of the closet than younger gays because of the social environment in which they were raised. Today's older gays were raised during the period from 1920 to 1950, which was a much more socially conservative era than the years after 1960. It has been only recently that the homosexual community has organized. Although some hostility and intolerance continues to be displayed toward gays and lesbian, same-sex orientation is more socially accepted than it was before 1960. According to one interviewee, it is difficult for a gay who has built a career on a fictional heterosexual image to come out of the closet. He continues to carry the stigma learned during his earlier years and he fears he will be fired or denied future promotions. If he does come out, he risks being labelled dishonest for the past deceptions.

### Retirement Planning

Some companies have implemented retirement planning programs to: help employees prepare for retirement; assist employees with decision making; and improve employee well-being and productivity (Morrison & Jedrziewski, 1988). They are not yet pervasive in the work world. However, they may become more common as the workforce ages and the needs and benefits become more salient. Their format varies from the distribution of relevant literature to individual counseling and group discussions. They most often include information about financial planning, but they can also include information about second careers and the management of anticipated leisure time.

Closeted older gays will be unable to benefit completely from these retirement planning sessions, because they often include discussions of family plans. The gay who has come out of the closet may continue to feel uncomfortable discussing his nontraditional lifestyle among heterosexuals.

## STRATEGIES FOR COPING

Lee and Brown explain in their chapter, "Hiring, Firing, and Promoting" (this volume), that homosexuals have no federal protection against discrimination based on sexual orientation. The homosexual employee is usually left to cope with perceived discrimination on his or her own, buttressed with the support of other gays and lesbians. Some cities and counties, and a few states, have laws prohibiting sexual orientation discrimination. In addition, some corporations have company policies prohibiting such discrimination (Lee & Brown, this volume). However, gay and lesbian employees often perceive hostility and intolerance despite these protections. Statements from interviewees and reports by others (Friend, 1990; Moses & Hawkins, 1986) indicate the following as ways in which gays and lesbians may attempt to cope with perceived intolerance in the workplace.

### Early Retirement

Given the stresses of concealing their same-sex orientation, many gays may perceive retirement as freedom (Moses & Hawkins, 1986). Consequently, they may choose early retirement when given the option. They no longer will need to endure the stress of hiding their true self under the fear of losing their means of living.

Many homosexuals may be more financially able to take early retirement than heterosexuals. Gays often have more disposable income than nongays (Lucco, 1987), and they often make plans and save funds to care for themselves during their older years for the reasons that follow. They usually have not had the financial responsibilities of raising and providing for children, permitting them to save more for retirement. In addition, they usually anticipate they will have to care for themselves because they lack family caregivers and they plan accordingly.

### Affirming One's Sexual Orientation

According to one interviewee, a gay employee who has come out of the closet will be better able to cope with the stresses of anticipated discrimination than a closeted gay. Such disclosure increases the chance of self-acceptance and allows him the opportunity to build a support network of gay friends. Similarly, Friend's (1990) theory of successful aging for gays and lesbians proposes that older gays and lesbians experience a high level of self-acceptance and psychological adjustment if they reconstruct "what it means to be gay or lesbian into something positive" (p. 107). Friend labels gays and lesbians who do reconstruct their homosexuality, "affirmative older gay and lesbian people." He contrasts this group with two other groups, "stereotypic older lesbian and gay people" and the "passing older lesbian and gay people." Those in the "stereotypic" group, according to Friend, internalize the negative stereotypes about them and experience guilt, low self-esteem, and anxiety. Those in the "passing" group "believe the heterosexist sentiments with which they were raised while also acknowledging and marginally accepting their homosexuality" (Friend, 1990, p. 105).

According to some researchers (Friend, 1990; Moses & Hawkins, 1986), older homosexuals may be better equipped psychologically than heterosexuals to cope with the negative stereotypes toward the elderly and older workers. According to these researchers, some older homosexual employees develop a "crisis competence." More specifically, coping with being gay early in life may fortify some older homosexuals against negative stereotypes in general (Moses & Hawkins, 1986). Friend (1990) proposes that "managing issues associated with sexual orientation involves dealing with the potential loss of family and friends. Therefore, some older lesbian and gay people may have already developed psychological skills for dealing with the losses which occur when family and friends move away or die" (p. 110). It is uncertain whether a theory of crisis competence applies to older homosexuals' ability to cope, given the gay community's focus on youth and physical appearance. Being gay may be effective as a buffer for the stigma of being old only if the person succeeded in accepting himself or herself early in life (Moses & Hawkins, 1986).

One interviewee recommended that employers use the following to help homosexuals feel accepted in the workplace and feel that they will not be punished for their sexual orientation: (1) The employer should adopt and publicize a policy that prohibits discrimination based on sexual orientation; and (2) The employer should establish a dialogue with gays and lesbians who have come out to identify concerns and needed practices.

## REFERENCES

American Association of Retired Persons. (n. d.). *Workers over 50: Old myths, new realities.* Washington, DC: Author.

Barrow, G. M. (1989). *Aging, the individual, and society.* New York: West.

Doering, M., Rhodes, S. R., & Schuster, M. (1983). *The aging worker.* Beverly Hills: Sage.

Friend, R. A. (1990). Older lesbian and gay people: A theory of successful aging. *Journal of Homosexuality, 20,* 99–118.

Hale, N. H. (1990). *The older worker.* San Francisco: Jossey-Bass.

Kelly, J. (1977). The aging male homosexual. In H. L. Gochros & J. S. Gochros (Eds.), *The sexually oppressed* (pp. 160–172). New York: Associated Press.

Lee, J. A., & Clemons, T. (1985). Factors affecting employment decisions about older workers. *Journal of Applied Psychology, 70,* 785–788.

Lucco, J. J. (1987). Planned retirement housing preferences of older homosexuals. *Journal of Homosexuality, 14,* 35–56.

Morrison, M. H., & Jedrziewski, M. K. (1988). Retirement planning: Everybody benefits. *Personnel Administrator, 33,* 74–80.

Moses, A. E., & Hawkins, R. O., Jr. (1986). *Counseling lesbian women and gay men.* Columbus, OH: Merrill.

Rhodes, S. R. (1983). Age-related differences in work attitudes and behavior: A review and conceptual analysis. *Psychological Bulletin, 93,* 328–367.

Robinson, P. K. (1986). Age, health, and job performance. In J. E. Birren, P. K. Robinson, & J. E. Livingston (Eds.), *Age, health, & employment* (pp. 63–77). Englewood Cliffs, NJ: Prentice-Hall.

Rosen, B., & Jerdee, T. H. (1976). The nature of job-related age stereotypes. *Journal of Applied Psychology, 61,* 180–183.

Salthouse, T. A. (1986). Functional age. In J. E. Birren, P. K. Robinson, & J. E. Livingston (Eds.), *Age, health, & employment* (pp. 78–92). Englewood Cliffs, NJ: Prentice-Hall.

Chapter 14

# Personal Reflections on Coming Out, Prejudice, and Homophobia in the Academic Workplace

**Ritch C. Savin-Williams**

I entered Cornell as a very young 28-year-old assistant professor. Similar to many in my profession, I was inadequately trained for my new job. No one taught me how to teach (except through passive, usually negative modeling); how to be a citizen of my department, university, and profession; how to blend the personal and the professional; or how to confront sexism, racism, or homophobia in the workplace. I was, however, well versed in how to be a researcher. You will probably discern in the course of this essay moments when I should have known better or should have expected other than what I did. The story I share with you concerning my personal experiences of being gay and a faculty member at a "major" university may at times be unique to my time and my setting, but it may ultimately be one shared to some degree by you at other times and other settings.

## THE CONTEXT

I live and work in a community that is clearly one of the least homophobic places in the United States. This is Ithaca, New York, where gay rights laws, domestic partnership ordinances, and anything else that guarantees the rights of gay men, lesbians, and bisexuals fly through the City Council with only one dissenting vote, cast by the lone Republican.

This haven disappears, however, when I venture just outside the city boundaries. I am more protected in the city of Ithaca than in the county of Tompkins. There I encounter rampant moral diatribes; it is believed that the American family will disappear if homosexuals get their way. This is not to imply that the citizens of Tompkins County are not good people because, indeed, they are. But I do not feel that my sexual behavior and orientation are acceptable, although as a person I find acceptance, friendliness, and interpersonal connections. They love the "sinner" (especially if they do not know the sin) but not the "sin." In issues of sexuality, religion frequently has a lot more to say than common sense, decency, or a loving attitude.

Within these two contexts, Cornell University finds its existence. This has been my workplace for the last 15 years. Cornell prides itself in being an independent, liberal university that prefers, almost at all costs, to avoid controversy. It is not a university that assumes leadership on issues of ethics or morality. For example, long after many universities, including midwestern state universities and several Catholic-oriented colleges, incorporated sexual orientation in their protected rights clauses, Cornell finally followed suit in May 1990. It was not accomplished after a prolonged campaign orchestrated by student, employee, and faculty groups in 1983, but after a change in leadership on the Board of Trustees. This happened rather quietly, with lobbying behind the scenes.

Convincing the Board of Trustees to protect the rights of gay members of the Cornell community was a long, frustrating process. In 1983, several student groups, including the Cornell Civil Liberties Union and the Lesbian and Gay Political Action and Discussion Group, presented to the Trustees a 53-page document presenting the case. More than 50 Cornell organizations, including the Student and the Employee Assemblies, faculty groups, alumni, and student programming boards, agreed. The Trustees tabled the proposal in August 1984, because the "existing procedures work"; there were few documented cases of discrimination based on sexual orientation. Trustees' Chair Noyes stated, "I think that's a behavioral preference of people. I think you make a broad statement on behavior and you end up regretting it later." Two months later they outright rejected a change in the bylaws. To appease us, Cornell President Rhodes issued a "Presidential Codicil" that had the legal effect of a Trustees policy statement. It stated that it is illegal to discriminate against gays and lesbians in the provision of educational services or in university employment at Cornell. We were appeased. Five years later, much to the surprise of most community members, the Board of Trustees voted unanimously to prohibit discrimination on the basis of sexual or affectional orientation. Why now? Because, as the new chair said, "It was time."

This history should not imply that we, of the unprotected class, were not protected. Cornell administrators and trustees simply feared alienating alumni and their financial gifts by being overt in their ethical and moral obligation.

Administrators at Cornell are also faculty, lulled by status and salary to assume new responsibilities. Thus, at any one particular moment in time an administrator may be extremely pro-gay but his (usually) or her successor may be very antigay. In large part, whether that person will be pro- or antigay depends on which one of the 11 colleges that form Cornell University he (usually) or she is from prior to becoming an administrator. At Cornell there are extremely liberal, even leftist departments and colleges. For example, the College of Human Ecology and the College of Arts and Sciences are clearly two of the left-wing leaning colleges. Departments such as Human Development (my own), Human Service Studies, Women's Studies, English, and Africana Studies are even further left. Balancing pro-gay sentiment are colleges such as Engineering, Agriculture, and Life Sciences, which house some of Cornell's most conservative members.

In any case, and in most cases, Cornell administrators and faculty, less so than students, know that it is not socially or politically correct to be overtly homophobic. Relatively few faculty, staff, or administrators come out publicly as antigay, although several make a point to do so. Many express their "uncomfortableness" behind closed doors.

## COMING OUT TO SELF

Relative to the time it took, this account of self-recognition will be fairly brief. I tell it primarily to give background to my status when I assumed my Cornell position. During my childhood and adolescence I was essentially, at least overtly, asexual. My attraction to males was clearly present but I made the very logical and common self-centered assumption that my attractions and feelings were shared by all guys. My delay in dating and lusting (a foreign concept to me at the time) was simply nothing more than that, a delay that would self-correct itself. I had no clue of what homosexuality was, what gay or lesbian people were, or what I was sexually. All I knew was that I wanted to find that "David" picture again in the dictionary (I could not remember that I saw it under "Michelangelo") and to discreetly look for male underwear sales in the catalogues. I did not have a label for what I felt but I knew that whatever "it" was was exciting and not to be shared.

What I interpreted at the time to be intense friendships with other guys I now understand, in retrospect, to have been crushes. They were always with boys, usually a year or two younger with dark hair.* The first was with Bob when I was in the fourth and fifth grades. A neighbor one year older, Bob and I

*I have since expanded my age range and hair color.

spent every free moment together playing baseball, talking baseball, and trading baseball cards. Unlike many of my gay male friends today, I still turn to the sports page first. I owe it all to Bob. When my family moved at the end of my fifth grade, I cried for reasons that were beyond my comprehension at the time.

I loved the attention that I received from guys, especially athletes, and I believe that such needs propelled me to participate in athletics in junior and senior high school. Of course, I had to because there were so few males in my high school of 96 in Clever, Missouri, that every moving male body was needed to position himself somewhere on a playing field. I loved the "male bonding," if you will allow me to use such a phrase, and being in "their" presence. The sex talk among my fellow 13 male classmates consisted of screwing women, screwing sheep, screwing pigs, and screwing calves, and not necessarily in that order. I had little desire for any of these activities. I had some vague notion of what jacking off meant but no notion of what a blow job might entail. I dated several girls, not seriously of course, but just enough to satisfy the big dating events of the school year. The smartest girl in my class was my usual date; we could talk far better than we could kiss. I needed to test whether my delay was over yet; it wasn't.

At the University of Missouri I tried to fall in love with several very nice and friendly women. I even dated one for two years and got as far as third base. We even talked marriage. The reality was that I fell in love with my male roommate of two years. There were several women who elicited sexual desire and perhaps, under different circumstances and pressures, I would have married one of them. Whether or not this would have been a good thing is a moot issue.

My first homosexual sex came as a result of being picked up while hitchhiking in Atlanta, Georgia. It was a very erotic experience. More than 20 years later I can still recall specific details of the car ride and parking. It was perceived by me, at the time, to be another example of my post-Young Republicans, pro-SDS willingness to experiment with life. My uncontrollable crying afterwards, I interpreted at the time, was because of the fear that I had done something that was very dangerous. With some hindsight, I now realize that the crying was primarily an expression of tremendous release; the fear was that I had finally experienced something that felt so right but which was construed by the world around me and myself as so wrong.

I made several meager attempts to come to terms with my attraction to men. I recall going to psychological services at the University of Missouri after my sophomore year and requesting that I talk with someone about my future. This was to be the summer of my "great awakening" but the psychologist squelched that in a hurry. In the last 15 minutes when I finally approached the "issue," after talking about my career problems, he asked whether or not I had tried homosexual sex. I said no. His sage advice was to try heterosexuality and that I did not need to return. I didn't, and that was my experience with counseling during my college years. I also recall attending a student gay liberation meeting, but that was "just to hear" a Republican speaker.

Graduate school at the University of Chicago was a beginning for my sexuality in several ways. I continued on occasion to date females and, in fact, had my first "home run" heterosexual sex. It was an exciting, pleasurable experience and one that I have no regrets about. But I kept falling in love with men, eventually having a relationship with a man my age that lasted for several years. Neither of us defined ourselves as gay or what we were doing as homosexuality. The label was still not applicable for me because of my preconceived notion, driven by the media, of what homosexuals were. The relationship ended because my "friend" decided he needed to pursue women; I was pressuring him for a definition of ourselves and our relationship. Afterwards I recall going to gay places in the city. I was curious but a coward. Sexual activity was slight and my identity confusing. I ended my graduate career believing that perhaps there was the possibility that I might be gay, but the reality of it was still years away.

## COMING OUT AT CORNELL

Once at Cornell, true to my form, I dated women. My work colleagues helped me do this. With the Cornell job came an initial round of dinners, hosted by senior faculty and their wives (sexism intended). I found myself one of two single people invited. The other was always a woman. We grew to be good friends because we were always eating together! I enjoyed the women I dated very much because of their warmth and sensitivity; they were frequently more like friends than potential lovers. Try as I could, even though dating beautiful women with great personalities and great ideologies, I just could not pull it (love) off. Without realizing it on a conscious level, I was, dramatically speaking, waging a war: the forces of my homoerotic lust versus my desire for acceptability and a straight lifestyle.

It was a slow process, and by September 1981 at the age of 33 it was time. Sitting on Libe Slope at Cornell looking across the city that was my home, realizing my attractions were not disappearing, and feeling rejected by yet another man that I had a crush on, I made my decision. It was a nice gentle cry, one of recognition and understanding. There was relief, of cosmic proportions, and fear, of the "uncharted territory" in my life. The self-recognition aspect of coming out took three decades of ignorance, avoidance, denial, avoidance, suppression, and more avoidance before "gay" was allowed to eke into my awareness. Coming out publicly took much less time.

My first public act was to attend a Gay People at Cornell (GayPac) student meeting, but this proved to be less of an event than I had anticipated. I felt so courageous but I had magnificently failed to come out! Because I was known as a faculty person supportive of minority and liberal causes, my presence was perceived, not as a personal declaration but as an ideological statement. By my third visit I was able to convince those present that I was indeed one of us. The community coming out process was solidified when I agreed to be interviewed for a local alternative newspaper story on homosexuality in Ithaca. Little did I realize at the time the impact of the interview: I lost control of who would know. I was out to anyone who cared to know.

Another major outing event was running in a fraternity race for charity in May 1982. I ran with a GayPac team; on the back of our T-shirts were two interlocking male symbols. Team members ran one mile to six spots in Collegetown, drank a beer, and then staggered back to the starting point where they could throw up. In essence, I had made a public announcement of my homosexuality to the Cornell community. Thus, my coming out to myself extended over decades while my public coming out was solidified in that one academic year, 1981–1982.

Several repercussions of my publicly coming out have become important in my development. I anticipated several disasters in coming out; all fizzled. For example, as a result of the newspaper article I offered my resignation to the local Unitarian Universalist Church as a junior high Sunday School teacher. I assumed parents would object to a gay person teaching their "impressionistic" youth. The religious education director was surprised by my assumption but agreed to check with parents. None had any objection and I continued teaching. Rather than disasters, I began to realize distinct advantages of being "out in the workplace!"

In the fraternity race crowd was a "pre-gay" man who 10 years later would become a national leader in the gay and lesbian legal rights movement. After the race he sought me out; we became friends and he began the torturous process of fighting his own internalized homophobia, of coming out to himself, and of committing his many talents to gay causes. Our friendship continues, as have many others that had as their beginning a common sexual identity.

Another repercussion of being out was that I was known, briefly (because several lesbian professors would soon end my solitary reign), as Cornell's "gay professor." I became an institutional repository for many things, including personal narratives of gay students who needed and wanted to share their stories. This would ultimately change my life, become the source of my most significant research, alter the content and style of my teaching, and lead me to seek a new degree and career in clinical psychology.

Another important development was experiencing the process of a senior member of our faculty coming to terms with his own homophobia. At first he found it difficult to even say the word "homosexual" (it came out with an emphasis on the first two syllables) when we talked about my teaching and research. I am now happy to report that he can use "gay" and "lesbian" correctly and, more importantly because of his national and international standing, he has altered his perspective on gay parenting. He had always maintained that the best living situation for children was with one father and one mother. Now he advocates: "Two adults who are crazy about the child." Two lesbians or two gay men can be excellent and sufficient parents; one must consider not just the mere structure of families but the quality of the parenting that adults provide for their child. Such parental units need not be one of each sex. He requests that I give him materials that I believe would be helpful for him to better understand issues of homosexuality and to keep him abreast of my research and teaching in the area. He has no problems touching me and interacting with me on an intimate level. I give this example primarily because it illustrates that one can become educated after age 70 about gay and lesbian issues.

Other colleagues in my department at Cornell have also taken the issue of homosexuality in stride. They are relaxed, not startled, by gay issues. One teaches a course and conducts research on relationships; as a matter of protocol she includes gay and lesbian couples. Her presentation of gay issues as one variation on a common theme conveys a very clear message to undergraduates that I believe is not lost. Another colleague has no hesitancy in her social history courses discussing issues of homosexuality, especially female-female attractions. A third faculty member routinely teaches about gay and lesbian families in her family course. With other faculty I can talk openly and candidly about my gay friendships and relationships. This is as it should and must be, but is rarely so in higher education.

Students assure me, however, that this is not the norm at Cornell. Most classes simply do not discuss homosexuality, even when it is an appropriate topic. Some, hopefully few, professors openly bait gay students, raising issues of morality and criminality. I hear horror stories of this classroom behavior from students concerning a very conservative, nationally known professor of government at Cornell. More commonly, the homophobia is subtle, taking the form of silencing issues on homosexuality.

These and many more experiences gave me hope that I could be gay and not lose respect and trust; that I could be gay and influence lives, both by personal interactions and by public policy; and that I could be gay and accrue personal and professional happiness and success. But my naive optimism was soon to suffer a personal but, fortunately, not professional setback.

## TEACHING, RESEARCH, AND PUBLIC SERVICE

In the midst of this coming out process, there was an absolute silence from faculty and administrators at Cornell regarding my sexuality. Perhaps they knew of my transformation, or they knew before I did, or it was just considered a personal issue with little relevance for our professional interactions. I knew that they knew but I did not know the degree to which I had or lacked their support.

The watershed year was the year prior to my tenure review process. The silence was tolerable because I assumed "no news is good news." I did not expect an embrace from my faculty colleagues; mere tolerance would suffice. Thus, when I was called into the department chair's office in the spring of 1982 I was not prepared for the stern, red-in-the-face, very nervous chair I encountered. We had entered the department at the same time and we had grown to be friendly colleagues. Being 30 years my senior, he had taken a rather fatherly attitude toward me. Others in the department felt that I was one of his "boys" and I prospered as a result. Thus, what he was about to say was especially shocking to me. He instructed me, "What you do under the bed covers is your own business but you had better not mention anything about that stuff in your classes." It was apparent even to me in my shocked state that the "that" referred to homosexuality. More calmly than I felt, I asked if he ever mentioned anything about his heterosexuality in his classes. He sputtered and said, "that was irrelevant." I noted that it was an assumption throughout his teaching and course readings that all perspectives were heterosexual. I believe he was not personally prepared for my challenge, in large part because I had never talked back and had always been complacent with him. He gave me additional warnings about how this would ruin my career and my position in the department as I came up for tenure. I was angry, insulted, and hurt. Our relationship essentially ended at that point. We were both too polite for open combat. Despite his outburst the tenure process went smoothly and successfully.

The next two chairs of the department were of the same generation as the homophobic one, but they were entirely of a different mindset. Although they did not feel particularly comfortable discussing homosexuality, nor did they even know how to talk about it, they were in all respects extremely supportive, assuring me tolerance if not outright acceptance of my teaching, research, and public service efforts regarding homosexuality.

Because of this encounter and the explicit instructions that I was not to bring this issue into the workplace, my stubbornness (a genetic heritage from my father) consumed me and I decided to bring homosexuality into the workplace. I realized that I could conduct gay research, teach gay courses, and perform public service for lesbians and gay men.

### Teaching

In the spring of 1984 I taught an upper-level seminar that did not have "homosexuality" in the title but was advertised as such. The 30 students enrolled included, as far as I can guess, 13 straight women, two straight men, nine lesbian and bisexual women, and six gay men. When the course was retitled "Developmental Theory and Research on Homosexuality" and became Cornell's first permanent course on homosexuality, 10 to 12 students enrolled each year, most of whom were straight women oriented toward a career in the helping professions. A few gay males, bisexual women, and lesbians might stop by, but almost never straight men. My sense was that few took the course because the word "homosexuality" appeared on transcripts. The dilemma for me became a political versus a practical one: If I eliminated the "H" word then I could reach more students with the course content. But would this be selling out?

I decided to "sell out" in the spring of 1991. The title of the course was changed to "Sexual Minorities and Human Development." The course was scheduled for a seminar room seating 15, but on the first day of class there were students spilling into the hallways. We went to another classroom, filling it to capacity with 55 students. The most delightful and surprising aspects of the enrollment increase were that fully one-third of the class was students of color and the presence of a significant number of straight men. The 35 women were evenly split between the totally straight and those with some bisexual interest; I have no convincing explanation as to why no lesbians took the course.

I followed this with a second gay-related course, "Sexual Minorities and Clinical Issues."* I limited the course to a dozen students because the class project was to write a book that would help clinicians, human service providers, and policymakers better the lives of lesbians, gay men, and bisexual persons from birth to death. Most students were either gay men or (primarily) straight women. The class dynamics were exceptionally entertaining and delightful—an excellent atmosphere for education.

I would feel less need to teach gay courses if I could be assured that gay content was integrated in all appropriate university courses. This incorporation of gay issues in mainstream courses does not imply that I would be satisfied with no gay courses in a university's curriculum. There is a clear need for courses that focus entirely on aspects of homosexuality or sexual minorities. They are needed because it is a legitimate field of study, it promotes gay scholarship and service, and it helps gay students gain a sense of history and identity.

Occasionally I am asked to give a guest "homosexual" lecture for another Cornell faculty person. This may be an overview lecture in which I do a "Homosexuality 101" in 50 minutes, or a specialized presentation in which I fit homosexuality into a focused discussion, such as giving an evolutionary perspective on homosexuality for a biology class. I appreciate these opportunities to make contact with students and to integrate homosexuality in a diversity of courses. Of course the ideal would be for faculty to integrate homosexual issues throughout their courses or for them to give their own lectures on homosexuality. By agreeing to do their task for them I fear that I give them an easy out. But if I did not give the guest lecture, I feel no one else would speak about the topic, thus contributing to the silencing of homosexuality at Cornell.

*My courses on sexual minorities have been approved without dissension by my department and college. Seminar courses are left to the discretion of faculty members. I have never received an objection to these courses from my department chair or fellow faculty.

My undergraduate advising policy is that at least one-third of my advisees must be minorities, which means students of color or gay students. As a result, I both enjoy advising undergraduate students and making a political statement. At least one-third of our students at Cornell should be minorities. This, of course, is not now the case.

## Research

My first gay research was conducted in 1983–1984, a study using an anonymous questionnaire to gather baseline information on gay male and lesbian identity development. This became my 1990 book, *Gay and Lesbian Youth: Expressions of Identity.* I heard no faculty objections. Departmental faculty generally assumed their usual stance: Whatever I did was fine with them. No one monitored, censored, supported, or particularly cared. This is the norm at Cornell. We are left to our research program, especially after tenure, with either little interference or encouragement. Thus, it is difficult to evaluate whether this new program of gay and lesbian research received any more or less response from my colleagues than my previous straight-related research programs. My sense is that it is somewhat difficult for colleagues to discuss my gay and lesbian research, but this may reflect more their lack of knowledge of the subject matter than a homophobic discomfort with homosexuality in general. Several colleagues are notable exceptions to this. As noted earlier, these same professors, not coincidentally I am sure, include aspects of sexual orientation in their research and teaching.

Both my gay and nongay books have been featured in department and college book display cases and publications. I present my "current research interests" each year to entering graduate students. Few, however, appear to share my research interests so I am on few graduate student dissertation committees. Although there is clearly a high negative correlation between my being out and the number of graduate students who work with me, I would be hard pressed to call this overt homophobia. If there is homophobia present then it is of a more subtle nature, such as their need not to associate with me for fear of career implications. Other factors might account for more of the variance (e.g., my clinical respecialization).

The inverse has also occurred and this is an extremely positive side of being out: Because of my known sexual identity and my research on this topic, four gay and lesbian graduate students have recently sought me out and asked me to be on their graduate committees. In advance I talked at length with them about the potential career repercussions of this decision; in three cases they wanted to move in this direction.

More implicitly, homophobia has been a major problem in three other research areas. First, it has been nearly impossible to receive funding for my gay research, unless I was to make it "AIDS related." Few foundations or agencies, private or governmental, have been the least bit interested. I have discovered the ingenuity of conducting grantless research; perhaps money is overrated.

Second, was the problem I encountered with Cornell's Human Subjects Committee regarding its approval of my initial gay research project. The chair of the committee wrote regarding my submission that "they" were concerned because there was no evidence that I was going to ensure that heterosexual subjects would not be given the questionnaire by "mistake." The implication seemed to be that this would be quite hurtful, psychologically, for such young adults. Apparently, the committee felt that the sexual orientation of straight students is so precarious, and precious, that it can be disrupted if it was to be assumed by someone that it was other than heterosexual. My somewhat sarcastic response was that I would be more than happy to comply if the committee would extend its deep concern to gay male, lesbian, and bisexual students such as to ensure that they would never encounter a questionnaire or would never be asked to participate in research that explicitly or implicitly assumed that they are heterosexual. The committee was not willing to do this, I would like to believe, because its members realized (a) the absurdity of their initial objection and (b) that such precautions have never been and probably could never be taken. Gay students have always been subjected to questionnaires that assumed a heterosexual stance. The committee "graciously" backed off and approved the research design. As far as I know, no straight students suffered debilitating psychological stress or trauma as a result of my research.

Third, has been the invisibility of gay research in mainstream psychology. This is less true in clinical psychology than in my other subdiscipline, developmental psychology. The number of pages devoted to gay research in the child and adolescent journals is minuscule. At the 1990 meeting of the international Society for Research in Adolescence not a single presentation, among literally hundreds of posters, symposiums, and invited addresses focused on lesbian, bisexual, or gay male issues. Textbooks on adolescence usually address "homosexuality" but the discussion is separated in a special, brief section located at the end of the book in a chapter on adolescent sexuality. The usual message is that some homosexual sex is to be expected among early adolescents. The prevalence and causes of homosexuality, societal attitudes toward homosexuality, and the high rates of suicide, substance abuse, and peer harassment among gays are also covered. The reality of actually being a gay adolescent is barely audible. The reader will discover absolutely nothing regarding how a gay youth lives her or his life. "Homosexual" appears to refer more to behavior than to an identity. With this silence a reader could easily assume that a gay adolescent must be just like all other youths in pubertal maturation, cognitions, emotions, family relations, social relationships, culture, identity, moral development, careers, and all of the other topics outlined in most such textbooks. This is simply not the case.*

Another example of the invisibility of gay issues in psychological research is illustrated by a recent article submitted for review in the mainstream and influential journal, *Developmental Psychology.* In this manuscript there is an assumption, which is not an exceptional stance in such research, that the only kind of sexual activity that adolescents engage in is heterosexual. Apparently, according to the measures used, an adolescent only dates, kisses, holds hands, makes-out, and goes all the way with members of the other sex. Interpretations of the results by the authors assumed that none of the randomly sampled adolescents were homosexual or bisexual or had experienced same-sex sexual behavior. Pubertal maturity served to make girls more attractive to boys (yes, sexism); perhaps it also served to make them more attractive to other girls—an alternative explanation not considered by the authors.

I do not blame the editors of the journals or the conference organizers, at least entirely, although their absurd demands that manuscripts include a "representative" or "random" sample of the gay population certainly stifle submissions and acceptances. Conference organizers should engage in "affirmative action" and invite plenary speakers to address issues of sexual identity or homosexuality. Apparently, homosexuality is not yet perceived to be important enough for such invitations to be extended.

There is also a more fundamental concern: With little monetary or institutional support for gay research and the internalized homophobia of potential researchers who fear taking the professional risk of conducting research on gay themes, homosexuality will remain invisible. It is my impression that there are many lesbian, bisexual, and gay male scholars in developmental psychology, but few teach or research in the area of their sexual orientation. Reasons for this are many and are suggested in other chapters of this book.

There is progress, once there are appropriate reminders. Professionals in the field of adolescent development will include the gay issue in books, encyclopedias, and conferences if they are reminded of their obligation—or, if we volunteer to write the chapter or present the paper. I do not believe that my colleagues "want" to be homophobic, but they are nevertheless by their negligence. Perhaps the stereotype of gays prowling on young people is too entrenched for those who teach and research adolescence to feel totally comfortable with adolescent homosexuality. "Forgetting" the topic feels safer.

### Public Service

My third job requirement is public service. This is because as an employee of New York State I have an obligation to transmit my knowledge to others. This is accomplished through publications, both for professional colleagues and the

*If you doubt this, then read *Gay and Lesbian Youth: Expressions of Identity.*

public at large; public speaking, such as lectures or workshops; and consultations, either for private individuals or agencies. For example, I have been asked on several occasions to conduct workshops or present papers on gay issues, such as for Planned Parenthood or therapist conferences. Community-based helping professionals have also asked for recommended readings for parents who discover that they have a gay child or for the adolescents themselves. In this I am fortunate to be associated with Cornell's public service extension division.

I also serve as a resource to the student and local newspapers whenever an issue related to homosexuality emerges on campus. I become their "resident expert," commenting on any gay-related issue, such as whether to ban ROTC from campus because of the military's discrimination against lesbians and gay men, accept an archival collection of human sexuality that contains primarily gay male and lesbian material, or include in the university bylaws an equal protection clause. Because I am gay I am expected to be an expert on all of these issues and to know the "gay line." I will usually comment on these issues, in order to engender discussion and because I feel if I do not then a gay perspective will be omitted altogether.

One advantage to being known as gay on campus is the substantial number of students and staff that I have the opportunity to meet and assist who are gay, lesbian, or bisexual. Many begin by setting appointments to talk about a class paper or speech or to complain about a faculty who has made homophobic comments in class or has assigned homophobic readings. I point out grievance procedures if they choose that route for the latter; for the former, I try to help in whatever way possible to serve as a resource person. Some of these individuals also become personal friends.

## IMAGINARY OR REAL DISCRIMINATION?

Perhaps the best example I have of the ambiguous quality of homophobia in my workplace is the events surrounding my recent promotion from associate to full professor. As scheduled, seven years after my tenure decision, I requested to be considered for promotion. The department's senior faculty strongly supported the promotion and sent it to the college dean, who is mandated to appoint an ad hoc committee of three, two of whom must be from outside the college. The ad hoc committee took a very long time to review (more than six months), returning a negative report, even though they had exactly the same data as my department.

Before this decision was made I went to the associate dean of the college to express reservations I had regarding potential candidates who might be appointed to the ad hoc committee. This is a secretive committee, so I had no access to who was on it. I told the associate dean that there were faculty at Cornell who potentially could be very homophobic. I gave names and reasons; not all faculty have been warmly receptive of my being so out on campus, so visible in the community, and so out in my profession as a representative of Cornell at the state and national levels. He spoke to the dean regarding my concerns.

When a negative decision is returned, the usual procedure is to give this information to the department and for the departmental faculty to make the case on whether they believe the decision should remain positive. In my case, the dean considered both reports, agreed with the department and not the ad hoc committee, and forwarded a positive decision to the university provost.

How the ad hoc committee decided on its negative decision is, of course, unknown to me and, as far as I know, I will never receive feedback regarding the basis of its decision. There may be justified reasons why the decision was negative, but what cannot be ignored, and this is essentially my point, is the possibility that homophobia played some part. Of course, this would be extremely subtle and unknown to me but as a gay man this is an issue that I must continually face and be willing to accept as a possibility as long as I have an academic career. If I stay in this profession, I need heterosexual allies in order to undercut the impact of homphobia on my professional life.

## FIGHTING AND LOSING TO INSTITUTIONAL HOMOPHOBIA: A CASE STUDY

In June 1990, during a casual conversation with a lesbian Cornell staff member, we noted that the Cornell Board of Trustees adopted a non-discrimination on the basis of sexual orientation clause long after many peer institutions had done so. Perhaps gay male, lesbian, and bisexual faculty and staff ought to form a group to pursue ways in which we might be affected by this new "right." I called several other staff and faculty members to gauge their interest. All were enthusiastic.

At the initial planning meeting we agreed to call a general community meeting, if for no other reason than as a symbolic gesture to add our visibility to the Cornell community. A memo was distributed to all 10,000 faculty and staff in the Cornell community, with the financial support of the University. The proposed agenda was:

1 Is there sufficient interest to form such a group?
2 The purpose of the group (e.g., political, social, support).
3 Targeted membership (e.g., heterosexual allies? alumni?).
4 The activities and functions of such a group.
5 Structural and organizational issues.
6 Meeting times and frequency.
7 Name of the group.

By sending the memo from the office of human relations, the university would give those staff and faculty who opposed such a group a place to call to express their objections. Four letters were received. One was an unsigned religiously based argument that condemned any connection of homosexuality with the university. A second letter expressed concern that university facilities were being used for such a meeting. The other two letters expressed questions regarding why they (i.e., straight) had received notification of the meeting.

Nearly 40 attended the first meeting with another 15 individuals calling to say that they were unable to attend because of scheduling problems. The organizing committee welcomed everyone to this historic event, believed to be the first such gathering at Cornell and one of the first nationally.

An open discussion elicited the following topics for future consideration:

- benefits extension to our "spouses"
- an interdisciplinary lesbian/gay studies program
- pressuring the trustees to rid the campus of ROTC
- discrimination and harassment against gays on campus
- networking with faculty and staff at local colleges
- supporting lesbian, gay, and bisexual students in their efforts
- expressing our needs, interpersonal and social, and feeling supported (we are not alone on this large campus)
- act as a "welcoming" committee to help attract other gay staff and faculty to campus
- a forum to address issues that affect our daily life at Cornell, especially to hear our stories and to share knowledge
- career support group
- as a symbolic gesture to make visible our presence on campus
- networking with other gay groups and with heterosexual allies in the community

We decided that a steering committee should be established to help in the initial stages of growth. This steering committee should be fluid, incorporating all those who wanted to contribute their energies and skills. We also decided to include social aspects in our meetings (e.g., have an informal time before meetings), get information to the local media, and develop a mailing list.

A 12-member volunteer steering committee met and suggested that we needed an open meeting in which individuals could tell their stories concerning how they have faced discrimination and harassment at Cornell as a result of their sexual orientation. If there were a consensus on critical issues, then we would invite Cornell administrators to address these issues. The main advantage of this approach was that it would also give us more information about ourselves and would provide an opportunity for us to share with each other our lives at Cornell.

The number of community members who attended the second meeting fell from 40 to 16. Many of the personal experiences shared involved subtle forms of homophobia, such as not receiving invitations for one's partner to social functions. Several staff felt that their jobs might be on the line if their sexual orientation were known; others reported that they were very "out" at work and that as a result had achieved some measure of acceptance and support. They were so out as to be untouchable in terms of possible overt harassment or discrimination. It was recognized that there were many gay faculty and staff who were not present for reasons of fear and uncertainty regarding what our mission and goals were. Discussion also centered on whether we were obliged to educate the Cornell community regarding gay issues. Some believed that it should be our primary mission; others felt that it was not our responsibility to educate straight people. We also discussed the need to keep names confidential in regard to press releases and to work for partner benefits.

At the third meeting eight were present. Questionnaires were sent to the nearly 70 people on the list to survey what they felt we should be doing as an organization. Thirty-one were returned, evenly split between males and females with nine faculty responding. The results were fairly clear:

**1** Our main mission should be to support each other and develop a community.
**2** We should sponsor social activities and be politically involved.
**3** We should give low priority to educating the heterosexual community and support gay and lesbian students.

Major issues we needed to address were to build community networking, fight discrimination, and work for housing, health care, and spousal and insurance benefits. Most gratifying was that 17 of those responding said they would be willing to serve on the steering committee.

But at the fourth meeting six were present. A dish-to-pass dinner was scheduled at my house. Our hope was that a social event would encourage participation. On a beautiful spring day five men and one woman ate together on my front deck for our fifth and last meeting.

A week later I wrote a farewell letter and suggested reasons why the group did not succeed:

> First, there was never really an issue that inspired us to organize. Second, there was a lack of dynamic leadership that would provide the necessary motivation and inspiration. Third, we lead very busy lives and we have many priorities; few of us had this organization as a top priority.

I volunteered to keep the mailing list and encouraged others to take up the mantle. We are still dormant two years later.

It was a good try but one that ultimately failed, except to raise the consciousness of ourselves and the university to our presence. It is important to remember that the vast majority of gay faculty and staff never responded to any of our letters or announcements; only 70 of 10,000 community members volunteered the information that they are lesbian, bisexual, or gay. Ultimately I believe it was subtle homophobia that killed us, part of which is our own internalized version of it. We live in a "respectable" university where keeping quiet and respectability are the norm. The university wants no controversy or embarrassment. We have obliged.

## FADING REMARKS

Homophobia exists in my workplace. The alternative of not being out is not an option, although I was closeted for my first five years at Cornell. I would rerun the fraternity race, reattend the GayPac meetings, and regrant the newspaper interview.

I will never know the extent to which homophobia has played a role in my academic career. For example, I do not know why I have not been appointed to particular committees, not been asked to take particular leadership responsibilities, or not invited to particular social events. There are many reasons why these situations might exist, and some may be legitimate while others may be based on my sexual orientation. These are risks of being out on the job and they can occur on many different levels, from local to international. They are ones that every gay man and woman who enters the field of academic scholarship must face.

From my perspective, many who enter a particular profession face potential discrimination, whether because of class, sex, race, religion, physical ability, or sexual orientation. The real test is what we make of the prejudice, the setbacks, the discrimination. I am not fond of the explicit and implicit homophobia that affects me in my workplace. But I would never return to the closet because the added benefits that I have received from being out overwhelm the negatives. For example, being known as an expert on homosexuality, I have been being asked to do interviews for local papers and radio talk shows, to help students with course papers and talks, to give guest lectures to faculty, and to counsel or advise community members on many issues of homosexuality. I like doing these. If I had not announced my homosexuality, I would probably have been lost in the mainstream of academic scholarship, another of the nameless professors who are alone in believing in their importance. My homosexuality has given me an identity in my profession, which is enjoyable in its own right. It has offered me opportunities to give back to a community that has given me so much. It is my gift from God.

Chapter 15

# Threat, Stress, and Adjustment: Mental Health and the Workplace for Gay and Lesbian Individuals

**John C. Gonsiorek**

## INTRODUCTION

In January 1975, the governing body of the American Psychological Association voted to oppose discrimination against gay and lesbian citizens and to support the 1973 action by the American Psychiatric Association, which removed homosexuality from the official list of mental disorders. While most mental health professionals are aware that the American Psychological Association's resolution supported the de-pathologizing of homosexuality, they are often not aware how far reaching this statement was, particularly pertaining to issues of employment.

The text of the American Psychological Association (1975) statement is as follows:

> The American Psychological Association supports the action taken on 15 December 1973 by the American Psychiatric Association removing homosexuality from the Association's official list of mental disorders. The American Psychological Association therefore adopts the following resolution: Homosexuality per se implies no

> impairment in judgment, stability, reliability, or general social or vocational capabilities.
>
> Regarding discrimination against homosexuals, the American Psychological Association adopts the following resolution concerning their civil and legal rights: The American Psychological Association deplores all public and private discrimination in such areas as employment, housing, public accommodation, and licensing against those who engage in or have engaged in homosexual activities and declares that no burden of proof of such judgment, capacity, or reliability shall be placed upon these individuals greater than that imposed on any other persons.

It has been ascribed to Freud, but is also a commonplace wisdom, that the two most sensitive barometers of mental health and psychological functioning are intimate relationships and work. Beginning with Evelyn Hooker's (1957) study that provided the first empirical evidence that homosexuality per se was not indicative of psychological disturbance, the next two decades witnessed a line of research addressing whether homosexuality per se was indicative of psychological disturbance. As recently reviewed by Gonsiorek (1991), the data overwhelmingly indicate that homosexuality is not indicative of mental illness and theories that continue to purport an illness model of homosexuality represent egregious distortions of scientific information about homosexuality in the service of hatred and bigotry.

In the mid 1970s, following the de-pathologizing of homosexuality, a new wave of lesbian and gay affirmative research developed that attempted to elucidate the psychological processes involved as lesbian and gay individuals navigate the development of a viable identity in a typically hostile society (see Gonsiorek & Rudolph, 1991). Other areas of considerable theoretical and empirical work within emerging lesbian and gay affirmative perspectives include: lesbian and gay relationships (Peplau, 1991); lesbian and gay parenting (Green & Bozett, 1991); the complicated issues of definition of sexual orientation (Gonsiorek & Weinrich, 1991); the social-psychological processes mediating prejudice (Herek, 1991); and the possibly biological nature of sexual orientation (Kirsch & Weinrich, 1991).

Somewhat surprisingly, research and theoretical efforts delineating the role of the workplace in the lives of gay and lesbian individuals have received considerably less attention. Levine and others (Levine, 1979, 1989; Levine & Leonard, 1984; Schneider, 1987) have researched and documented discrimination against lesbian and gay workers. Legal aspects of this discrimination have been described (Hedgpeth, 1979/1980; Knutson, 1979; Rivera, 1991). There are periodic attempts to link occupational choice and sexual orientation (Whitam & Dizon, 1979; Whitam & Mathy, 1986), and equally regular refutations of such a linkage (Murray, 1991; Neuringer, 1989). Etringer, Hillerbrand, and Hetherington (1990) investigated a number of career decision-making factors and found a complex relationship between gender and sexual orientation (e.g., gay males had the most uncertainty about career choice and lesbian women the lowest). It can safely be said that this area is rudimentary in its development, except for the documentation of the existence of discrimination based on sexual orientation, which is robust (see above, and Bell & Weinberg, 1978).

The reasons for this are not difficult to understand. At a time when only two states and a handful of municipalities offer civil rights protection for lesbian and gay citizens, employment discrimination is the variant of bias that can produce the quickest economic ruin. Along with physical assault, common in its own right (see Herek, 1991), job discrimination continues to pose one of the gravest civil rights threat in the lives of lesbian and gay citizens. In such an environment, research poses a significant threat to the research subjects and so is difficult to do. The current volume is therefore a particularly welcome addition to the field.

This chapter explores the application of what has been learned in the past 20 years about the psychological lives of gay and lesbian individuals living in a hostile society to the work environment. Information about the developmental experiences of lesbians and gay men will be applied to the work environment. These developmental events and the unique minority statuses of lesbian and gay individuals will be outlined. Certain themes that have been developed in this discussion will then be applied to the work environment. Case examples will be utilized to illustrate various points.

## UNIQUE DEVELOPMENTAL EVENTS IN THE LIVES OF GAY AND LESBIAN INDIVIDUALS

The empirical basis for the demise of the illness model of homosexuality rested on a considerable body of research, which found that on psychological test instruments measuring psychopathology, gay and lesbian individuals could not be reliably differentiated from their heterosexual counterparts. Therefore, evidence for an intrinsic psychopathology of homosexuality was deemed lacking. Further, evidence for consistent personality variables, pathological or normal, which could reliably characterize homosexual individuals was also lacking.

Epidemiological studies, however, suggest a subset of homosexual individuals who, particularly in adolescence and young adulthood, have a greater than average likelihood of attempted suicide and perhaps chemical abuse (see Gonsiorek, 1991). It is also noteworthy that comparable epidemiological findings are common in other politically or socially oppressed minority groups. The most parsimonious explanation of this data is that while homosexuality per se (or any minority status) is not related to psychopathology, there are particular stresses in the lives of some gay and lesbian individuals that apparently result, particularly in adolescence and young adulthood, in higher rates of certain kinds of symptomatology. It is also noteworthy that by the later years, these differences can no longer be found: gay and lesbian seniors give no evidence of increased rates of symptomatology.

Much of the theorizing during the 1980s regarding homosexual identities focused on creating models that could explain such findings, as well as describe the psychological processes involved in developing a positive and affirmative identity as a lesbian or gay individual.

The initial wave of theories suggested that lesbian and gay individuals progressed through a series of stages typically occurring in adolescence or young adulthood. While these various theories differ in the number and description of stages, they generally describe an initial stage where recognition of same-sex feelings is blocked or denied, progressing through a variety of defensive strategies that may require significant psychological resources for their maintenance. Some individuals maintain these defensive strategies indefinitely, constricting same-sex feelings but also incurring constriction in general functioning and distortions in sense of self. For most individuals, however, a gradual recognition of same-sex interests emerges, often accompanied by a period of crisis in which much of this increased symptomatology occurs. The individual in degrees begins to gradually tolerate the existence of significant same-sex feelings.

This is usually followed by a period of emotional and behavioral experimentation with same-sex sexuality and often an increasing sense of normalcy about same-sex feelings. Some models postulate a second crisis after the dissolution of a first relationship in which a reemergence of ambivalent feelings about being lesbian or gay occurs. As the individual eventually begins to accept his or her same-sex feelings, a sense of identity as gay or lesbian is successfully accepted and integrated as a positive aspect of the self. The models vary on the particulars of these later stages, but most theoreticians note that while the process can be described in discreet stages, it is more unpredictable with stops, starts, and backtracking. In particular, denial of same-sex feelings, or other sorts of psychological defensive strategies to block them, may weave in and out, periodically interrupting this developmental process.

This "coming out" process, as it has been termed, represents a shift in the individual's core sexual identity and can be accompanied by dramatic levels of emotional distress. Individuals may temporarily display virtually any psychiatric symptom, especially if they are without support or adequate information about sexuality. The best predictor of an individual's long-term adjustment during this phase is his or her level of functioning prior to this process, rather than the presenting symptomatology. Most gay and lesbian individuals weather these crises and emerge several years later with minimal or no symptomatology.

As some have noted (see Gonsiorek, 1988), this process for males appears to be more abrupt and likely to be associated with psychiatric symptoms whereas the process for women may be characterized by greater fluidity and ambiguity. It may well be the case that differences in the pacing of identity development are influenced by sex role socialization. Because women are allowed a wider range of behavioral and emotional interactions with other women, they may experience emerging sexual and emotional intimacy as "mere friendship." Because men are confined to more narrow patterns of expression, longing for emotional and physical contact with other males is apt to be perceived as clearly "homosexual."

Also consistent with traditional sex role socialization, males are prone to sexualizing distress during the coming out process and women appear more likely to respond with reflection and self-absorption. For example, Sears (1989) noted that "important differences among males and females and the meanings constructed around these sexual feelings and experiences are evident. Lesbian participants, more often than gay men, attached emotional-romantic meaning to same-sex relationships prior to engaging in homosexual behavior, defined the term homosexual in an emotional romantic context, and denied the legitimacy of their own sexual feelings. . . . Some scholars have concluded that lesbians have more in common with heterosexual women than with gay men" (p. 437). One European theoretician summarized the idea in the following way: "The psychological discourse on lesbian sexuality differs from the one about gay male sexuality. It is of a more exploratory nature" (Schippers, 1990, p. 14).

Probably the most psychologically rich model was articulated by Malyon (1981, 1982a, 1982b). Malyon theorized that gay and lesbian persons, like heterosexuals, are raised with culturally sanctioned anti-homosexual biases. Such biases mobilize other psychological processes that extend beyond the development of prejudice. Children who will eventually be bisexual or homosexual often develop an awareness of being different at an early age. They may not understand the sexual nature or precise meaning of their differentness but soon learn it is regarded negatively. As these individuals develop and mature, they reach a fuller understanding of the nature of this difference and the considerable negative societal reaction to it. These negative feelings may be incorporated into the self-image, resulting in varying degrees of internalized homophobia. Negative feelings about one's sexual orientation may be overgeneralized to encompass the entire self. The effects of this may range from a mild tendency toward self-doubt in the face of prejudice to overt self-hatred and self-destructive behavior. Gonsiorek and Rudolph (1991) further amplified and refined these ideas within a self-psychology perspective (see also Gonsiorek, 1988; Savin-Williams, this volume).

It should also be noted that these generalizations are more or less true of any single individual depending on the flexibility of his or her sex role and other aspects of personality structure and personal history. Perhaps most importantly, one would expect such developmental events to be highly sensitive to cultural, class, socioeconomic, racial, and ethnic variation. In fact, the 1980s witnessed considerable theoretical development in applying this identity development model to racially and ethnically diverse populations (see Gonsiorek, 1991).

This developmental perspective stresses the relationship between the individual, social forces, and sense of self. The entire developmental process and outcomes within the sense of self can vary greatly as the social forces that shape them vary. For example, both the nature of homophobia and concepts of maleness and femaleness can vary along socioeconomic, educational, class, racial, and ethnic lines. For nonwhite, non-English speaking groups, the process of developing a gay and lesbian identity can be considerably more complicated.

Many theoreticians speak of double or triple minority statuses that must be accommodated by gay and lesbian individuals from different racial and ethnic backgrounds. For example, Gock (1985) describes the perceived choice of having to identify with the homosexual community "and so address expression of intimacy" versus the ethnic minority community "and so retain cultural groundedness." Morales (1983) describes this as "a conflict of allegiance" and offers a four-stage model on how ethnic lesbian and gay individuals resolve conflicts of multiple identities. Espin (1987) synthesized a number of models in her attempt to describe the psychological processes involved in integrating various disparaged identities. The task for such individuals is quite complicated; namely the integration of multiple minority identities in a context where all are disparaged and in which one minority group typically disparages the others.

Another important concept is that the manifestations of internalized homophobia can be expressed in a variety of ways. Overt manifestations may include individuals consciously viewing themselves as evil, second class, or inferior on account of their homosexuality. Such individuals may engage in substance abuse or other self-destructive or abusive behaviors. However, because overt internalized homophobia is so psychologically painful and destabilizing, it is less prevalent than covert forms. Few persons who have not been seriously damaged by earlier childhood events can tolerate such conscious self-deprecation.

Covert forms of internalized homophobia are often the most common. Such individuals may appear to accept themselves and their same-sex orientation, but sabotage their own lives in a variety of subtle ways. For example, such individuals may abandon career or educational goals with the excuse that external bigotry will keep them from their objectives. Internalized homophobia can also take the form of excessively tolerating discriminatory or abusive behavior from others. When gay and lesbian persons are met with bigotry and oppression, as they invariably are, they are forced to make a choice. Neutrality is not among the options. To say no, either behaviorally or symbolically, is self-affirming; to tolerate second-class status is to, in effect, affirm a view of oneself as inferior.

The coming out process is an additional developmental event in the lives of lesbian and gay individuals, superimposed on whatever psychological and developmental processes are particular to the individual. In adulthood, there are other processes in later periods that are relatively unique to lives of gay and lesbian persons. Chief among these is the management of disclosure. As will be described later, the management of disclosure has special significance for gay and lesbian individuals because gay and lesbian people are the only minority group whose disclosure of their minority status is optional and not thrust on them. Therefore management of a full range of options concerning disclosure is required, often demanding considerable psychological sophistication and well-tuned reality testing. In other words, gay and lesbian persons must develop the skills to perform a complex "cost-benefit analysis" when faced with external bigotry and oppression. They can err by not standing up for themselves and thereby undermining their sense of self-worth; or they can err by allowing themselves to be provoked into rash ill-advised disclosure, also with negative consequences.

Similarly, the degree of self-disclosure will determine the extent and depth of one's support system as a gay or lesbian individual. Disclosing insufficiently incurs a constriction of one's potential social support system. Disclosing too much exposes oneself to a greater degree of harshness and hostility from the external disparaging world. As can be easily imagined, individuals who have a significant degree of internalized homophobia have a difficult time with this process. Overtly, such individuals may view themselves as inferior and not deserving of an adequate support system. More subtly, such individuals may set themselves up for rejection by poorly planned and impulsive disclosure in an environment that is likely to produce a harsh response. These ideas will be further developed later in this chapter.

## THE UNIQUE MINORITY STATUS OF GAY AND LESBIAN INDIVIDUALS

As alluded to earlier, gay and lesbian individuals have unique features in their minority status. Unlike racial and ethnic minorities, sexual orientation is a minority status whose disclosure is optional, except perhaps in the most gender atypical individuals, who are a minority of gay and lesbian individuals. Even in this group, management of gender atypical behavior is usually a skill that one can usually acquire. Racial and ethnic minorities typically have little choice in disclosure: it is made for them by appearance.

While this reduction in options can initially expose the racial and ethnic minority individual to the full force of bigotry and ostracism, later consequences can be perhaps ameliorating. The predictability of prejudice can create cohesive bonds among racial and ethnic individuals whose inherent diversity might otherwise impair cohesion. Psychologically, the range of options is simplified. For racial and ethnic minority individuals, the prejudice is there, and it will be directed toward them: the main options then revolve around how best to respond. With gay and lesbian individuals, disclosure of minority status usually is optional; the choices are more complex. One need not necessarily disclose: the psychological task involves not only considering a range of responses should disclosure occur, but also weighing the pros and cons of nondisclosure.

Further, cohesion and unification are more elusive as one's minority status peers may choose not to disclose and may not be available as support.

A second crucial feature is that the economic oppression that is often the core of bigotry toward racial and ethnic minorities is considerably less predictable with gay and lesbian individuals. While gay and lesbian individuals can be and are economically devastated by prejudice, many are not. Lesbian women face consistent economic oppression primarily because they are women, not lesbians. Within gay and lesbian communities then, male-female differences can become noteworthy around economic issues. Gay white males whose minority status is not known can enjoy the most enfranchised status in the economic hierarchy whereas lesbians will be discriminated against as women, thus dividing gay men and lesbians on an economic basis. Nonwhite lesbians and gay men face economic and other discrimination due to color, creating further divisions in gay and lesbian communities. Predictable economic discrimination can be a powerful unifying force, one lacking in the economically divided (along gender and color lines) gay and lesbian communities where optional disclosure, with its variable overt discrimination, further weakens cohesion.

It is interesting to speculate how these factors play out with religious minorities. Religious minorities can be construed as having a quasi-optional minority status. One could remain undisclosed although this usually interferes with the ability to practice one's faith, and runs counter to group pride, perhaps evangelizing requirements, and pressures to bear witness. It is perhaps not surprising in light of this analysis that many religious minorities such as Seventh Day Adventists, Mormons, and Jews as a group highly value ambition, economic success, careers, and education. One might conclude that such groups correctly recognize that economic bias can be the most debilitating. Group norms then serve to ameliorate potential economic deprivation.

A final and perhaps the most crucial difference is that gay and lesbian individuals are the only minority status organized horizontally, not vertically. In other words, it is a minority status that is not intergenerational. Racial and ethnic minority individuals are born into racial and ethnic minority families. Religious minorities are often born into religious minority families or if they convert, it is often into a community where family and social support are highly valued and well developed. Gay and lesbian individuals are born into heterosexual families and are raised with heterosexual norms. Therefore, the ameliorating influence that parents, grandparents, and other relatives and peer communities can have in training the individual to handle the strains of minority status, inculcate group norms, and provide support are not only absent but frequently replaced by lack of understanding, confusion, and at times outright rejection by one's family and original community.

It is not surprising, therefore, to observe that attempts by gay and lesbian communities to create intergenerational bonds have met with the most irrational reactions. The majority culture correctly intuits that should intergenerational bonds develop within the gay and lesbian communities, such communities would be greatly strengthened. For example, there has been great resistance to gay and lesbian individuals being parents and perhaps creating the possibility of having a support system in the next generation, albeit one that would be no more gay and lesbian than the general population, but deeply bonded nonetheless. Attempts by the gay and lesbian communities to provide outreach and services for gay and lesbian adolescents typically are met with the most violent reactions, and charges of pederasty.

The net effect of these unique features of gay and lesbian minority status is that gay and lesbian individuals may appear on the surface to have a "better deal" than other minority groups. They can "choose" to disclose or not to disclose, which to other minorities may seem like a luxury. Overt economic oppression is either highly inconsistent, in the case of gay males; or along gender lines in the case of lesbian women, who are thereby afforded some solidarity and comradeship with women in general; or along racial/ethnic lines.

Underneath these apparent "advantages," there are some distinct disadvantages. The lack of intergenerational support and transmission of community wisdom in handling the minority status is lacking and the "option" of disclosure not only produces a lack of cohesion, but also introduces levels of complexity to the psychological decision-making process, which can balance and at times outweigh the "luxury" of having the option of disclosure.

The intent of this discussion is not to suggest that individuals of different minority statuses have a better or worse deal on account of that minority status. Rather, different minority statuses experience different combinations of assets and liabilities in dealing with the oppressive forces arrayed against them. Gay and lesbian individuals are faced with a variety of factors in their minority status that can be easily overlooked because they are atypical. Finally, it is important to recognize, with any minority group member, regardless of the nature of the status, the particular acuity of oppression varies from individual to individual and across time for the same individual. Handling one's minority status, or minority statuses in those individuals who have multiple statuses, is a moving target as the nature and severity of a disparaging environment change over time, and as one's life experience in handling this disparagement changes one over time.

It is interesting to note how the gay and lesbian communities have developed since the beginnings of gay and lesbian liberation in the early 1970s, when bar and other "entertainment" milieu, with a scattering of political organizations, were virtually the only organized social structures available. Lesbian and gay religious organizations have recently been among the fastest growing institutions in the gay and lesbian communities. Not far behind has been the development of gay and lesbian business and athletic organizations. While there has been little organized discourse on the unique features of lesbian and gay minority statuses among lesbian and gay individuals, it is noteworthy that gay and lesbian communities appear to have correctly intuited which institutional structures within the community might best ameliorate the particular stresses inherent in gay and lesbian minority statuses.

As a rule, religious organizations tend to value cohesion, and personal and institutional support for their members; and regardless of theological differences advocate mutuality, cooperation, and justice. Lesbian and gay business networks are often overtly organized around the principle of pooling expertise and providing support to lesbian and gay individuals facing the unique stresses in their various job environments; and in creating economic (and thereby political) clout via community cohesion. Sports organizations tend to facilitate cohesion, teamwork, management of difference, and often evolve social relationships.

Such developments are noteworthy because they are counterintuitive, given the hostile role religion has usually played in the lives of gay and lesbian individuals; the stereotypical incongruity between sports and homosexuality, especially for males; and the unfriendliness of the corporate world toward gay and lesbian individuals. One would not expect religious belief, sports, and business affiliation to be organizing principles for the gay and lesbian communities; one might have predicted instead that political clubs of various persuasions would be expected. However, such organizations with their focused goal orientation, minimal personal support, and lesser norm building for their members would not serve the psychological needs of the nascent gay and lesbian communities at this point in time.

## DILEMMAS FACING GAY AND LESBIAN INDIVIDUALS IN THE WORKPLACE AND THEIR PSYCHOLOGICAL RAMIFICATIONS

In this section, case examples are used to illustrate common psycho-social dilemmas in the work lives of lesbian and gay people. These examples are drawn from the author's clinical practice and consultations to other mental health professionals. Almost none of these individuals sought mental health services presenting with vocational problems. These problems newly developed on the job while the person was focusing on other concerns; or had occurred previously and were brought up after other initial complaints had been handled. It is not clear what this reflects; perhaps a covert expectation that trouble in the work environment is to be expected for lesbian and gay citizens.

### The Reality of External Oppression

Sexual orientation is one of the last minority statuses in which those who are bigoted feel no compunction about expressing such bigotry. Although there has been some development of a sense that homophobia, like racism, sexism, and other variants of prejudice are inappropriate, this is often confined to more educated or worldly circles. In the job environments of most U.S. citizens, homophobic bigotry remains a form of hatred with the least constraints on it. This is particularly true in those bigoted individuals who believe themselves to have a religious authority in support of their beliefs, who may believe that expression of such bigotry is not only a right but an obligation.

More common, perhaps, is simple ignorance and misunderstanding. For example, as gay and lesbian relationships are less understood and saddled with misinformation, even a worker who is known to be lesbian or gay faces an uphill battle discussing with coworkers mundane events. Questions about the basic nature of a same-sex relationship are raised that have no counterpart in heterosexual individuals.

### Case Example A

Marian had been at her job in the accounting section of a large corporation for some months. Early in her time there she let it be known in a low key way she was lesbian. Other than a few coworkers occasionally referencing that they had been following with interest a local lesbian custody case that was very much in the news, there was little discussion or acknowledgment of her as lesbian. One day at lunch, Marian decided to casually talk about a canoe trip she and her lover made over the weekend, as her coworkers were talking about their weekend activities. Conversation abruptly came to a halt, until one of the more extroverted individuals began asking Marian questions along the lines of who did the cooking in the relationship, fixed the car, etc. She came away from the situation exhausted, feeling as though she were an alien species being examined under a microscope.

It can be difficult for nonminority individuals to appreciate how fatiguing and demoralizing it can be to have to explain oneself to others at unpredictable times and circumstances. It can be difficult for minority individuals to accurately judge if they are being "hypersensitive," and reading situations accurately.

External oppression remains a common reality for gay and lesbian individuals. The vast majority of U.S. citizens who happen to be gay or lesbian, do not have civil rights protection unless they live in Massachusetts, Wisconsin, or a handful of municipalities that have degrees of employment protection varying from extensive to minimal.

### Case Example B

Peter had worked for more than 12 years in the technical end of a high-tech firm since his graduation from college. His work was respected, and his technical skills were such that the most difficult challenges were often assigned to him. His sexuality was not generally known at work although he had disclosed his sexual orientation to a few close coworkers. His section was reorganized and a new manager was assigned who was a fundamentalist Christian. Through the office grapevine, this manager discovered Peter's homosexuality, and immediately fired him, stating that it was an infringement of his civil rights and freedom of religion to have to work with a pervert.

Peter hired an attorney and attempted to redress the situation. He found that his personnel file had a number of recent entries by this manager claiming that Peter was insubordinate. The corporation, which had awarded Peter a number of commendations and salary increases because of the quality of his work, responded to his legal action by stating that the only thing they would be willing to do would be to not mention "insubordinate behavior" in future letters of reference on account of his previously exemplary work. Not a single coworker from the 12 years of employment was willing to assist Peter. Living in a municipality with no gay rights protection, he had no alternative but to seek employment elsewhere.

Increasingly, however, external homophobia is more subtle. The following example also illustrates the tensions of managing multiple disparaged identities for a racial minority gay male.

### Case Example C

Ted was an openly gay, extroverted, and energetic African-American gay male working in the claims section of a large insurance company. Over his six years at the company, they had transformed from a sleepy, traditional insurance vendor, to one of the more aggressive and innovative managed care companies in the area. Ted responded to these challenges enthusiastically and received a number of promotions, eventually becoming manager of a section. One of his new subordinates was an individual notorious for his bigotry and unabashed expression of it. When Ted's promotion was announced at a staff meeting, this individual loudly proclaimed, "I won't be taking orders from that cocksucker," which was met with nervous laughter. In the days following, Ted filed a complaint with personnel about this individual.

After a few weeks the complaint had gone nowhere. Ted requested a meeting with his immediate supervisor and personnel officials, in which he was told he was being hypersensitive and was perhaps not cut out for this level of management. Discouraged, Ted attempted to make the best of it. A few weeks later, when giving feedback to this individual as well as a number of others, Ted was met with a comment from this person, "What do you expect from a dumb nigger?" The corporation's response to this remark was to immediately fire the individual. Although Ted was relieved, he attempted to point out to the director of personnel the disparity in their view of these two comments. He was privately told by the director of personnel, who was also African-American, that he had obviously grown insensitive to "real nature" of racism and dismissed his concerns. Interestingly, the company involved had a written policy preventing discrimination on the basis of race and ethnicity, as well as sexual orientation.

It is important to note that a heterocentric perspective may appear on the surface to be more benign than a virulently homophobic one. In terms of its pragmatic effects, however, a perspective that values only heterosexual couples may be as discriminatory as one that actively disparages homosexual individuals.

### Case Example D

Marjorie worked in the legal department of a large corporation. Because her undergraduate background was in a technical area similar to one in which the corporation specialized, she began to advance in the corporate structure beyond the confines of being an attorney. She did not disclose she was lesbian. At work, her "being single" in the mind of her employer did not appear to pose a problem until she received a promotion to assistant vice president of a division within the corporation. Comments began to be increasingly made from her peers and superiors that someone "of her stature" needed to demonstrate the "stability" that family life entailed. It began to be apparent to her that much of the corporate entertainment with potential clients involved spouse pairs and there was little room for "single" executives.

In line for another promotion, she was officially given the reason when she did not receive it, that she had not developed an adequate experience base in her current position and "needed to mature" in the position for another year or two before her next promotion. She was told privately that until she was married, she would be unable to fulfill the obligations of interacting with corporate clients. Her supervisor told her that her being a woman was no impediment and that other corporations had found that other female executives who entertained with their husbands were just as effective as male executives who entertained with their wives. After considering the situation for some months, Marjorie informed her immediate superior that she was lesbian and that she was willing to do the required corporate entertainment with her long-term female spouse or single, whatever the corporation wished. She was assured that being lesbian would pose no barriers to further advancement.

She found over the ensuing years, however, that she was offered only lateral moves and eventually decided to transfer to a less prestigious division that required less corporate entertainment. It became clear to her that not only was heterosexual marriage a requirement for advancement beyond a certain level in the corporation, but also that "stable" heterosexual marriage was required. She ran into a number of peers who reported quite bitterly that following their divorces, they seemed to be frozen in terms of advancement.

These case examples pose challenges for gay and lesbian individuals in ascertaining the way discrimination works and in making an appropriate response. This task becomes complicated for those individuals who have significant residuals of internalized homophobia. Both overt and subtle expressions of homophobia or heterosexism can psychologically resonate for them in a way that diminishes their ability to respond effectively and act in their own best interests.

Another source of problems is the propensity of such situations to exacerbate relationship conflicts. Gay and lesbian couples often differ on the degree to which each member of the couple has disclosed in the work environment. This may be because of attitudinal differences between the two about disclosure; or realistic dangers in different job environments. For example, a self-employed dentist may have a lesser risk of problems in employment with disclosure than an individual who works as an elementary school teacher in a conservative school district. Tensions within lesbian and gay couples can sometimes be sparked or worsened when one member of the couple is significantly more or less politicized around disclosure than the other; or when other realistic concerns like financial security become entwined with decisions about disclosure. This can create a situation where even in the home environment, the gay and lesbian employee does not get full support of his or her spouse but instead finds the challenges at work creating challenges in the relationship.

As mentioned above, management of disclosure is an extra developmental event in the lives of gay and lesbian adults. When to disclose, to whom to disclose, how and under what circumstances, as well as when not to disclose, are a series of skills that every gay and lesbian person is challenged to master. This process varies over time: as the nature of the external environment changes, the rules of disclosure management also change. In fact, perhaps the cardinal rule of effective disclosure management is to recognize that one solution will not suffice for all situations. While disclosure management can be done well, there always exists a "wild-card" element in it, to the extent that there will always be individuals to whom one discloses, who, for reasons that cannot be anticipated, respond in ways that were not expected. Acknowledgment of this "wild-card" element is part of the skill of disclosure management.

This discussion has so far focused on effective responses in the context of a particular job. Even less predictable are the effects of disclosure on long-range career options. Perhaps the only thing that is predictable is that some degree of career restriction and diminishment of choice is likely for most gay and lesbian people in the current socio-political climate.

Disclosure management can present another difficulty, what might be called a heart versus head problem. Some individuals may develop well-honed skills at disclosure management; in a rational, objective sense they can correctly ascertain with a high level of success what responses will be in their objective "best interests." However, particularly as individuals age, they may become more cognizant of the subtle emotional price tags of aspects of disclosure management, even when nondisclosure is the "right" (i.e., rational), thing to do.

### Case Example E

Arthur was a middle-aged professor in a large, religiously affiliated college. A number of faculty and administration knew he was gay and this posed no problem for them, with the understanding that Arthur kept it "discreet." To other gay and lesbian faculty and staff, Arthur was a master at management disclosure. He weathered attacks from both conservative colleagues who tried to use his homosexuality against him, and radical gay liberation students who tried to ''out'' him, with grace and equanimity. He had become chairperson of his department and achieved national prominence in his field.

When a high-ranking position in the administration of the college became vacant, Arthur was asked in a public forum to apply for the position by a conservative member of the clergy who had earlier been one of his opponents. The general consensus was that this was a genuine offer based on respect for Arthur's competence. To everyone's surprise, Arthur not only did not apply for the position, but also made a public statement that he could not apply for the position in the governance of an institution so homophobic and sexist as this, that he preferred to be a ''free agent for institutional change,'' and so he publicly came out.

Arthur had been talking for some years to colleagues about his growing dissatisfaction with the compromises he had made. Most of his colleagues dismissed his concerns as academic or a harmless crisis of middle age, but to Arthur they ran very deep. He befriended a number of students and faculty over the years, some of whom were gay or lesbian and had suffered terribly as a result of the church's sexism and intolerance of homosexuality. The more Arthur acquired success, the more discordant his role in a religious institution became. He considered this dilemma in his usual cautious way and recognized that while as a tenured professor he could not be fired, he could certainly be frozen into oblivion should he come out publicly. He did so anyway.

For some people, and at some points in life, issues of value and meaning can be more important than ''objective success.'' In a sense, the most developed kind of disclosure management also involves knowing when deciding with the head should give way to deciding with the heart.

## Misinterpretation of Other Situations as External Homophobia

Other issues may mimic externalized homophobia. Effective disclosure management involves picking one's fights very carefully; otherwise, exhaustion and ensuing impaired judgment can result. It is particularly important to differentiate what is *not* external homophobia.

### Case Example F

Kate was new in her nursing position. She had been hired with much anticipation as she had completed her master's training in a new and innovative area, at a prestigious university. The hospital had made her an attractive offer and seemed welcoming to her. She had been open to the hiring committee that she was lesbian. It appeared to her that this was not a problem for them. They seemed to welcome diversity on the staff. Kate was then surprised when during one of the first social events among staff, one of her colleagues who had been on the hiring committee expounded, rather pointedly it seemed to Kate, that she was ''fed up'' with how selfish childless people were.

At first, Kate did not take the comment personally but this individual repeatedly came back to the subject in a way that Kate felt was directed at her. As she was the only person without children and the only lesbian on the unit, she began to be concerned that the work environment might be homophobic. She spoke to another of the hiring committee members, who encouraged her to directly confront the colleague in question and attempt to resolve the matter. Kate did this and found there was a serious issue here, but not the one she thought. The colleague in question, while genuinely welcoming of Kate, had also become jealous because the demands of childrearing had made it impossible for her to obtain a master's degree. While this individual had genuinely looked forward to professional interactions with Kate, she found herself becoming increasingly jealous of Kate's skills and confidence. Further, the colleague had a sister who was childless with whom the colleague had a longstanding competitive relationship. This sibling received a promotion in a similar health care field around the same time Kate was hired. Kate and the colleague reached an understanding and their relationship warmed appreciably.

It is important for gay and lesbian individuals to realize that, even among heterosexuals, having or not having children creates differences in life circumstances that can be as big or greater a factor than sexual orientation. It is also important for heterosexual individuals to realize that being lesbian or gay only peripherally predicts whether one is or has been a parent. Many lesbian individuals, and to a lesser extent gay males, have been heterosexually married with children. Other gay and lesbian individuals, particularly the latter, choose to have their own children outside a heterosexual marriage. Finally, increasing numbers of lesbian and gay persons desire, for concerns related to generativity and others, to have children in their lives and do so through adoption, foster parenting, becoming godparents, and comparable activities. Simply stated, individuals of various sexual orientations would do well to make as few assumptions about each other as possible, not only regarding childlessness but also other variables.

Work environments that are competitive, or even noncompetitive environments during tough economic times, can create tensions between staff in which some individuals may say or do things to hurt rather than because they ardently believe them. In a culture that condones and facilitates sexism, racism, homophobia, class bias, and religious and other bigotries, individuals with positive feelings toward each other can, under stressful circumstances, lash out through the vehicle of such culturally sanctioned prejudices. In other words, not every prejudicial remark or action represents a permanent attitudinal disposition.

The behavior remains nonetheless harmful to the targeted individual. Intentionality is not required for bigotry and ignorance to exist and to wound. On the other hand, the reality of bigotry and its damage does not necessarily predict intentionality, long-term attitude, or willingness and ability to change.

### Manifestations of Internalized Homophobia

As discussed earlier, most gay and lesbian individuals to some extent internalize the societal denigration of homosexual individuals. Particularly in times of high external oppression, there are also individuals who had especially oppressive experiences regarding their sexual orientation or who have had earlier assaults to their self-esteem not related to sexual orientation (see Gonsiorek & Rudolph, 1991). This internalized homophobia can be played out in the work environment.

#### Case Example G

Bill was an openly gay graduate student who was offered a long sought after fellowship for study abroad with a prestigious expert in his field. His graduate department was supportive of this period of study abroad and facilitated the integration of this two-year fellowship with his graduate studies. The finances of the fellowship were generous and everything appeared conducive. Inexplicably, Bill announced to his department chair that he was having second thoughts about going. He offered a weak excuse that it might be "more hassle than it was worth" to spend two years abroad. He made a comment in passing to his advisor, "What's a faggot like me going to do in that high class place?"

The advisor persuaded Bill to accept the offer, which was to begin in five months, and to go into therapy before he left. The advisor pointed out to Bill his observation that whenever he had a major success, he seemed to get down on himself, especially regarding his sexuality. He persuaded Bill to accept the offer with the understanding that if he still felt like not going at the end of the five months, he would respect that.

In most cases, internalized homophobia is not quite as transparent.

#### Case Example H

Chris was known as one of the best troubleshooters with technical equipment in the utility where she worked. She was not promoted, however, because of excessive sick leave for back problems. A perceptive physician noted that periodically Chris became perfectionistic about her work and did not leave until a particular piece of equipment was running to her satisfaction. Rather than wait until the next day when coworkers could assist her with the project, she would tackle it alone after hours, frequently lifting machinery, which was meant to be managed by two or three people, by herself. As a result, she had irritated a disk and periodically aggravated this problem by the same behavior, despite competent instruction by the physician on ways to avoid further injury. When she did sustain a back injury, she became self-denigrating at her "weakness." When she returned to work it was with the resolve to work harder.

The physician made a referral for a psychological evaluation, which suggested that Chris, who was closeted about being lesbian, socially isolated, and uncomfortable with her sexual orientation, also had many unresolved issues about physical abuse in her family and significant disturbances in her self-esteem.

## Sexual Harassment of Gay and Lesbian Individuals

Sexual harassment is painful and disorienting. Lesbian and gay victims of harassment represent some unique features. If the harassment is heterosexual in nature, this quality may make it feel especially intrusive or disorienting. For those individuals who have not disclosed in the work environment, they may feel conflicted if they believe that disclosing their sexual orientation might discourage this harassment. Ironically, this belief is not even always accurate. In some situations, individuals who are out may receive sexual harassment specifically on that account due to homophobia, a belief that heterosexual sex will cure them, or perception that because the individual is lesbian or gay, the harassment ''doesn't really count and is only fun.''

For some bigoted individuals, knowledge that person is lesbian or gay appears to incite higher degrees of sexual harassment based on the myth that lesbian women ''really just haven't had good sex with the right man yet'' or that gay men eagerly wish the body of any heterosexual man who offered it. It should be noted that men and women can be targets of sexual harassment, from either men or women, and regardless of the sexual orientation of the harasser.

### Case Example I

A supervisor in a factory assembly line was well known for his propensity for inappropriate sexual innuendo toward attractive college-age males. However, as he was married, ''a family man,'' and active in his church, he would shrug off the situations as ''horsing around'' when challenged. When the supervisor ascertained that younger males happened to be gay, he was particularly rapacious and would badger and sexually harass such men to the point of physical assault. He silenced his victims with threats of disclosure, a powerful threat in that conservative community.

### Case Example J

Karla was the first woman to work on the road maintenance crew of a semirural/semisuburban county outside a major metropolitan area. There was considerable sexual innuendo from some male coworkers. She disclosed to a number of them that she was lesbian in an attempt to discourage them from asking her on dates. This had the effect of increasing the frequency and the virulence of their sexual harassment. When she complained to a supervisor, she was told she was imagining things because ''what would any sane man want with a dyke?''

### Case Example K

Paul was a quiet and unassuming gay man who was known as a good listener. He had been recently hired by a small architectural firm. His supervisor was a divorced woman, about 15 years his senior, to whom he disclosed his homosexuality. His supervisor befriended him and began to confide in him her impressions, often not complimentary, of other employees. Paul was uncomfortable with this but valued her friendship and felt she was mentoring him, which she did in many substantive ways. At one point, Paul, in response to her hints, volunteered to babysit her children one evening. Requests to babysit became frequent as did increasing requests that he spend the night the times he did babysit. As was typical for him, he had a difficult time saying no, even though he was increasingly uncomfortable with the situation.

Eventually, his supervisor suggested he share a bed with her when he slept over after babysitting. Paul became very upset at this and spoke to the owner of the firm. Paul was then fired for trying to sexually compromise the supervisor.

Sexist assumptions that sexual harassment is only something men do can interact with homophobia, as above. Sexual harassment and external homophobia can interact in complicated ways.

### Case Example L

John was a middle-aged man who worked as a manager in a family owned business in a small town. While out with this friends and participating in gay social life in a nearby city, he was closeted at work. One of his heterosexually married female employees saw him when they were both at a gay bar in a nearby city and she assured him that it made no difference to her. A few months later, John was forced to fire this employee when it was discovered she embezzled money from the business. She then sued the company and claimed that John had sexually harassed her and promised her the money as a reward for sexual favors.

While the family owning the business believed John in the matter, his relationship with them became so strained that he eventually left the position. The female employee's attorney had privately stated to John in the hallway during one of the depositions, "Well, I guess we have you over the barrel on this one, don't we?" The employee herself told John that if he made any attempt to block the settlement offered by the company, she would have him "run out of town for being queer."

Ironically, disclosure of sexual orientation by the gay and lesbian individual in such situations, which might logically strengthen their cases, often has the effect of backfiring by reducing their credibility and rendering them further suspect.

## SUGGESTIONS

### Gay and Lesbian Citizens Must Negotiate Complicated Challenges

Such challenges take the forms of: variable and unpredictable levels of external bigotry, psychological consequences of growing up in a disparaging society in the form of internalized homophobia, and issues that can occasionally mimic the above. These tasks are difficult enough for any disparaged minority groups; however, without the protection afforded by civil rights legislation, gay and lesbian citizens are at an enormous disadvantage. Civil rights protection in the areas of employment, housing, public accommodations, and the like is an essential step in normalizing the work environment for gay and lesbian citizens. To the extent that these issues become a mental health concern for lesbian and gay citizens, this is due primarily to inequity in public policy.

### Disclosure Management Is an Important Skill for All Gay and Lesbian Individuals, Particularly in the Work Environment

It is not useful to conceptualize this as a "mental health problem" but rather a developmental process requiring pragmatic skills that can be behaviorally mastered, akin to assertiveness training, public speaking skills, and the like. Concepts of external and internal homophobia can be useful in understanding the interplay between a disparaging society and disparaged gay and lesbian citizens.

It is important, however, that this concept not be used to repathologize gay and lesbian individuals. To state that external homophobia mobilizes whatever degree of internal homophobia exists in the gay or lesbian person is a truism and ultimately as trivial as stating that any individual has some areas of conflict stemming from their family of origin. In both situations, for some people this can become a mental health problem. For most people it is not, but is rather an existential challenge to be mastered.

### Perhaps the Greatest Specific Challenge Facing the Lesbian and Gay Communities at This Point in History Is the Development of Cross-Generational Supportive Institutions

The current generation of lesbian and gay citizens entering middle age is the first to have articulated the value of disclosure and to have en masse attempted to lead lives as openly gay and lesbian. Much trial and error learning and some occasional genuine wisdom have been accrued. It is the right, responsibility, and obligation of gay and lesbian communities to create institutions to transmit this learning to, and to support, gay and lesbian youth.

### Taking the Broadest Perspective, the Overall Challenge Facing Gay and Lesbian Communities Is to Create and Maintain an Ethical Place in Society

Work and relationships are the main vehicles in which this occurs. This transition from ostracism and disparagement to integration and productivity will, as with comparable situations, be accompanied by mistakes on the part of both gay and lesbian and heterosexual individuals. Minority and majority status individuals are challenged to meet these tensions with as much equanimity and humanity as they are capable of, and not to wallow in facile and familiar stereotypes or quick judgments about the other. For majority communities, this is a question of justice, fair play, and the degree to which society is truly civilized. For minority communities, this is an issue of simple survival.

## REFERENCES

American Psychological Association (1975). Minutes of the Council of Representatives. *American Psychologist, 30,* 633.

Bell, A., & Weinberg, M. S. (1978). *Homosexualities.* New York: Simon & Schuster.

Espin, O. M. (1987). Issues of identity in the psychology of Latina lesbians. In Boston Lesbian Psychologies Collective (Eds.), *Lesbian psychologies: Explorations and challenges* (pp. 35–51). Urbana, IL: University of Illinois Press.

Etringer, B. D., Hillerbrand, E., & Hetherington, C. (1990). The influence of sexual orientation on career decision-making: A research note. *Journal of Homosexuality, 19*(4), 103–111.

Gock, T. S. (1985). *Psychotherapy with Asian/Pacific gay men: Psychological issues, treatment approaches and therapeutic guidelines.* Paper presented at the Asian American Psychological Association, Los Angeles, CA.

Gonsiorek, J. C. (1988). Mental health issues of gay and lesbian adolescents. *Journal of Adolescent Health Care, 9,* 114–122.

Gonsiorek, J. C. (1991). The empirical basis for the demise of the illness model of homosexuality. In J. C. Gonsiorek & J. D. Weinrich (Eds.), *Homosexuality: Research implications for public policy.* Newbury Park, CA: Sage.

Gonsiorek, J. C., & Rudolph, J. R. (1991). Homosexual identity: Coming out and other developmental events. In J. C. Gonsiorek & J. D. Weinrich (Eds.), *Homosexuality: Research implications for public policy.* Newbury Park, CA: Sage.

Gonsiorek, J. C., & Weinrich, J. D. (1991). The definition and scope of sexual orientation. In J. C. Gonsiorek & J. D. Weinrich (Eds.), *Homosexuality: Research implications for public policy.* Newbury Park, CA: Sage.

Green, G. D., & Bozett, F. W. (1991). Lesbian mothers and gay fathers. In J. C. Gonsiorek & J. D. Weinrich (Eds.), *Homosexuality: Research implications for public policy.* Newbury Park, CA: Sage.

Herek, G. M. (1991). Stigma, prejudice and violence against lesbians and gay men. In J. C. Gonsiorek & J. D. Weinrich (Eds.), *Homosexuality: Research implications for public policy.* Newbury Park, CA: Sage.

Hedgpeth, J. M. (1979/1980). Employment discrimination law and the rights of gay persons. *Journal of Homosexuality, 5*(1/2), 67–78.

Hooker, E. A. (1957). The adjustment of the overt male homosexual. *Journal of Projective Techniques, 21,* 17–31.

Kirsch, J. A. W., & Weinrich, J. D. (1991). Homosexuality, nature and biology: Is homosexuality natural? Does it matter? In J. C. Gonsiorek & J. D. Weinrich (Eds.), *Homosexuality: Research implications for public policy.* Newbury Park, CA: Sage.

Knutson, D. C. (1979). Job security for gays: Legal aspects. In B. Berzon & R. Leighten (Eds.), *Positively gay.* Millbrae, CA: Celestial Arts.

Levine, M. P. (1979). Employment discrimination against gay men. *International Review of Modern Sociology, 9,* 151–163.

Levine, M. P. (1989). The status of gay men in the workplace. In M. Kimmel & M. Messner (Eds.), *Men's lives.* New York: Macmillan.

Levine, M. P., & Leonard, R. (1984). Discrimination against lesbians in the work force. *Signs, 8,* 700–710.

Malyon, A. K. (1981). The homosexual adolescent: Developmental issues and social bias. *Child Welfare, 60,* 321–330.

Malyon, A. K. (1982a). Biphasic aspects of homosexual identity formation. *Psychotherapy: Theory, Research & Practice, 19,* 335–340.

Malyon, A. K. (1982b). Psychotherapeutic implications of internalized homophobia in gay men. In J. C. Gonsiorek (Ed.), *Homosexuality and psychotherapy: A practitioner's handbook of affirmative models* (pp. 59–69). New York: Haworth.

Morales, E. (1983). *Third world gays and lesbians: A process of multiple identities.* Paper presented at the American Psychological Association, Anaheim, CA.

Murray, S. O. (1991). "Homosexual occupations" in Mesoamerica? *Journal of Homosexuality, 21*(4), 57–65.

Neuringer, O. (1989). On the question of homosexuality in actors. *Archives of Sexual Behavior, 18,* 523–529.

Peplau, L. A. (1991). Lesbian and gay relationships. In J. C. Gonsiorek & J. D. Weinrich (Eds.), *Homosexuality: Research implications for public policy.* Newbury Park, CA: Sage.

Rivera, R. R. (1991). Sexual orientation and the law. In J. C. Gonsiorek & J. D. Weinrich (Eds.), *Homosexuality: Research implications for public policy.* Newbury Park, CA: Sage.

Schippers, J. (1990, August). *Gay affirmative counseling and psychotherapy in The Netherlands.* Paper presented at meeting of the American Psychological Association, Boston, MA.

Schneider, B. E. (1987). Coming out at work. *Work and Occupation, 15,* 463–487.

Sears, J. T. (1989). The impact of gender and race on growing up lesbian and gay in the South. *National Women's Studies Association Journal, 1,* 422–457.

Whitam, F. J., & Dizon, M. J. (1979). Occupational choice and sexual orientation in cross-cultural perspective. *International Review of Modern Sociology, 9,* 137–149.

Whitam, F. J., & Mathy, R. (1986). *Male homosexuality in four societies.* New York: Praeger.

# Index